The Match I Remember

Days Without Sunset
The Game Goes On
British Boxing
Gods With Gloves On

THE
MATCH I REMEMBER

by

Denzil Batchelor

WERNER LAURIE

LONDON

COPYRIGHT 1950

Printed and bound by Odhams (Watford) Ltd., St. Albans Rd., Watford, Herts
for T. Werner Laurie Ltd., 187 Piccadilly, London, W.1.

CONTENTS

LIST OF ILLUSTRATIONS

ACKNOWLEDGMENTS

Grateful acknowledgment is made to the following for
permission to reproduce the photographs in this book:
P.A.—Reuter Photos Ltd. for those facing pages 16, 17 ;
Picture Post Library for those facing pages 48, 49, 144 and
Central Press Photos Ltd. for those facing pages 176, 177

Introduction

THIS book began as a daydream on the banks of the Mississippi. I was enjoying a holiday in America (and *enjoying* is the operative word) till I met an Englishman who by no means regarded it as a privilege to live in the earthly paradise where his daily steak was as big as the gesture of a fisherman telling a lie about his bad luck. He was, mind you, quite broad-minded about the tribulations and agonies of exile. He ate his steaks resignedly. He did not argue about being asked to pay the equivalent of a shilling for a very fine Havana cigar. He gritted his teeth and drank his Scotch with the panache and more than the fortitude of Mr. Darling faced with his son's medicine in Act I of *Peter Pan*.

Being interested in sport, he managed to patch up his broken heart by dropping in, now and then, for a glimpse of Joe Louis at the Garden, ingratiating himself with the man in the next seat by explaining what Bruce Woodcock would do to Joe if ever he got the chance.

Not a bad life in its way—but there was no Lord's. Indeed, unless you went to California and became intimate with those athletes of the British film colony whose contracts called for a strictly limited poundage, there was no cricket to be watched at all.

We sat smoking our Henry Clay cigars, watching dusk settle over the Mississippi, not the Colossus of New Orleans, but the young stripling of Minneapolis, and we tried to pretend that the magic of the half-light had switched the personalities of Old Man River and Sabrina herself. When the sun rose we should see, not a crazy river-house full of Negroes on the bend of the stream or a fleet of tugs toting timber to the south, but Worcester Cathedral and the green cricket ground below, and the first match of an Australian tour in full swing. As we pretended, the vision began to take on life and colour

and three dimensions, if not four. We were watching again
the game we loved.

Only—which game?

The best games, of course. The unforgettable games. Ah,
but which were they?

And my friend remembered a terrific finish at the Oval in
1933, when Yorkshire scraped the 135 needed against Surrey
with three wickets in hand, after two of their most successful
batsmen had been missed. And two years later there was
South Africa's first victory against England at Lord's; embellished with Cameron's 90, hit in an hour and three-
quarters, perhaps the finest *non-century* ever made in a Test
match.

To which I retorted, "Nonsense, Larwood's 98 at Sydney
in '33 was that."

And so battle was joined. Using the unfair advantage of
antiquity, my friend trumped my ace (the first England-
Australia Victory Game in 1945) with Fowler's match. I ri-
posted with Cobden's match: the greatest of all Oxford
versus Cambridge contests. He vigorously suggested that, this
having taken place in 1870, I couldn't have had a very clear
view of it. We agreed about that. . . .

Finally our evening closed amicably on a note of specula-
tion. Which *were* the greatest games, in the opinion of those
who had actually played in them? Which game would Hobbs
choose, or O'Reilly, or Denis Compton or "Plum" Warner?
Why didn't I find out?

So, when I got back to England, I did find out. I worried
every cricketer of my aquaintance to pick his match; and to
tell me as much about it from the inside as he could remember. The results were most encouraging. Cricketers have
good memories of the matches that mattered to them. Some
are too good. One player gave me a long impassioned description of the tactics adopted by the greatest bowler on the other
side during his own most unforgettable innings: and when I
looked up the records I found that this bowler was not playing.

By and large, however, the heroes produced the testimony;
they nominated their own immortal games. It remained for

me to write the epics. There was a slight problem here. Was I to paint the picture as if I had been there? Some of the games I had watched, but not all. Nevertheless the narrative would be unreadable if it was to be speckled with such admissions as, "Unfortunately my informant was buckling on his pads in the dressing-room at the moment, and I was not present, so I am unable to describe to you the amazing stroke that won this ever memorable match."

No, I decided I must regard this book as a work of dramatized history: sometimes seen enacted by its editor, sometimes brought to life by patient research. It is as such I present it.

And, if it comes to that, if you did not see me at the match you remember, are you sure some magic spell had not changed me for a few hours into Father Time on the weather-vane at Lord's, or into the hour hand of the clock at Sydney? Many much more improbable things have happened in the long saga of the glorious uncertainty of cricket, as you well know.

My explanation is made. It remains only to dedicate this book to my chosen XI, ready and willing to do battle with the best team Mars can put into the field; and to my old and excellent friend, the Twelfth Man.

Now let us walk out to the middle, you and I. The bails are in the pockets of our long white coats. We put them on the stumps with the air of high priests performing a ritual. I toss the cherry-red ball to the fast bowler, already pacing off his run to the wicket. We settle down to watch (I hope absorbedly); and impartially, of course—impartially, to the very end of the chapter.

Chapter One

THE ASHES COME HOME

(J. B. HOBBS)

HE was always as svelte as a fox terrier, but today he is lean as a hound. The alert expression on his face is sharper than ever: the eyes have a far-sighted look about them which you sometimes find in the eyes of African hunters or trackers of big game. F. C. Selous will be a name that immediately comes to mind. But if you put the man in flannels and crown him with the blue cap he wore in the field, he would still be more like the Jack Hobbs we knew of old than the figure that represents him in the waxwork museum.

He comes to his place of business in Fleet Street twice a week, and at Tests you will find him sitting in the Press Annexe—not the Box—at Lord's. He is genial and never severe when the cricket is bad enough to make eloquently despairing those of us who couldn't in our prime have kept Lindwall out of our wicket for all the wealth of Lombard Street.

The far-seeing eyes have a long way to look back. They survey the earliest days when he played for St. Matthew's Church Choir at Cambridge, with that first game of all in front of the servants' quarters at Jesus College where his father was groundsman, and the boys learned to play with a straight bat in the form of a stump against a tennis ball, a tennis post serving as a wicket. He remembers making 90 in a schoolboy game, when he was given out l.b.w., a decision so flagrant that the local paper, from the loftiest of motives, corrected it, and gave the young batsman a printed certificate of having scored 90 *not out*. There followed years as grounds-man and as coach, with one golden day when his father enjoyed a last evening of pride and delight as he heard on his death-bed the details of a great century in John Berry Hobbs's first professional engagement against Herts Club and Ground. That was the occasion for which he was paid ten shillings and expenses.

Then came the call. It came in April, 1903, and it summoned him to the Oval, to twenty minutes at a net, with an invitation to play in a trial match next day. Ah, that first innings under the shadow of the gasometers, when every ball was as important as any bowled before lunch on the first day of a Test match, because one mistake might bring an end to a career carefully and secretly planned almost from the day the infant was held up in his father's arms to get a glimpse of Spofforth bowling for the Australians in '86! That all-important innings took root and bore a harvest. The young player scored 37 before Philip Mead, then striving to establish himself as a Surrey bowler and with no ambitions in the direction of batsmanship, caused him to play on.

Thenceforward the great career is unrolled, wide, handsome and clear-cut to the horizon. The first season began gloriously with an 88 against a Gentlemen's team led by W. G., and a century in the first inter-county match. There was also a score of 94 on his first appearance against the Australians. This great innings ended when Clem Hill, with only one stump in sight, threw down the wicket from the boundary, to be rewarded with what Hobbs has always believed was a positively scandalous decision of run-out. A few more runs would have secured for the young player a collection, probably amounting to £100. It was slim consolation to read in next day's papers that he had given two chances, and to realize that in fact he had given four.

By now the career was in full bloom. There followed the first visit to Australia in 1907 when the name of Hobbs first came to be respected as an opening batsman in Test match circles.

Then there were the great games of 1911, which had as highlight the Melbourne match when on a perfect wicket in heavy atmosphere Barnes took five of the first six Australian wickets to fall. ("Not Trumper's," he once said to me. "I missed his stumps by a coat of varnish. . . . What was the secret of it all, sir? Well, to tell the truth"—the voice sank in a conspiratorial whisper—"*I was bowling rather well.*") That match ended with an unbeaten century for Jack, coolly accumulated after having been consummately beaten and all but bowled by Cotter in his second over.

Never in history did England have a more trustworthy opening batsman than the John Berry Hobbs of this tour. In three successive Test Matches he scored centuries. He was, in those days (I have C. B. Fry's assurance for it) a different batsman from the Hobbs who dominated the game from Launceston to Leeds in postwar years. He was a pugnacious forward player with the points of a ballet dancer. In the August of his day, he was cagey, but statesmanlike. He might mercilessly destroy an enemy attack, but it would be done by shrewd co-ordination between the intelligence directorate and the mobile arm, with smoke and surprise weapons—the heavy armour would play a minor part.

Yet, in spite of everything, the match of matches in Jack's lifetime of experience belongs to the wrong side of a curtain as impenetrable as iron—the curtain that separates youth from experience and maturity. It isn't even the match that he and Sutcliffe won, not so much against the most dangerous bowling in the world as against the most dangerous wicket.

It's the final Test Match of 1926—the Test in which England strove to win the first victory gained over the ancient enemy since before the First World War. It was a Test upon which everything hinged; for the first time since Stoddart and '95 a rubber of five games stood to be won or lost in the last match of the series.

The draws that had gone before would have frozen the interest of any race more phlegmatic on the subject of cricket. The first game had been reduced to a few gelid overs enshrined in the heart of a Nottingham rainstorm. In the second, Bardsley carried his bat through the Australian innings and made defeat impossible, though England had the better of the draw. At Leeds, with Collins ill and Bardsley captaining Australia, there was one more indecisive game.

England would almost certainly have lost it if George Macaulay, picked for his bowling, had not proved at number nine the most trustworthy batsman on the side. The fourth match was also drawn, being at Manchester.

By now certain things were clear at last. Fred Root, who from early in the tour, with the help of a leg field, teased and hypnotized the Australian batsmen into a petrified impotence, was adjudged to have worked his final sleight of hand on this majestic batting combination. In his place the attack devolved upon a new fast bowler, Harold Larwood, supported by the mighty Tate and George Geary.

Most important of all, came a change in leadership. In the first four Test matches, Arthur Carr had captained England. His leadership had been of the MacLaren rather than of the Warner school: he believed in the view-halloo and the drumhead court-martial. He lost face when he put the Australians in to bat at Leeds, missed Macartney at slip off the third ball of the match, and stayed in the field to watch the enemy remorselessly amass a score which rendered them impregnable on a wet wicket never made villainous by sunshine working on sodden turf.

Out he went for the Fifth Test match, and in came A. P. F. Chapman, the *preux chevalier* of English cricket, light-hearted, valiant, ready to fight it out and readier yet to take the advice of the newest recruit to the side, Wilfred Rhodes, a co-opted member of the Selection Committee, who had been playing in Test matches before he was born.

People said the reconstituted side only lacked the presence of a young, almost unrecognized genius named Walter Hammond, whose qualification for Gloucestershire was unfortunately the object of disapproving official scrutiny, to add up to the most impressive side since Warner's team of 1911.

The Australian team had its troubles, too. In the previous tour it had fielded the classic opening pair of bowlers renowned throughout Christendom for their sheer destructive diabolism. Since then Ted Macdonald, of the flawless, streamlined action and arrowy flight, had seceded to Lancashire; and Jack Gregory had lost his fervour and his buoyancy. He reached the Oval without a single Test match wicket to his credit, though he celebrated his thirty-first birthday by bowling down the stumps of Hendren on the first day of the game. The alternative to Gregory as a strewer of thunderbolts was Sam Everett, barely eminent as a Grade cricketer, and not to be considered for a Test match. With John Ryder rightly written off as the sort of bowler needed to get a batsman's eye in with half an hour's net practice, and "Stork" Hendry out of form and health, the attack resolved itself upon Mailey and Grimmett with Arthur Richardson and Charlie Macartney as spare parts, and Collins himself—good for a belly-laugh whenever he went sombrely to the bowling crease in Sydney—as next candidate on the list as a change bowler.

Moreover, the batting was weaker than it had been in the past. The omission from the touring side of Kippax, then at his superb best, was keenly felt. Neither Andrews nor Taylor fulfilled the hopes he had aroused in Sydney: the former less of a Porthos, the latter not quite the d'Artagnan they had seemed to rose-coloured spectacles Down Under.

Nevertheless, there were abundant possibilities in the team: Woodfull, then regarded by the superstitious as totally unbowlable; Ponsford, the world's only scorer of quadruple centuries; the mercurial Macartney; Bardsley, with some smack of age about him, but still vehement and dominating; and Herby Collins himself, lean and mahogany-cheeked, cold as ice in a crisis, and, like the embryo penciller he was, ever ready to pit himself against the field when the book called for it. You couldn't tell how close-penned such a side must be before it would crack into submission.

August 14 began well, Chapman producing a lucky coin from the breast pocket of his blazer and winning the toss with it. On a bland morning with little breeze blowing, Jack Hobbs and Herbert Sutcliffe went out to open the innings against Gregory and Grimmett.

The wicket had just enough variety and pace to keep the game from getting tedious; but it was benevolent enough at heart. Certainly there was nothing in the early Australian bowling to suggest that England had a right to adopt an attitude indicating that their backs were to the wall. Now and then Hobbs, when brandishing his off-drive, would use his feet against Mailey almost skittishly. Now and then, too, he would swish a short ball from Grimmett round the corner, and Bardsley or Ponsford would amble along the outfield with the slow perseverence of a goods train.

Sutcliffe for the most part kept his ground, sternly cutting anything short of a length through the slips, and not yet indulging in his favourite stroke at all: the flaying cover drive.

In about as many minutes the two had scored 53 runs, when, quite against the run of the play, Hobbs swiped over a full pitch from Mailey which cut down his stumps as if they had been the wicket of a preparatory schoolboy.

Of all the Australian bowlers Arthur Mailey was working hardest against the collar. He had reason to. It seems that he had spent the night before the game began dancing to even his jubilant heart's content, but being caught by the Australian manager returning to the hotel in white tie and tails at breakfast time. Fortunately, Mailey got his breath back first and asked for sentence to be suspended until close of play. On the way to the ground he had knelt on the floor of his taxi, his hands clasped in prayer. If God would allow Collins to lose the toss and himself to get six wickets he would never be naughty again. He spent the day bowling hard enough to rank as God's formidable ally—and with six wickets in the bag, he spent the following night dancing.

His defeat of Hobbs was a major blow to English hopes. The master was top of the averages and very easily the major factor in morale in the English batting strength.

In came Woolley, looking as usual as if he had strayed out of a Gainsborough canvas. He began to play in his usual mood of lyric elegance. He leant forward to a long hop from Gregory; and there was the ball chiming from his bat towards the fine leg boundary. He leant forward again, and an off-drive sang in a full-throated tenor through the anchored covers. He leant forward a third time, and Mailey had hit his wicket askew with a googly.

Nor was Hendren's Cockney impudence to prevail where

the airs and graces did not suffice. A ball from Gregory swinging away to the slips went from his twinkling bat on to his wicket. At lunch time the three great members of the Old Guard were back in the pavilion, and we had barely 100 runs on the board.

The enemy was Mailey. Down the length of his career this consummate master of the googly had never prided himself on the immaculateness of his length. Indeed, he had cherished a sentimental affection for its lifelong irregularity; rather as a parent has a fondness for a wayward child, surpassing his esteem for the admirable behaviour of his church-going, bundy-punching brothers. But on this morning, when Australia was at bay for the first time for nearly twenty years, Mailey bowled with the accuracy of an academician as well as with the imagination of an Impressionist. He looked slow from the ring, but not in the middle. He would twist his googly fast enough to buzz like a hornet through the air.

And, at his best, his powers of deception were limitless. I once umpired in a game where a Sheffield Shield wicket-keeper jumped in front of first slip to take his break; which (the batsman having missed it by two feet) was ultimately collected by a bewildered long leg. All through August 14 Arthur Mailey was bowling a bit better than his best.

But he wasn't to have things all his own way. After lunch, Chapman came out to counter-attack. He hit rocketing drives into the deep field. He used his quick feet and his prodigious reach to punish the insidious stuff before it had its chance to develop venom off the pitch. In the end he died as he lived, by the sword: Oldfield stumped him while he was spreadeagled in an attempt to give the deep field further exercise.

The rest of the English batting was of small calibre. Tate was dropped at 12 but continued for a quarter of an hour on his jolly way as if he were batting in a village match with a breeze from the Channel acting upon him like a tonic. The great Rhodes set about the job like a Yorkshireman. It wasn't to him a needle match, so exciting that you played with your nerves first and your batting technique afterwards. It was just another game of cricket; and he played his

Jack Hobbs leaps out to drive. The full flourish of bat and the left foot off the ground are signs of a technique less restrained than the present-day "flat-footed" shuffling into position for a drive.

Herbert Sutcliffe in action against the Australians in 1930.

steady strokes to Gregory's forked lightning and Grimmett's black magic with bat first, and with his wide pads as a never-forgotten second line of defence.

As the innings wore on, however, it was clear that only Sutcliffe stood between England and a dismal score. His off-driving was trenchant. He hit the short ball to leg austerely but emphatically. When he was sixth out, after batting for longer than he generally took to make a century, it was apparent that any runs the tail could scrape together must be regarded as in the nature of bonuses. The bulwark lost his wicket unluckily: a ball skidded from his pads to his face; and I think there must have been tears in his eyes which prevented him from following the flight of the huge leg-break with which Mailey trimmed his stumps next ball.

Two hundred and eighty was a poor enough score on a point-device wicket in the first innings of a timeless Test match, but if the occasion was too much for our batsmen it appeared to have the Australians on tenterhooks, too. Bardsley had not got the pace of the pitch before he flicked at a ball from Larwood, and Strudwick took an exultant catch. A great moment this for that smallest and best of English wicket-keepers. He had played in each of the earlier Tests, but had been dropped in favour of George Brown to strengthen the English batting in the final game. Then Brown had injured his hand, and little "Struddy" had been given at the end of his career his first chance to appear in an Australian Test on the ground upon which he had almost taken root in a lifetime of devoted service. Be very sure he was not going to drop any chances offered by any Australian opening batsmen.

Before the day's play ended three more grandmasters had joined Bardsley in the balcony outside the Australian dressing-room. Macartney's brief innings, though less than the label of his great name warranted, had a certain sparkle —it was *demi-mousseux*. He of all men was likeliest to turn the game Australia's way; and England had made a percep-tible advance towards victory when he played a lamentable long-hop from Stevens into his wicket.

Then Ponsford started off on an ill-judged trot up the

pitch to see Strudwick flip the bails off from a brilliant return by Larwood. And just before the day's play ended, the swart and menacing Andrews had a stump knocked out of the ground by our fast bowler.

Four for 60 was a far from imposing answer even to England's uninspiring score. We broke off at the weekend feeling that our noses were just in front; not far enough ahead to justify any singing of "Land of Hope and Glory," but at least well enough placed for there to be no recriminations about having thrown away the golden opportunity that winning the toss had given us.

On the Monday, Australia at once counter-attacked. Collins was the leader: if a man so deeply entrenched, so flat-footedly resolute to stay put at all costs can be described as the leader of any such action. A remarkable player was Herbie Collins. Slim, far from garrulous, with the eyes of a watchful fox in the narrow dead-pan of his mask, he combined the gambling instincts of the born poker-player with the resolute caution of the born bookmaker. No man, not Woodfull nor Bruce Mitchell, has ever been better suited to the task of imperturbably defending his wicket until every opposing bowler has bowled the sap out of his system.

On such occasions as his duty demanded it of him, he was ready to present the bleakest bat in the game to the juiciest bowling. This was just such an occasion. Unemotionally he watched Woodfull the unbowlable bowled by Rhodes—as had happened on the only previous occasion on which the two had met. Like a dowager faced by a solecism, he kept his nose in the air when Arthur Richardson, attempting to hit Rhodes into the upper strata of the pavilion, was deftly caught at mid-off.

Nor did the ice-pack melt from his game when Jack Gregory did what Richardson had failed to do. He took his life (and his country's) in his hands and risked the stake on pretty well every ball bowled to him. Tate's accuracy was astonishing, considering how much fierceness he was contriving to spur out of an unargumentative wicket. Yet Gregory was ready for him: ready to hook him over square-leg's head with a mashie shot: and once to volley him past the bowler with an aristocratic straight drive. For a giant, he used his feet particularly astutely; to defend as well as to attack. He was not afraid, once in a while, to set off as if with a war-whoop down the pitch to scalp a defenceless-looking ball from Rhodes, and then to stride back and proffer a half-cock shot in the end. At last he fell to Tate: but not until he had hit ten boundaries and put his side back in the picture.

Collins, thin-lipped, coolly suspicious to the last, followed him almost at once. He edged an outswinger from Larwood gently into Stevens's hands, knee-high in the slips. He had batted for nearly four hours and had been respectfully hated by almost every man on the ground. Finally, he was cheered all the way back to the pavilion by the most rigid little Englander present.

We clapped; with the departure of Collins, we quite incorrectly imagined the virtual end of the Australian innings. The tail-enders might cock a snook or two at our unwavering bowling, but they would surely retire respectfully as soon as the whip was cracked in earnest. Nothing of the sort. Oldfield and Grimmett batted like a clear-cut opening pair with all the patience and all the repertoire of strokes expected of pastmasters. They did what even Gregory and Collins could not do: for a few overs they reduced the English bowling to impotent raggedness. Tate alone seemed calm and dominant, and to Tate it fell to bring the innings to an end, but not before it had shaded the English total.

An hour's play was left: the most crucial in the match. One wicket now, and the game had swung Australia's way. On such an occasion, experience and the superhuman calm which only experience can bring are the best gifts a batsman can ask of the gods. Hobbs and Sutcliffe set about their task as blandly as if they were having a pipe-opener in the nets. The crowd's heart missed a beat when Richardson, with the pavilion behind him, yelped in appeal till his glasses bounced upon his forehead. But Hobbs looked down his lean nose disinterestedly. There was a pat to mid-on here; a dab through the slips there. A short run, so skil-

fully taken that there was no element of risk: and once
or twice a firm, clean drive that made extra-cover spin about
and take to his heels. In the hour came 49 runs, and not
a ghost of a chance: the game was inching its way to
England's side once more.

Next morning, before the tug-of-war was resumed, with
both sides taking the strain, nature took a hand in a way
that had a right to raise optimism in the Australian
enclosure higher than it had soared since the game began.
On the night after the second day's play, rain fell over
South London like a pall. You could sail paper yachts on
what had been Clapham Common. In Wimbledon, boys
paddled in the gutters; and in Streatham, the parched
zinnias in back gardens welcomed a reprieve, and soon were
waterlogged and hapless. The Camberwell Beauty had the
curl washed out of her hair. At the Oval, the wicket was
left sodden enough, but as soon as the morning sun got to
work on it (at least an hour and a half before lunch), it
degenerated into something like downright malevolence.
The ball popped and slithered, and only a master of the
gluepot could hope to have the quickness of eye and the
co-ordination of hand and foot to cope with such a wicket.
Not an Australian batsman in recent memory, except
Trumper, could have begun to shape on it: even though it
was but an electroplate copy of his own minted Melbourne
"sticky." But Hobbs and Sutcliffe were, so to speak, born
and bred in a briar bush. They took a knock or two,
certainly, but not very many—far fewer than they gave.
Hobbs, in particular, reached before lunch a technical proficiency not seen before during this game—or indeed, in this
series. His chief opponent was Arthur Richardson, bowling
his off-breaks, with the pavilion behind him and a densely
packed leg field. Hobbs was able to lay the ball dead in the
middle of them, or draw back and punch it wide and away
beyond mid-wicket, or even, once in a while, to use his
feet and lunge into the off-drive.

If Collins had risked more Macartney (off whom neither
batsmen relished risking scoring shots) and cut down on
his Richardson, or if the off-breaker had bowled over the

wicket with Andrews at silly point, it is hard to see how Australia could have failed to break through.

As things were, the opening pair not only survived: they played strokes with horsepower enough to penetrate to the sodden boundary. At lunchtime the score was 161: and Hobbs had made 99. Fantastically enough, he had never before made a Test match century against Australia on his own home ground. The rumour of imminent history brought the Prince of Wales, the Prime Minister and most of his Cabinet to the Oval during the afternoon, as in an earlier generation, the news that Grace was abounding at Lord's emptied the clubs of the eminent into a tinkling procession of hansoms down the length of St. John's Wood Road.

The worshippers reached the shrine in time for the climax, and no more. There was an anxious quarter of an hour during which 10 runs were added: then came a dab and a short single, and the century was consummated. Then, in the next over, Gregory skimmed the bails from Hobbs's wicket with a ball which history would never have forgiven him for bowling a few minutes earlier.

The great century possessed every romantic grace you could ask for. It was made (and the first of its kind at that) by the veteran on his own ground: it was made at the very moment when most direly needed, and it was made in the face of towering obstacles. A writer of school stories could not have given his hero a more fitting or a more punctual triumph according to the tenets of his art.

After Hobbs left, the strength of the English innings was centred on Sutcliffe. Others came, went through the motions, and passed on their way. Rhodes contrived to be dropped in the slips by Gregory: an escape few men can have enjoyed. By the time the innings ended before lunch on the fourth day, the next best thing we had seen to the batting of the opening pair was a hearty exercise in fast-footed slogging by the Elizabethan Tate.

Sutcliffe's innings, however, was one of the major glories of our cricketing history between the wars. He had come in with that horrid hour to survive on Monday evening. He had quietly set about getting his eye in while the ball was wet and

the wicket lifeless for an hour on the Tuesday morning.
Then he had almost scornfully repelled charge after charge
of the Australian attack when the pitch was grim enough to
have commanded that his wicket be forfeit. He had stayed
on after losing his great partner; not varying his business
technique, not lowering his dividend. He had stayed in while
the wicket regained its credit, even though Woolley and
Hendren, Chapman and Rhodes could not stay with him.
In the end, he was bowled (by Mailey's most insidious googly)
in the last over of Tuesday, when the crowd was getting up,
putting on its coat and moving off on its way home, behind
the bowler's arm.

On the Wednesday afternoon, when Mailey had toppled
over Larwood's bails and hypnotized Strudwick into playing
a genteel catch into the iron hands of Tommy Andrews, the
rain fell for the second time in the game. There was a long
pause, from before lunch till after three o'clock. Then, at
last, as the sun struck through the billowy grey clouds,
Chester and Young went out to peer at the pitch and decree
the resumption of battle.

Four hundred and fifteen was the little trifle Australia
were set: and it is a tribute to their national characteristic
of courage in time of crisis that most of the groundlings in
the Oval crowd were still uneasy when Larwood made his
first over from the Vauxhall end prance and caracole to left
and right of the batsman's stump.

At once, things began to happen suddenly, violently and
dramatically enough. Larwood whistled by Woodfull; there
was the flash of a bat and a dolly catch in the slips—where
no slip was. Over came Geary into the gap; there went the
stroke again—with the ball clutched safely just below the
fieldman's larynx.

And now Macartney. If any man could stop the rot it
was he. But that day was not Macartney's day. He gave a
sketch for a masterpiece, and then he, too, popped the ball
almost down Geary's throat in the slips.

There was always Bardsley—the great Warren, to these old
eyes so indistinguishable (facially, be it understood, not in the
matter of batting style) from the equally great George Robey.

He was the one man left on the side who might bat the sun under the horizon—bat till August was out—bat till Australia was in sight of the unattainable horizon. More so than Collins, more so than any of the great ghosts of the past, Bardsley was the retriever of the impossible position, the reorganizer of routed armies into the firm, unbending line.

Hadn't he batted through a Test innings already in this series, and seventeen years ago didn't he score a century in each innings of a Lord's Test in an age when no one was demanding a fourth stump, the main theme of this season's correspondence in *The Times*?

But against the magnificent Bardsley, another giant had come forth from his tent, the fabulous Rhodes himself. Soon he had even Bardsley groping into a befuddled stroke; and as the ball flew in a gentle parabola into the slips, Warren Bardsley trotted off for the pavilion without so much as a backward look to confirm his fate.

There was a little breezy assault and battery from husky, dusky Tommy Andrews, which ended with a massive leg hit off Larwood taken by Tate with both feet off the ground and one arm stretched to the limit.

Arthur Richardson did not finish before showing that there were boundaries to be hit. He cracked what might have set out to be a yorker from Rhodes disdainfully to the on. Next ball, he tried the same stroke again—and there went his leg stump see-sawing in its socket.

Towards the end, Gregory and Oldfield showed a swash-buckling flourish or two. The fast bowler hit a glorious brassie-shot off Tate, which Sutcliffe imperturbably pulled down at mid-on.

The game ended when Geary wasted a perfect masterpiece of a ball, a ball which should have been saved up for the next Australian tour, on the shivering bails of the innocent Mailey.

Then came the scramble for souvenirs, the rush of the crowd over the ground, and the long hours of milling and cheering underneath the windows of the players' dressing-rooms.

The Ashes were won back. The rubber was England's for the first time for fourteen years. As twilight fell, the senior gasometer winked; the Younger's Scotch Ale pub and Archbishop Tennisson's School linked arms around the Oval and hugged that vast circumference.

As the moon came up over Kennington, strange figures kicked up printless heels across "the middle": Silver Billy and Terrible Billy, Julius Caesar and H. H. Stephenson. Some of the tribal gods of Surrey waved tall grey beaver hats. All of them bore in their transparent hands huge and heavy mugs foaming with that brew that Nyren boasted would put the souls of three butchers into one weaver. They danced, and they sang songs we have forgotten; they caroused. And on the edge of the ground they gathered for one last toast: to Hobbs, the Surrey cricketer, without whose century the immortal game could not have been won. Then they vanished in the glare of the Kennington street lamps.

And years hence, there on the very spot where they gathered for that final bumper, the memorial gates spring up to tell the future of Hobbs's greatness as a cricketer. It is indeed a remarkable coincidence.

The Ashes Come Home

(AUGUST 14—18, 1926)

ENGLAND

FIRST INNINGS				SECOND INNINGS		
Hobbs, J. B., b Mailey	...	...	37	b Gregory	100
Sutcliffe, H., b Mailey	...	...	76	b Mailey	161
Woolley, F. E., b Mailey	...	...	18	lbw, b Richardson ...	27
Hendren, E. A. P., b Gregory	...	...	8	b Grimmett	15
Chapman, A. P. F., st Oldfield, b Mailey	... ...	49	b Richardson	19
Stevens, G. T. S., c Andrews, b Mailey	... ...	17	c Mailey, b Grimmett ...	22
Rhodes, W. R., c Oldfield, b Mailey	28	lbw, b Grimmett	14
Tate, M. W., b Grimmett	... ...	23	not out	33
Larwood, H., c Andrews, b Grimmett	0	b Mailey	5
Geary, G., run out ...	... ...	9	c Oldfield, b Gregory ...	1
Strudwick, H., not out	... ...	4	c Andrews, b Mailey ...	2
Extras (b 6, lb 5) ...	... ...	11	Extras (b 19, lb 18) ...	37
			280		**436**

AUSTRALIA

FIRST INNINGS			SECOND INNINGS		
Woodfull, W. M., b Rhodes ...	...	35	c Geary, b Larwood	...	0
Bardsley, W., c Strudwick, b Larwood ...	... ...	2	c Woolley, b Rhodes ...	21
Macartney, C. G., b Stevens ...	...	25	c Geary, b Larwood ...	16
Ponsford, W. H., run out ...	...	2	c Larwood, b Rhodes ...	12
Collins, H. L., c Stevens, b Larwood	61	c Woolley, b Rhodes ...	4
Andrews, T. J. E., b Larwood ...	...	3	c Tate, b Larwood ...	15
Richardson, A. J., c Geary, b Rhodes	16	b Rhodes	4
Gregory, J. M., c Stevens, b Tate ...	73	c Sutcliffe, b Tate ...	9
Oldfield, W. M., not out ...	...	33	b Stevens	23
Grimmett, C. V., b Tate ...	...	35	not out	8
Mailey, W. A., c Strudwick, b Tate	0	b Geary	6
Extras (b 5, lb 12) ...	... ...	17	Extras (lb)	7
		302			**125**

Bowling Analysis

AUSTRALIA

	O.	M.	R.	W.		O.	M.	R.	W.
Gregory	...	15	4	31	1	... ...	18	1	58	2
Grimmett	...	33	12	74	2	... ...	55	17	108	3
Mailey	...	33.5	3	138	6	... ...	42.5	6	128	3
Macartney	...	6	3	16	0	... ...	26	16	24	0
Richardson	...	7	2	10	0	... ...	41	12	81	2

ENGLAND

	O.	M.	R.	W.		O.	M.	R.	W.
Tate	...	37.1	17	40	3	... ...	9	4	12	1
Larwood	...	34	11	82	3	... ...	14	3	34	3
Geary	...	27	8	43	0	... ...	6.3	2	15	1
Stevens	...	29	3	85	1	... ...	3	0	13	1
Rhodes	...	25	15	35	2	... ...	20	9	44	4

Chapter Two

THE PRINCE OF PUDSEY

(HERBERT SUTCLIFFE)

I ONCE heard a Yorkshireman cross-questioned as to his ultimate beliefs. He was, of course, as canny as could be. Why should one strip oneself to the buff of one's fundamentals for the frivolous amusement of some southerner with time to waste on conversation? But in the end he capitulated. And when he spoke out, he spoke without shame. "Of course I believe in God. In God: and in Herbert Sutcliffe." It was an adequate Yorkshireman's creed; blunt, forthright, unequivocal.

The only footnote the occasion demands is that this pronunciamento was made the summer *after* Hutton had made 364 against Australia at the Oval. And doubtless you know what Yorkshire thinks of the man from Pudsey who watched Sutcliffe as one who gazes at one of the Seven Wonders of the World.

You also remember, surely, the story of the return of the small boy, dispatched home from outside the door of the public bar with the message that father won't be back until close of play. "Father, I've news for thi. T'hoose is burned down, and muther never posted t'insurance, and both t'twins is doost and ashes."

"Ah—and ah've news for *thi*: Hooton's out."

Nevertheless, in Yorkshire God reigns; and there is also Herbert Sutcliffe. Hutton's a likely lad, too: one of these days, perhaps—but don't interrupt a man when he's at worship.

Today, Herbert, only a trifle plumper at fifty-five than he was when he dominated the landscape from Sydney Harbour Bridge to Headingley, is a mellow business magnate in the paper trade who speaks in warm terms, good enough for a reference, of D. R. Jardine, secretary to his firm. He is prosperous, imposing, genial: a likely target for a knighthood for his services to industry. He is ideally suited to his appointment as a member of the National Committee of Inquiry into Gambling: he is human. No doubt, in his salad days he recognized the way to the more modest windows of the Tote as exactly as he has always disregarded the signpost that points the bettor's road to ruin.

The envious may suggest that this success story has left Herbert unduly sleek, tinctured with pomposity or self-importance. Nothing could be further from the truth. He remains the same self-possessed, unpretentious high-grade citizen for whose sake (and in whose absence) I once heard an Australian Prime Minister's daughter declare her readiness to leave home and throw her nightdress over the windmill.

It is by a narrow margin that Herbert misses sharing the strangest of all cricket records: the record of having played in the first-class game before the First World War and after the Second World War. He was the best batsman in the Yorkshire Second Eleven in the season of 1914; and he was fit to open for the Players in 1940. But by accident this is one record he avoided, leaving the unique distinction to W. H. Ashdown of Kent.

Herbert of Pudsey—Long John Tunnicliffe's town—inherited his cricketing skill from his father to such an extent that he was playing for the county second team at the age of sixteen. Then the First World War intervened. Sutcliffe joined the Sherwood Foresters, and later won a commission on the field with a Yorkshire regiment. He first played for the county in 1919, and at once proved his mettle, heading the averages above Holmes and Hirst, Denton and Rhodes and Kilner. "Old Ebor" judged him on that first summer's play to be even more attractive to watch than the new recruit, Percy Holmes. Sutcliffe was preferred for his clinking driving powers; but Holmes's defence was thought to be the sounder.

Within five years he had left Holmes behind, as Hobbs left Sandham behind. Great opening batsman as he was for

Yorkshire, Test matches were his *forte*. They were tailored to suit his style; bringing out the concentration and attention to detail and gift for persistent chivalric hostility in a way that was beyond the resources of county cricket.

And if Sutcliffe was essentially a Test match player, so, too, was he essentially a Test match player in Australia. The timeless Test suited him as it suited Woodfull or Collins; not that (like them) he was comparatively short of strokes—he bristled with them—but because he had more patience mixed up with his artistry than most players.

It's a high compliment to him that Australian patriots speak of his batting at peril of their blood pressure. They admit he was well-nigh "ungetoutable," but when you have said that, they consider you have bestowed all the praise you need. Niggling. Paltry. Pettifogging. I have heard Herbert's game touched off in such terms by partial critics who would cross their hearts and swear that he never scored more than five per cent of his runs in front of the wicket in any major innings of his life. Indeed, I once heard a comparatively broad-minded Australian, doing his best to assess Sutcliffe's worth objectively, declare that he admired him as an opening bat to such an extent that he considered him almost in Bill Woodfull's class.

Heresy! Horrid heresy! Why, I remember seeing Herbert Sutcliffe hit a hundred in two hours for Yorkshire against the Rest of England, an innings iridescent with straight drives, glowing like a cathedral window with flashes into the deep field. When I put to him a bowdlerized version of the Australian-on-the-Hill's opinion of him, he was majestically pained. How can such things be, his manner seemed to ask. And he explained, as impartially as Old Ebor would have explained to any such ignorant critic, that his favourite stroke all through his career had been the cover-drive. After that came—not the dabbed cut, or tippy deflection to the on —but the full-blooded pull past square-leg, counting four runs. This second stroke, he added, was most enjoyable when one's victim was a fast bowler, bumping down an unconsidered short one. "Such as Gubby Allen," he added, thoughtfully. Gubby Allen, who some of us think kept

Herbert Sutcliffe out of his team in 1936-37, which may have cost us the Third Test match on the Melbourne glue-pot, which, undoubtedly, put an end to our excellent hopes of winning the rubber. . . .

For Herbert Sutcliffe had only Jack Hobbs as his peer in batting on those virtually unplayable surfaces. None of the Australians of the past thirty years was fit to buckle the pads of either of them when it came to this sort of game: not Macartney, not Bradman. And the time that Herbert Sutcliffe showed his greatest skill in this branch of art was the match that he chooses to look back on as the towering peak of his career.

The Third Test of A. P. F. Chapman's tour. . . . The game which, lasting a week, spanned the years 1928 and 1929. The game which England pulled out of the fire after it had seemed certain Australia must win by a comfortable 200 runs at least. The game in which Walter Hammond hit a double century, but which should bear the name from now to eternity—*Sutcliffe's Match*.

The team Percy Chapman took to Australia twenty-two years back was the strongest England put into the field between the two wars, and perhaps calls for higher praise than that. It is idle to compare it with the classic side of 1902, for there is no common factor by which the two teams can be measured; but it stands up very favourably to contrast with the side that won the Ashes, by the same wide margin of four games to one, in 1911-12. The Hobbs and Rhodes of the earlier side, magnificent as they were, can hardly have weighed heavier in the balance than the Hobbs and Sutcliffe of Chapman's team. And, for my part, I should prefer to have batting for me, Hammond, Jardine, Hendren and Chapman than George Gunn, J. W. Hearne, Mead and Douglas: even allowing for the fact that the former had only to score their runs off à Beckett, Hendry, Grimmett, Oxenham and Blackie, while the latter had to face Cotter, Hordern, Armstrong and Matthews, the only man in the world who ever did the hat-trick twice in a Test match.

On balance, you may opt for the older team's bowling strength, but not by much. The names of Barnes and

Foster have an imperial ring; but after that you come to bowlers whom you might, or might not, have chosen for the best of England sides after the First World War. I hope this rating is not unfair to young Jack Hearne, J. W. H. T. Douglas, Hitch, and a Woolley who was usually kept till third change. Certainly (even conceding that Barnes and Foster have the edge on Larwood and Tate) I prefer our second wave of attack: White, Geary and Hammond.

Chapman's team had won victory after victory on the way to the Third Test. It had set the pattern as early as the First Test at Brisbane, which it won by 675 runs, a margin so huge that one looks again at the score card to make sure that it was really England that prevailed. That match saw the last of Jack Gregory and Charles Kelleway as Test cricketers, while in the Second Test, Ponsford had a bone broken in his left hand by a ball from Larwood which kept him out of the field for the rest of the season.

Thus it was that, when the two sides faced each other at Melbourne on December 29—a dull day that brightened before noon—Australia, at the nadir of her fortunes, was in process of whistling up a new generation of cricketers, while England still relied on the body of men who had put them on top at the Oval in '26. There were only three of the Australian Old Guard left from that match: Woodfull, Grimmett and Oldfield. England had seven—everyone except Hammond, Jardine, Duckworth and J. C. White. Anyone knowing the psychological make-up of the two countries would, on digesting these facts, predict that Australia was on the threshold of a long period of success. And he'd have been right: she was to lose that game and the next by decreasing margins; and after that only one of the next seven rubbers.

And yet, strangely enough, her first batch of newcomers didn't provide the team with the power it needed. None of the new draft of bowlers was to make history. The most interesting of the younger generation of batsmen was a young man who'd been dropped after his failure in the First Test and brought back when Australia had failed again in the Second; in this Melbourne game he made runs in both innings, and shaped so well that critics said he would be a tower of strength to his side for years to come. If, however, you'd told the most optimistic of those critics that he would be knighted for his prowess as a cricketer before retiring from the game, you would probably have been laughed at.

When the teams came to grips in the match which might cost Australia the Ashes, Chapman called "heads" and lost the toss for the second time running. John Ryder decided to bat. "Decided" is the operative word; for at Melbourne there is special force in W. G.'s adage that no captain should ever put the other side in first—though he should sometimes think very hard about it. That Melbourne wicket can be a box of tricks before lunch; and especially on the first day of a match. But on this day it was as good as gold; it was great-hearted bowling rather than geological curiosity that brought about the early downfall.

Larwood's first over was a thing of brimstone, and Tate was coming off the pitch with an elastic jerk that made the slips lick their lips hungrily. Neither Woodfull—at that stage believed by responsible scientific opinion to be unbowlable—nor Victor Richardson, looking more like an officer of the Grenadiers than any Australian has a right to look—gave an appearance of having indulged in any long-term planning to speak of. Woodfull's back-lift was, as usual, a matter for microscopic measurement, but when he had scored 3 he snicked a ball miraculously through the network of slips for whose sake Tate was exerting himself.

And there was George Duckworth, his rosy face flung back, howling an appeal against Victor (who had perfunctorily played forward at Larwood) as melodiously as a pack of hounds in full music. In no time the crowd was mimicking Duckworth, a habit it kept up to the game's end.

Swiftly came further disasters. Jardine unemotionally pouched Woodfull off Tate, and half an hour later zoomed up from the gully to take a right-handed catch that ended "Stork" Hendry's efforts to play Larwood by guess or by God.

Another wicket now, and Australia would be fighting a rearguard action. The bowlers were tensely ferocious as jungle beasts on the pounce. Geary and Hammond, who had relieved the faster men, were relieved in their turn; and Tate almost made a mouthful of a skier from Kippax behind mid-on.

The field were on tiptoe for the most minimum chance. Hobbs made three strides and a jack-knife snap of action to cut off a cover-drive from Kippax that had a moral right to four runs. Chapman was a two-way human telescope in the slips. Still the run-getting rippled on. A single to Kippax past third man. A two to Ryder from an off-drive. And, little by little, the bowlers were losing the initiative. The fast men's fury was spent, and Geary and White hadn't quite their murderous edge. A hundred up—a hundred and fifty—two beautiful blooming hundreds. The boys clinging to the awnings of the Melbourne stands risked their lives by letting go to clap till their palms ached.

In the end Kippax was the first to go. He had been plying hooks and glides to the leg boundary. Three came from an over; and then a long hop from Larwood was swept away within reach of Jardine's sure fingertips at long-leg.

The second day brought the crowds in with midsummer weather, and Australia set for a huge score; it was no surprise that 62,000 should think it worth sitting all but singeing in the breathless sunshine. They saw some indigestibly slow cricket. Almost at once Ryder proffered a catch as gentle as a caress to Hendren at short-leg. After that came a partnership between à Beckett and Bradman which only the blindest patriotism could fail to recognize as tedious indeed. Bradman was unable to pick holes in a tight-drawn defence. The hard-flogged drive was stopped by Sutcliffe in the deep; the big-shouldered hew to leg was cut off by Tate. One apiece; and if he could have varied the angle by a fraction, there was a boundary in each.

à Beckett produced a few crackling drives. His stance was a curiosity of cricket; a strange, deep, ducking crouch, from which he emerged to stand up like a Guardsman on parade when he aimed his stroke at the ball.

There were few pulse-quickening incidents. Once Duckworth flung the ball up in triumph before incredulously being told by the umpire that he had not caught à Beckett.

After that, he had only to clear his throat for the crowd to quack at him fortissimo, or to count ten in slow time.

Now and then as his innings matured there were hints of the sheer destructive power that was to be Bradman's special quality when his game came of age. In his three hours' lease of the wicket he hit nine fours, most of them showing animal vigour rather than applied magic. The best came from a sage and savage hook off Hammond's short ball; but the next ball, a yorker, wiped out his wicket from under him.

The finest thing about the first innings, surpassing Kippax's silvery skill or Ryder's downright power, was Tate's bowling: it never flagged nor lost hostility till the last ball was bowled.

Before the day's end the great crowd had been rewarded by what was then considered the most beautiful scenic effect in Australia: the sight of Jack Hobbs's back. He scored his three thousandth run in Test matches during his stay at the wicket with a glorious sweep to leg off Grimmett, but he was never happy against à Beckett, and Oldfield's smart catch was not against the run of the play.

The third day's cricket was as close-fought as ever. It devolved into an unrelenting struggle between Hammond, at his imperious best, and the First and Second Conspirators, Blackie and Hendry. Sutcliffe was in the picture, too; but for once discreetly in the background—a modest Horatio to a flamboyant Hamlet. He persisted for three and a half hours before being caught in two minds by a ball from Blackie which came back to hit the stumps.

But Hammond survived the heat of the day. Hendry's pace off the wicket and ability to turn the ball either way never ruffled his majesty. He was too august to be intimidated by Blackie's flawless length and sharp-toothed backbreak. He particularly relished the bowling of Oxenham. He hit twelve runs off one of his overs; and shortly after reaching his century brought the crowd to its feet with the stroke of the day against this bowler—a straight drive off his back foot which reached the sight screen almost before the deep fieldsmen had spun round to chase the blur. When he fell next morning after six and a half hours of impeccable batting, it was some consolation to his admirers that he should have perished in the high Roman fashion. He volleyed one of his mighty straight drives at Blackie, and à Beckett moved like a whippet behind the bowler to shoot out at full length and take the ball in his hands an inch or two from the ground.

After Hammond, the innings dwindled to an anticlimax. Jardine's runs were a by-product of an innings designed to make the clocks run down rather than to blunt the pencils of the scorers.

In his last spell of bowling Blackie had his reward. Three hundred and fifty-one runs were on the board when he took the ball; by the time he had finished with it he had added four wickets to his bag for another 34 runs, and England were all out for a token lead of 20. If the weather lasted, it was still anybody's game. But it was also clearly a game that was going to persist longer than any Melbourne summer could decently be expected to last.

Australia's second innings began with a superb but not a sustained effort by Tate and Larwood. The great fast bowler crashed down Richardson's stumps with the second ball of his second over; while Woodfull, with his score at 3, all but touched a ball from him into his wicket. Those who knew their William Maldon soberly agreed that nothing now remained to worry about—the preliminaries to a century had been undergone.

There was a reluctance on Chapman's part to keep his shock troops in action for any length of time. After an over or two of Larwood (with a wicket to underline his passionate hostility), White appeared in his stead: like a lawyer serving writs in place of a man-eating highwayman. Before the day's play was over Tate had again beaten the unbowlable Woodfull, but the wicket still stood in one piece. Inasmuch as any bowler worried this Meccano-constructed opening batsman, it was Tate. He snapped and reared at his thighs all through the plodding, faultless century that was consummated by the broiling morning of the fifth day, and ended with a catch at the wicket as soon as Tate replaced Geary with the second Australian hundred on the

board. No one of taste and discernment could luxuriate in
a typical Woodfull innings, but it could be a magnum opus
for all that. To the aesthetic, better half an hour of Kippax,
with glimmering off-drive and diamond cut, than half a lifetime (as it seemed) of a Woodfull innings. But, over a
decade, there were enough Australian statisticians to feel the
force of the contrary argument.

After the long, uphill pull of Woodfull, the occasional
firefly sparkle of Bradman, the jack-o'-lantern. The magnifico had not yet broadened out into the *Roi Soleil* period.
The touch wasn't as certain; the imaginative pugnacity
hadn't quite developed. But his play had, already, glimpses
of other-world magic. He defended as dumpishly as anyone
else, but now and then he cut and thrust, and laughed puck-
ishly as he dabbed the ball into vacant spaces on the on-side.
He had a brief and glittering partnership with Oxenham;
and in his four-hour stay came to play even Tate on man-to-
man terms. By the time Duckworth cut him off in his prime
from a fine ball off hard-working George Geary, the pundits
were reproving the young for suggesting that a successor to
Charlie Macartney had been found.

Towards the end of the innings Jack White came into
his magnificent own. In the whole match he bowled 113
overs, and had only 171 runs hit (though *hit* is too aggressive a word) off him. When a thunderstorm broke over
Melbourne in the small hours of the sixth day, and a heavy
shower fell at half-past eleven, it was his gloomy privilege
to finish off the Australian innings in a matter of minutes.

There was no fun at all in playing executioner, for it
simply meant that it was his own side's turn next. The sun,
that incalculable Melbourne jack-in-the-box, popped up from
behind the coiffure of clouds. At once the crocodile-slime of
the Melbourne wicket began to thicken to the consistency of
glue. In the pavilion the grand old men of Australian
cricket, Hugh Trumble, Clem Hill, Warwick Armstrong and
Joe Darling, set about debating the question of how many
England could hope to make. Eighty was High Field.
Around 60 was a conservative estimate. If anyone had suggested that they might make the 332 needed for victory,

there would have fallen the sort of hush that descends on Anglo-Saxon conversations when someone has the bad taste to touch on miracles or other acts of God.

Out came umpires Hele and Elder, and in their wake the players.

The bowling was opened by à Beckett and Hendry, and from the first overs you could tell how it would be. The rampant half-volleys hit Hobbs and Sutcliffe violent blows from neck to hip; the good length balls sailed over their heads.

Well, it was a challenge—and no two men in the English team relished this sort of fight more heartily than Jack and Herbert. It was typical of them that they went to work unpadded, except as to the legs. Better be limber and take whatever knocks were coming their way than muffled up for safety with less chance of an activity that might yet save the day for England.

For, as the Australian pavilion froze against England's chances, our first pair opened their hearts to hope. "Why not?" murmured Jack Hobbs, patting a pock-mark out of the pitch. "You only have to play one ball at a time," said Herbert Sutcliffe, looking about for a divot the size of a crown piece which a vast spinner from Hendry had prised out of the pitch.

One ball at a time. It was enough. A howl that died away in a sigh echoed round the ground as Hobbs cut Hendry's spring-heeled spinner into the slips where à Beckett juggled and spilt the catch on the treacherous turf. Not a member in the pavilion but was murmuring: "Dayspring mishandled cometh not again," when Hobbs had a second escape as Bradman failed by a foot to reach an uppish swing off Oxenham.

But except for these desperate moments the batting never faltered. à Beckett and Hendry gave way to Grimmett and Oxenham, and soon the most dangerous bowler in the side, wily Don Blackie, was spinning them the width of the pitch at buzzing speed.

Herbert Sutcliffe was bruised on the shoulder, the forearm, the biceps, the ribs; but he continued to play strokes, and to use his feet in their well-sprigged boots to preserve his life and his wicket. Now and then a ball would emerge out of the nightmare which wasn't predestined to hit you—which it was safe for you to hit. There went a crisp chop-shot off Oxenham through the fieldsmen tilted forward on the edge of the pitch: two well-merited runs in that one. And here came an overpitched one from Grimmett. He could trust himself not to slip as he stepped out to cuff that wide of Victor Richardson to the square-leg boundary. Then would follow an over of corporal punishment, and a second, and a third. But your wicket stood still, and the loose ball still came in by the slow freight now and then.

Moreover, a man was heartened, sustained and elevated into a world-despising batsman high above such petty assaults, by something that began life as a thin suspicion in the mind, and grew up to be a stalwart article of faith. *These Australian bowlers didn't know how to use this wicket that had virtually guaranteed them a cast-iron certainty of victory.* What was the good of hitting a chap in his ribs—or bowling one he could duck and the wicket-keeper had to catch high above his head? What was the good of it? What was wanted—what you'd think couldn't be missed on this gift of a wicket—was the ball that forced the batsman to spar, and to poke up the catches for which the fieldsmen were clustering like vultures around carrion. Blackie continued to bowl an immaculate length that gave the stumps a breathing space; and à Beckett was wheeling them down wide of the off stump.

There went a fool of a ball that rose up almost perpendicularly and ripped Jack Hobbs's cap off by the peak! But where was the ball that ripped the bails off his wicket? Peel would have been bowling it for the past hour—or the great Wilfred Rhodes. But it wasn't on exhibition today. Arrogance is a grand thing in the hour of supreme crisis. It may transmute a martyr into a hero. Herbert Sutcliffe began to bat in a mood of modest arrogance: courteous and urbane as ever, but at last blandly contemptuous of the foe. They could plaster him—they could batter him—they would never get him out. And there, with the compliments of Pudsey, went another leg-glide for two off Blackie—the

Devil Don who, in Sutcliffe's view, was the most formidable of all the enemy.

And meanwhile, there was old Jack signalling for a new bat. Out came a cupboardful of them, and he tested one or two gravely, and then sent them in again—to continue with the blade he was already using. But the messenger staggering under his load went back with more than his cargo. He carried a message, possibly of match-winning importance. It was to Percy Chapman, captain of the team, in the window of the dressing-room—and it suggested that the batting order should be changed, Hammond preserved for next day, and the dour and defensive Jardine be instructed to put on his pads and prepare to go in as soon as the first wicket fell.

The advice was taken. Jardine joined Sutcliffe, when, after two and a quarter hours at the wicket, with the score standing at 105, Hobbs played forward to Blackie, and was given out l.b.w.

Sutcliffe and Jardine: concrete of nerve, clear-eyed, breathing easily; how could you get either of them out in a time of national peril? The storm of the Australian attack broke in foam upon their rocklike defences.

By curtain-fall the wicket had much improved, and Herbert Sutcliffe's score stood at 83; he had already bettered off his own bat the score which the greatest sages of Australian cricket had supposed his side could aspire to.

The wicket rolled out honest and benevolent for the last day's cricket. Inexorably, grimly, England advanced on her prey. On that lovely pitch, ripe for runs, Herbert Sutcliffe and Douglas Jardine continued to plod forward with the massive determination that had been the perfect mood in which to fight the previous evening's rearguard action. Jardine had done what was expected of him like a Scotsman with a mission. He continued to play as if every ball might contain some infection deadly to batsmanship. There were four sombre maiden overs on end before Grimmett bowled him off his conscientious pads: the death such a man with such a vocation might have chosen in his prayers.

By this time victory was in sight. Hammond was able to shape strokes as if a cricket match had broken out on the battle-scarred playing pitch. He went for a frisk down the wicket, pushed a ball from Grimmett to the off, and was run out by the mobile Oldfield.

And then at last, with the game—*his* game—won, Herbert Sutcliffe modestly retired a few minutes before it was time for the curtain calls. He stepped firmly in front of his wicket and swished for the square-leg boundary. Grimmett's faster ball came through—you could hear the thud against the boot. The bowler's long arms went up and there was the thin, eldritch squeal he gave by way of an appeal. And there was Herbert Sutcliffe marching to the pavilion like a disciplined officer of a light infantry regiment, handsomely bustling to an appointment with his colonel, his girl friend, or a firing squad. Well-brushed head up, bat tucked smartly under the right arm—and the well-drilled feet marching at the quick-step. You would not have thought he had undergone the withering nervous strain of an innings six and a half hours long—an innings without a fault. He had turned those gnarled, weatherwise faces watching from the Committee window inside out. He had held out through thick and thin, till his side, with six wickets in hand, were within 14 runs of victory. He had done everything that could be asked of him, except actually win the match.

For a little while it seemed as if he had been expected to do this, too. A few minutes before tea Oxenham comprehensively bowled Patsy Hendren, who had scored an invaluable 45 after having survived the shock of seeing himself missed at long-on by Bradman. With only two more runs on the board Chapman and Tate had joined him in the dressing-room.

The crowd began to revive—perhaps the stock of miracles allotted to this game hadn't yet run out. As Duckworth came in they greeted him with mocking laughter that somehow had enough heart to survive until he took guard.

A ball or two later there was nothing for them to laugh at. Perhaps in the spirit in which a captain goes down with his ship, Ryder put himself on to bowl what was likely to be the last over of the game. George Geary faced him squarely, picked off his shorter ball with the full face of the bat, and watched unmoved as Bradman chased it despairingly to the leg boundary. By three wickets England had won the Third Test match, and with it the rubber game in Australia for the first time for seventeen years.

Hammond had played one of the most imposing innings in Test history; Hobbs had batted as only Hobbs could bat on such a wicket. Tate had bowled valiantly; Larwood had shown magic flashes of form, and Geary and White had deserved well of their country. But it had been Herbert Sutcliffe's match: his cool but battered hands had wrung the victory from an iron enemy.

His tour had not been crowned with prodigious personal success. The critics were shaking their heads and gloomily computing that the great firm of Hobbs and Sutcliffe had passed their golden best. He himself had not, before this game, hit a single century during the tour. There were critics, and not carping critics either, who believed that in his mid-thirties Herbert Sutcliffe had his best cricket behind him. Well, he was to score two more centuries against the Old Enemy. He was to head, by a prodigious margin, the English batting averages in 1930. He was to retire from Test cricket at last with the highest English batting average against Australia; and with only Bradman among the foe above him. It would not be stretching things to say that he was the most consistent and most successful Test match batsman England ever put into the field.

Today, where'er he walks, the small boys pinch each other furiously, jerk inky thumbs, and dare each other to try for autographs. That, fifteen years after one's retirement from the international field, is enduring fame. What Cabinet Ministers or best sellers or famous actresses of the mid-thirties have been asked to sign their names on the margin of last week's twopenny speedway magazine?

And now Herbert sits in judgment on Our Betters. Remembering, perhaps, the odds they were offering in the pavilion at Melbourne more than twenty years ago: ten to one against England getting 200; fifty to one no individual century; and write your own ticket about the side's chances of winning the Impossible Test match.

The Prince of Pudsey

AUSTRALIA

FIRST INNINGS		SECOND INNINGS	
Woodfull, W. M., c Jardine, b Tate	7	c Duckworth, b Tate ...	107
Richardson, V., c Duckworth, b Larwood	3	b Larwood	5
Hendry, H. L., c Jardine, b Larwood	23	st Duckworth, b White ...	12
Kippax, A. F., c Jardine, b Larwood	100	b Tate	41
Ryder, J., c Hendren, b Tate ...	112	b Geary	5
Bradman, D. G., b Hammond ...	79	c Duckworth, b Geary ...	112
Oldfield, W. A., b Geary	3	b White	7
à Beckett, E. L., c Duckworth, b White	41	b White	6
Oxenham, R. K., b Geary	15	b White	39
Grimmett, C. V., c Duckworth, b Geary	5	not out	4
Blackie, D. J., not out	2	b White	0
Extras (b 4, lb 3)	7	Extras (b 6, lb 7) ...	13
	397		351

ENGLAND

FIRST INNINGS		SECOND INNINGS	
Hobbs, J. B., c Oldfield, b à Beckett	20	lbw, b Blackie	49
Sutcliffe, H., b Blackie	58	lbw, b Grimmett	135
Hammond, W. R., c à Beckett, b Blackie	200	run out	32
Chapman, A. P. F., b Blackie ...	24	c Woodfull, b Ryder ...	5
Hendren, E., c à Beckett, b Hendry	19	b Oxenham	45
Jardine, D. R., c and b Blackie ...	62	b Grimmett	33
Larwood, H., c and b Blackie ...	0		
Geary, G., lbw, b Grimmett ...	1	not out	4
Tate, M. W., c Kippax, b Grimmett	21	run out	0
Duckworth, G., b Blackie	3	not out	0
White, J. C., not out	8		
Extras (b 1)	1	Extras (b 15, lb 14) ...	29
	417	(7 wkts.) ...	332

Bowling Analysis

ENGLAND

	O.	M.	R.	W.		O.	M.	R.	W.
Larwood	37	3	127	3		16	3	37	1
Tate	46	17	87	2		47	15	70	2
Geary	31.5	4	83	3		30	4	94	2
Hammond	8	4	19	1		16	6	30	0
White	57	30	64	1		56.5	20	107	5
Jardine	1	0	10	0					

AUSTRALIA

	O.	M.	R.	W.		O.	M.	R.	W.
à Beckett	37	7	92	1		22	5	39	0
Hendry	20	8	35	1		23	5	33	0
Grimmett	55	14	114	2		42	12	96	2
Oxenham	35	11	67	0		28	10	44	1
Blackie	44	13	94	6		39	11	75	1
Ryder	4	0	14	0		5.5	1	16	1

Chapter Three

THE APOTHEOSIS OF THE HARLEQUIN CAP

(SIR PELHAM WARNER)

THEY say that when Sir Pelham Warner first came to play at Lord's (for Rugby against Marlborough) he was so small and so young that he had to be lifted over the turnstiles. They say that by the time he came to leave "the middle" there, thirty-four years later, he knew every sparrow in the outfield by its Christian name.

Certainly throughout my boyhood, it was impossible to think of Lord's without thinking of "Plum." To begin with, he was high on the list of cricketers who came to mind because of specialities of costume, or idiosyncracies of behaviour. Others included the Hon. F. S. G. Calthorpe, who could be perfectly depicted by any caricaturist as a pair of long arms in the sleeves of a billowy silk shirt, buttoned at the wrists. Again, when I think of Phil Mead, I see him plucking at the peak of his cap and engaging in that little dance routine of a double-shuffle between balls. And I see Plum, as I see Douglas Jardine, in a Harlequin cap. One of these caps brought comfort and inspiration to the crowd at Lord's, while the other brought high blood-pressure and a wish to sever connection with the Empire to the Sydney Hill.

The Happy Warrior in the Harlequin cap figures in so many great matches of my memory and of my reading. There was the Australian tour of 1903-4 when he, who had never played in an Australian Test before, led the first M.C.C. side to the Commonwealth and brought back the Ashes. At Adelaide he made 79 overnight, his nearest to a century against Australia, and next morning was caught at once by Hughie Trumble ("that old camel"), who alone on earth had an arm long enough to reach the screaming drive that should have carried him into the eighties.

Then came the South African tour of 1905-6 in which Plum found himself up against Schwarz and Faulkner, Snooke and Vogler: a quartette strong enough to stun any good man as would a new interpretation of revealed religion. It was enough to persuade an old-established batsman to retire from business, but Plum stuck to the game and in 1911 returned to Australia, to score a century in the first game of the tour and then become so ill that he never played in another match. After that came the first of the World Wars, during which Captain Warner declared that he believed it was time he gave up first-class cricket, to be met with a reproachful admonishment from his sergeant-major: "Oh no, sir—why, you've got the straightest bat between Dan and Beersheba."

In the early years after the First World War, Plum's health was much less good than it was to become twenty years later, and the innings in this period best remembered was played against the handicap of repeated attacks of cramp even more than against the very formidable bowling of the A.I.F. team. Plum struggled through to a century that gave Middlesex a first innings lead and saved the game in the end, but only after he had collapsed at the wicket several times and been helped off the field with his score at 82. Cyril Docker, the Australian fast bowler of that day, tells me that what really depressed Plum was neither cramp nor the Australian bowling but a mistake in the scoreboard, debiting him with one perfectly legitimate run which he had earned with the sweat of his forearms. Keeping his score meticulously, he knew that an injustice was being done him, and stood his ground resolutely until his total had been advanced by one.

The years roll on. One remembers gratefully the climax of a career that always seemed to be floodlit with glory at the precise moments when triumphs were most memorable. To the very end, to the last crowning ball at Lord's of that halcyon season of 1920, he preserved the qualities by which he will be so long remembered. He was, even in his forty-eighth year, a limber, supple figure in every movement; and above all, the dapper master of fast bowling with special graces on the leg side. Charles Fry tells me that when he originally came into first-class cricket Plum was an off-side player who eschewed strokes to leg almost as religiously as Walter Hammond himself a few decades later.

But the passing of the years, and the mastery of the googly, changed all that. By the time Pelham Warner was at the peak of his career he was the model on-side player of a generation. But there was a spick-and-span look about all his play. He played forward down the line of the ball in real life as in one of G. W. Beldam's instructional photographs. He had a straight drive with a bloom on it. And he could play back with an air: a dead-ball shot that somehow persuaded you that the charge for entertainment tax was justified.

Again, he was—for Englishmen particularly—the model captain. He wasn't authoritarian, but he was in command. His greatest gift (according to one of his Middlesex team) was his ability to make every man in the fielding side appreciate that he was in the thick of the game—in the heart of battle. With Plum in command there wasn't an inner and outer ring of fieldsmen; there were eleven men pulling against the enemy like a tug-of-war team.

And finally, with his extensive and peculiar knowledge of the game and his deep and romantic passion for it, he had a dowser's skill at divining buried talent. He would note a little boy in a mid-September game for under-fifteens, and the name he jotted down to add to the Lord's ground staff next April would be Denis Compton. He foresaw Edrich. He watched Ian Peebles rolling them out of the back of his hand at Aubrey Faulkner's cricket school—and there was Peebles picked for the Gentlemen at the Oval before he had even played in a first-class game, and persevered with after a run of unrewarding trials.

Well enough—but what in the name of patriotism, made him note with approval the action of a gangling young Australian in a pick-up game in the Services, and invite him to play in one of the big charity matches he was arranging at Lord's as the First World War drew to a close? True, the boy was a nephew of an Australian captain of the past and the cousin of a vehement Australian second-wicket batsman, but if Plum Warner hadn't unearthed him to make his mark in that first big game, it is always possible J. M. Gregory wouldn't have been discovered in time to riddle our wickets with his thunderbolts in the first Test series of the peace.

Out of the many thousand matches Sir Pelham Warner has played in, selected for, written about, or merely watched and gossiped at in the past half-century, two are embossed upon his memory. The first is that famous First Test of 1906 against South Africa; the second is his final County Championship match in 1920 which won Middlesex the overlordship for only the third time in the history of the competition.

The First Test match between Warner's team and P. W. Sherwell's at Johannesburg was as close as a game can be, and hard fought from the first brain-wracking over from Schwarz to the full pitch which Sherwell hit to the boundary to win the match for his side by a single wicket.

It was a game which England should have won, and won again. True, on the first day on that red-dusty Wanderers' ground at Johannesburg, the ten thousand spectators thronging the cycle-track under the tall gum-trees had almost as much to shake hands about as to shake heads over. Only Crawford was able to judge the double-faced googlies with which Schwarz (who never varied his magic with the leg-break) and Faulkner (who mixed them) engineered the side's collapse. Only Crawford—and the summer before he had been a Repton schoolboy.

The old-timers chewed their quids and grinned sardonically. Three out for 15—side out for 184; it was the next best thing to a collapse. With a side that bats so well that you can almost turn it upside down, South Africa has every right to celebrate tonight under those southern stars which Mr. Kipling has compared with cattle's eyes in the lamplight. But by the time stumps are drawn, South Africa's teeth are drawn, too. Seven are out for 71, and only Dave Nourse, that

dogged left-hander, playing one ball at a time, has been able
to cope with the unfaltering length and direction of Lees
and Blythe.

Next morning England finished the first innings to gain a
lead of 93. Then Pelham Warner himself, redoubtably cool,
kept even Faulkner at bay and nosed out opportunities for
scoring all round the wicket; while Crawford, standing up as
straight as a statue, lashed out with his intimidating drive
until Nourse hit his wicket with a googly. After that Faulkner went through the side with the speed and grace of the
Prince Regent dashing through the dog-rosy lanes between
St. James's and the Brighton front. Good bowling had that
team of all-star batsmen uncorked: seven of them were tried
and each got at least a couple of wickets.

By the end of the day's play Warner had snapped up
Tancred, and for the second time in the match Walter Lees
had taken Hathorn's wicket. Eight of them were left to be
got out; and 216 runs still needed. It was anybody's match.

At first, next morning, it seemed as if it must be England's. Four wickets fell quickly. The great Jimmy Sinclair,
six foot four, and the only really bright batsman in the
Dark Continent, was one of them. The crowd was on its toes
as he came in: he was always the man to wipe the smile off
the scoreboard. Hadn't he hit the Australian bowlers—
Saunders and Howell and Noble and such great folk—eight
times out of the Newlands ground a year or two back?
Watch him do it again! But this time it doesn't happen.
Lees bowls him an unexceptionable ball against which the
giant develops a cast-iron prejudice as it keeps punctual
appointment with the pitch. With his little swagger-stick of
a bat held almost at handle's length, he swings his vasty
mashie shot for a gum-tree over the long-on boundary. It's
a rising ball, and buzzing as it lifts. F. L. Lane, behind the
bowler senses the catch and is moving like a sprinter after
it before it is over the umpire's head. He has to spring for it
and shoot up his left hand, but the ball sticks; and the likeliest man of all to hit the England bowlers off their length
is walking thoughtfully back to the pavilion.

After this, as one would have expected, South Africa's

approach to victory became stealthy, but the hunt after runs continued unabated and inexorable. Neither Lees nor Blythe had quite the keen-stropped edge of the first innings, but their perseverance was above praise, and the fielding was spring-heeled stuff. The long partnership between Nourse and White was as grand a duet as ever was played out on a matting wicket. Nourse, the match-winner, played back with a bat that seemed as wide as a barn-door, and uncoiled his whippy wrists in that power-drive without follow-through that goes past point's left ear like the rumour of a wasp. Only once does he falter, and then second slip cannot quite pluck the catch out of the sky.

And White's innings is worthy of his reputation as being the prince of South African stylists. On the fast, true matting wicket his firm, clear-cut off-drives remind even the footsore bowlers and weary fieldsmen of Reggie Spooner, all light and felicity and beatitude, teaching the airs and graces to folk who have come off the cobbled streets to the green lawns of Aigburth.

But Relf's impeccable length and neatly cut off-break skim off White's bails at last, and Hayes knocks down Vogler's wicket, and Reggie Schwarz, that deft off-driver and paladin among rugby half-backs, taps the ball within reach of the bowler; and the last two batsmen are together with 45 runs to get.

In such circumstances you could hardly wish for a more commanding last man than Percy Sherwell. He is a batsman good enough to make his century in Test cricket: indeed, in the following year he is to make it—and at Lord's, and as opening batsman at that. You would not suppose this good fellow, captaining the side, too, is playing in his first Test match. As he hits his first ball unconcernedly for four, an English fieldsman is heard to wonder why they couldn't have kept the chap at the Royal School of Mines in Camborne, where he worked for years, spending his happy summers playing cricket for Cornwall. Or, if that wouldn't satisfy him, why couldn't he had stuck to his lawn tennis, at which he was South Africa's champion a year or two back? But no—it had to be cricket; and there he went again, cleaving Crawford through the slips with that fine late-cut of his. Whoever heard of a last-man-in who specialized in the late-cut? The thing was immoral.

But immoral or not, the thing was happening under the very eyes of the spectators. Not 45 runs were wanted now—only 25. And the runs were coming quickly, quicker than at any other time during the innings. A couple to Nourse off Colin Blythe: hooked boldly off a turning ball on the leg stump. A nice square chop off Walter Lees: run for the second one—run like a Springbok!

The crowd has woken up at last to the possibility of South Africa pulling off a cricket miracle. By now the bowlers are tired; and the loss of Schofield Haigh, suddenly taken ill on the last day, is sorely felt. But the fieldsmen are still there on the mark and ready to leave it at a split-second's notice to chase the farthest hit or spring for the impossible catch.

Then with 8 runs needed, there goes Percy Sherwell tickling Crawford's fastest ball through the slips. A couple of inches either way and that would have been the end of the match, and the ten thousand delirious customers would have been cheering in a different key altogether.

As it is, Crawford gives place to A. E. Relf, the prop and support of Sussex: fast-medium with a composed and comfortable action, a swerver with the new ball and a master of the one that goes with the arm as well as the one that whips back from outside the off peg. Now or never, Relf! And he bowls one outside the leg stump to Dave Nourse of all men, and round it goes to fine-leg for three quick-scampered runs. Observe—there's no nursing the bowling for Dave. Sherwell can be trusted to do as much as his partner to win or save their game. He plays two grand balls from Relf with the centre of his bat, and disdains the third. But the next is a full-pitch to leg, and there is a swish and a crack and the ball is across the square-leg boundary and the crowd hurling its hats in the air and streaming across the ground to carry its heroes shoulder high to the pavilion.

That was January, 1906, and even Plum Warner, who has played his cricket everywhere from Philadelphia to Auckland, had to wait fourteen years before taking part in a game to

Sir Pelham Warner, President of the M.C.C.

A characteristic Compton hook.

compare with it for excitement and importance. The second imperishable memory of his cricket career is, of course, the game Middlesex won against Surrey in the last days of August, 1920, a game which had to be won if the team were to capture the County Championship in Pelham Warner's last season in cricket.

In brilliant June, and even in the most sodden July for years, nothing seemed less likely than that they would meet with such distinction. They began the season with a heavy defeat from an Oxford side, which was later to be beaten by an innings by the M.C.C. and to have the worse of a drawn game against Cambridge. By mid-June, Nottinghamshire had beaten them at Trent Bridge and Lancashire and Yorkshire had led them on the first innings. In mid-July the side were halfway down the list, and they still weren't regarded as having an outside chance of winning the championship when, as late as July 27, they lost by 4 runs to the very moderate Essex side at Leyton.

The stoicism with which that defeat was sustained deserved a reward, for on the first day, P. F. Warner had to leave his innings unfinished and hurry off to Lord's to attend a meeting of the Selection Committee, at work on the Australian tour. Then, in the last innings of the game, it seemed that the ironies had relented. Middlesex were set 118 to win, and, on a turning wicket, it fell to Warner to carry his side to within sight of victory. He scored 46 quite flawlessly, farmed the bowling with elfin skill and then had his wicket skittled by a magnificent ball from Johnny Douglas, his old vice-captain and comrade in arms, after a lost game had seemed won.

He came back to the pavilion smiling, even though he must have known that only some such miracle as winning every one of its remaining nine matches would give his side a chance for the championship. How can you win nine matches running in an English summer? The weather quadruples the odds against you, even supposing that such sides as Yorkshire, Surrey, Nottinghamshire and Kent are not obstacles enough in their own rights.

But, in fact, Middlesex *did* win nine matches off the reel;

and if they'd so much as drawn one of these games it would have cost them the championship. They didn't win them easily either. Kent, Yorkshire and Surrey lead them on the first innings. Kent started the last day's play needing only 29, with four wickets in hand. In rain, which hampered the bowlers, they seemed certain to get the runs; but Hendren turned the game by brilliantly running out Humphreys, and young Jack Hearne (two steps and a skip) wheedled out eight Kent batsmen for 26. When Freeman's leg-bail shivered and fell, Kent were 5 runs behind.

The Yorkshire match at Bradford is an even closer call— one run closer. With Kilner ill and unable to bat on the last day, Yorkshire have 58 to get when Waddington comes buoyantly from the pavilion to join E. R. Wilson in a last-wicket stand that would have been enough, let us say, to turn most Middlesex captains' hair white. The two men cuffed the ears of the Middlesex bowling with disrespectful zest, buffeting their way in an hour to within a boundary's width of victory. Mark well that the Middlesex captain chooses Stevens to bowl the crucial over that follows: a death-or-glory hero of the forlorn hope if ever there was one. Last year he was a schoolboy, but also a member of the Gentlemen's team at Lord's. He is as unruffled as he looks, this tall, handsome cavalier of a figure, and his leg-break slips under Abe Waddington's bat and the North goes into mourning.

Thereafter there were four matches without a break, three of them at Lord's. Even so, when Pelham Warner beats P. G. H. Fender in the toss on the morning of the last match, he realizes that if Lancashire beats Worcester at Old Trafford (as they do) nothing less than total victory will be any good to Middlesex.

The crowd realize it, too. Never before have so many people come to watch a county match at Lord's. They cheer lustily as C. H. L. Skeet, slim and debonair, and short, square H. W. Lee come out to face Hitch's flashing bowling and the hard-working Rushby, accurate as an accountant and endowed with lethal quantities of spin. They say at Oxford that Skeet got his Blue for fielding. He is the best cover-point since Vernon Royle—and today his well-sprung wrists are not to earn him runs. Ducat takes him neatly in the slips off Rushby, bowling with the pavilion behind him.

Never mind—it will be Lee and Hearne, then! The wicket is fast and true; as if tailor-made for Lee, crouching over his bat like a stamp collector over a specimen. But in three-quarters of an hour he is gone and Hearne, too, to the tamest of caught-and-bowleds, and Hitch's fires are still not banked, and tall, long-nosed, almost chinless Percy Fender, with the frizz of hair on top, is bowling conjuring tricks that have the batsmen groping.

Hendren and Warner are together now, and the score-board shows three wickets down for 35. Moreover, it is still half an hour till lunch. Surely the afternoon will be one of delirious excitement? Surely the only way to overcome these early disasters is to club the bowling into coma, for quite apart from the tactical mission of rushing up a massive score, there is the strategic task of getting out one of the strongest batting sides in England twice in three days. Getting them out—Hobbs and Sandham, Miles Howell, Shepherd, Ducat and Fender—with what? With about the weakest bowling any side ever sent in to tilt for the Championship. Huge Jack Durston, tall and thickset as any giant ever balanced on a beanstalk, has vastly improved in pace and accuracy. Beside him, Jack Hearne is as a miniature painter beside a master of murals. No man bowled a more civilized googly; but his quick-spun leg-break is rarely in evidence.

After Durston and Hearne there are G. T. S. Stevens, who can, when the mood seizes him, bowl his slowish spinners to roll up a side of blood royal on a feather bed. You must expect violence to be used successfully on this type of bowler when the luck is running against him. There are also Lee and Nigel Haig. All in all, it is an attack which, even remembered in this starvecrow age, seems appallingly meagre.

No wonder then, that Hendren and Warner attempt no cut-and-thrust forays when they come together with the score at three wickets for 35. They are playing, not to win the Championship, but to get their side out of a scrape. Only in this way can the Championship be won. Run by run they push the total forward. On such a glorious wicket it must have been galling to Hendren not to leap out and volley a huge pull at that long-hop of Fender's, but the ball comes fizzing from the wicket, and there is Bill Hitch, square as a barn door, at short-leg with hands that could close over a snipe. Instead, Hendren perishes in the high Roman fashion: playing back and playing on. By the close of play Middlesex's score stands at 253 for eight wickets: and Plum is still there, with 70 not out. G. T. S. Stevens is the second hero. Missed at slip off Hitch when 7, he goes on to bat with dash and resolution.

Even so—253 for eight: it is hard to imagine it as match-winning.

The world is blaming Pelham Warner for having played an innings slow enough to have cost his side the match and all that goes with it. But in the Middlesex dressing-room, Murrell, the wicket-keeper, cheers his captain by remarking that 250 runs always take a lot of getting: there is a last day to this match as well as a first.

In point of fact, Warner's 79, made in four and a half hours, is of crucial value to his side. It saves a collapse, which would give Surrey so great a moral advantage so early in the game that it is hard to imagine that they could have failed to win within a couple of days. As it is, Durston, from the Nursery end, and Haig are able to come into action on the Monday morning against Hobbs and Sandham with the knowledge that no more than a miracle is needed to give the side a chance.

Monday is Andrew Sandham's day. That brief figure with the long, impassive face stands cool and gentle, at the wicket, deflecting Durston between first slip and the wicket-keeper with pin-pointing exactness. He feathers Haig down to fine-leg. He throttles Hearne's googly and throws out his left leg to send the whistling blade within inches of his instep in propelling an underpitched corkscrew from Stevens beyond the reach of small, scudding Hendren on the boundary. Ducat, a sergeant-major in stroke production, gives him moral support, although Murrell should have stumped him before he reaches 50, and slip spills a catch in the mid-70's.

The Apotheosis of the Harlequin Cap

There is something saurian about Sandham. He has a lizard's stony immobility; and when he moves he is back to the impassive before you can blink an unhurried eyelid. On this day, with Hobbs soon sunk in that sandbank of a mid-off, Frank Mann, and Howell and Shepherd caught at the wicket sparring at Durston's nip off the pitch, he might be forgiven for making himself into a Maginot Line. But he doesn't. He plays with beautiful freedom. Repeatedly he uses his feet to Hearne, forcing him through the covers, while lesser batsmen are aiming bewildered stabs at him.

There are rear-rank defenders who might help to push the score along, but the bowling is too accurate to monkey with. Ducat alone appears rooted at the crease. Though frequently beaten by Stevens he goes for runs eagerly and cuts and drives so well that he helps Sandham to add 99 runs in an hour: after that early frolic is over he is able to slash for the gap between cover and mid-off and bring off lightfoot sorties that end with whisking the fast bowling away in a graceful arc which mid-wicket follows much as an astronomer follows the sparkling red gleam of a shooting star. He hits Durston to the boundary four times in an over, but in the end Durston contrives his downfall.

After that it is Sandham — Sandham — Sandham — till Surrey declares, 73 runs ahead, three-quarters of an hour before stumps are drawn. Sandham steering Durston wide of first-slip. Sandham turning Lee towards mid-wicket and breaking into his trot for the first run as he finishes his follow-through. Sandham hitting Stevens past the bowler with the gravity of a judge making it penal servitude. The highlight of his innings is, however, his cutting. Not even Percy Holmes surpassed him in this branch of craftsmanship.

Fender's plot to bustle a wicket or two on the Monday evening fails. If it hadn't—if Skeet or Lee, playing with dour concentration, had mistimed a ball from Hitch or Rushby— Surrey's position when the last day's play began would have been quite impregnable.

As it is, Middlesex begins the last day 46 runs behind. They have to wipe this out, rush up enough runs to give Surrey a total big enough to force them into taking risks,

and then rattle them out. All in a day. The odds against all
this happening on the last day of *any* cricket match must be
immense. The odds against it happening on the last day of
the final, vital match of the season, and Plum Warner's last
season at that—well, perhaps all this background of romantic
melodrama really shortens the odds against the miracle. It
puts too much weight on the shoulders of all but the most
experienced campaigners and, therefore, lightens the task
of the coolest man on the field. The tension calls for leadership even more than for any of the cricketing skills; and
there is only one Pelham Warner in the game. Anyway, as
Skeet and Lee play Hitch and Rushby so that chocolate
spots begin to develop in the precise middle of their blades,
news came from Manchester which adds a gleam of determination to the stern and steady eyes of the Middlesex
spearhead. Despite the heavy dew which had kept the score
down to under 200 in each innings, Lancashire have made
light of the task set them by Worcester. Long before lunch
it is known that only victory will do: and there in the
middle are Skeet and Lee firmly fighting their way ahead,
past objective after objective.

You can't, in such an hour of crisis, ask for a better man
to serve you than Harry Lee. He watches the ball onto his
bat, and from no long distance either, but his tucked-up
position does not prevent him from making strokes with
tremendous power behind them. On this day, when his best
is called for, he gives better than his best. He takes the
initiative from Fender and hits him confidently and hard,
making Miles Howell skim the ground at long-off, while
Sandham moves with the silent fleetness of an electric
machine to cut off the boundary from the heavily clubbed
hook off Reay. His hooking is, indeed, breathtaking. He
repeatedly takes the risk of being out l.b.w.; and fortune
favours him as he deserves.

Skeet is a little less certain. There is an early tentative-
ness while the dew is on the wicket, and now and then a
stroke or two that is less than perfectly rounded. But soon
enough confidence grows out of survival. The free-swung
drive travels occasionally into the deep-field, and there is a

neatness and dispatch about the leg hitting. It is unimaginable that this dominating batsman should be ninth man in for the University side.

Skeet and Lee cram on full sail. When Hitch, with the new ball, bowls one and causes the other to be caught at slip, Middlesex, for the first time since the match began, have a right to look the clock in the face. Afterwards it is runs at all costs for a brief interlude of slapstick, with the certainty of an early declaration followed by the most serious chapter in all the epic. There are a few stalwart drives from monumental Frank Mann, and a little brisk tip-and-run by G. T. S. Stevens, whose partnership with his captain produces the fastest scoring of the innings.

Then comes the declaration; leaving Surrey 244 to make in a few minutes more than three hours.

The beginning isn't propitious. Hobbs and Sandham start as calmly as ever, as if there isn't anything in the situation that calls for Herculean efforts. Each over yields its 3 or 4 nicely contrived runs; and at each over's end the famous pair potter out of their creases, heads down, tapping in complete absorption with the base of their bats at spots on the wicket.

And then at 22 half Surrey crashes when Hobbs falls. He fails to get over a ball from Haig, and Lee throws the catch up in the slips with an instinctive gesture of triumph. The sustained rumble of applause tells that the spectators have suddenly glimpsed the possibility of a happy ending beyond the dreams of the most incurable romantic.

Miles Howell, short and elegant, plays for three-quarters of an hour the challenging cricket called for in this hour from the immaculate amateur. Then Stevens, in his first over, beats him in the air and on the ground—one had almost said under the ground. Murrell flicks off the bails with the air of a pretty girl who hands the conjuror back his cloak and topper and shares in the applause.

Three good ones gone; but the score stands halfway to victory as Shepherd and Sandham parry and drive the best of the bowling with jovial unconcern. Shepherd, tall, russet-faced, solid, is the finest driver in the team, next to Hobbs. He is runner-up to P. A. Perrin, the recognized best cricketer who never played for England—only a rigidity in the field keeps him out of the side. Today he smites unemotionally on all sides, and his downfall is the turning point of the match. He hits a towering straight drive from Stevens designed to land first bounce on the Nursery ground. Hendren forestalls it. He scuds in, then backs away and takes the ball with outstretched hands within the shadow of the sightscreen.

The flank is turned; thereafter it is only a question of rolling up the line. Sandham, looking more than ever like Lestrade, nose down to a dubious clue, places a full pitch from Hearne squarely in the bowler's undeserving palms. And then Stevens puts the tail to the sword. Ten minutes before time he bowls Strudwick over the top of those ramparts of pads above which the little wicket-keeper's eyes peer like the eyes of a Foreign Legionary on sentry-go. The match is over: and the Championship is won.

After that there is such a chairing and a cheering as has never been seen on the ground since the turves were laid over the market garden by young Thomas Lord, down from Scotland after his father has blotted his copybook by backing the wrong horse in the '45.

And so, after more than a quarter of a century of cricket, Pelham Warner enjoys the crowning triumph of his life. He has done much since then: selected and inspired English teams; kept the game he loves alive and at home when the glass of the windows of the Long Room shivered to the explosion of V weapons; and—hardest task of all—remained a perennial optimist in the face of ever-mounting Australian supremacy.

But I like to think that sometimes, when Committee meetings are over and a light or two glimmers from the houses around the ground and swallows jink hard-winged in the gathering twilight, that he stands in the dusk and lets his memory drift back to the greatest day of all. The day that Hendren caught Shepherd before the sightscreen, and Stevens bowled his queer leg-breaks to Surrey's destruction, so that in the last hour the impossible match was won. The day upon which, beyond nightfall and eclipsing the evening star, the cloudless sun of memory lingers yet.

The Apotheosis of the Harlequin Cap

(JANUARY 2—4, 1906)

M.C.C.

FIRST INNINGS		SECOND INNINGS	
Warner, P. F., c Snooke, b Schwarz...	6	b Vogler	51
Lane, F L., c Schwarz, b Faulkner ...	1	b Snooke	3
Denton, c Faulkner, b Schwarz ...	0	b Faulkner	34
Wynyard, Capt. E. G., st Sherwell, b Schwarz	29	b Vogler	0
Hayes, c and b Vogler	20	c Schwarz, b Snooke ...	3
Crawford, J. N., c Nourse, b Sinclair,	44	b Nourse	43
Relf, b White	8	c Sherwell, b Faulkner ...	17
Haigh, b Faulkner	23	lbw, b Nourse	0
Board, not out	9	lbw, b Faulkner	7
Lees, st Sherwell, b White	11	not out	1
Blythe, b Sinclair	17	b Faulkner	0
Extras(b 6, lb 9, nb 1)	16	Extras (b 23, lb 8) ...	31
	184		190

SOUTH AFRICA

FIRST INNINGS		SECOND INNINGS	
Tancred, L. J., c Board, b Lees ...	3	c Warner, b Blythe ...	10
Shalders, W. A., c Haigh, b Blythe	4	run out	38
Hathorn, M., b Lees	5	c Crawford, b Lees	4
White, G. C., c Blythe, b Lees ...	8	b Relf	81
Snooke, S. J., c Board, b Blythe ...	19	lbw, b Lees	9
Sinclair, J. H., c and b Lees	0	c Fane, b Lees	5
Faulkner, G. A., b Blythe ...	4	run out	6
Nourse, A. D., not out	18	not out	93
Vogler, b Crawford	14	b Hayes	2
Schwarz, R. O., c Relf, b Crawford	5	c and b Relf	2
Sherwell, P. W., lbw, b Lees ...	1	not out	22
Extras (b 9, lb 1)	10	Extras (b 6, lb 2, nb 7) ...	15
	91		287

Bowling Analysis

SOUTH AFRICA

	O.	M.	R.	W.			O.	M.	R.	W.
Schwarz	21	5	72	3	...	...	8	1	24	0
Faulkner	22	7	35	2	...	...	12.5	5	26	4
Sinclair	11	1	36	2	...	...	5	1	25	0
Vogler	3	0	10	1	...	...	11	3	24	2
White	5	1	13	2	...	...	4	0	15	0
Nourse	1	0	2	0	...	...	6	4	7	2
Snooke	...	...	...	...	...	...	12	4	38	2

M.C.C.

	O.	M.	R.	W.			O.	M.	R.	W.
Lees	23.1	10	34	5	...	...	33	10	74	3
Blythe	16	5	33	3	...	...	28	12	50	1
Crawford	7	1	14	2	...	...	17	4	49	0
Haigh	...	...	...	...	...	...	1	0	9	0
Relf	...	...	...	...	...	...	27.5	7	47	2
Wynyard	...	...	...	...	...	...	3	0	15	0
Hayes	...	...	...	...	...	...	9	1	28	1

The Apotheosis of the Harlequin Cap

(AUGUST 28—31, 1920)

MIDDLESEX

FIRST INNINGS		SECOND INNINGS	
Skeet, C. H. L., c Ducat, b Rushby	2	c Fender, b Hitch	106
Lee, H. W., c Hitch, b Fender ...	12	b Hitch	108
Hearne, J. W., c and b Hitch ...	15	lbw, b Rushby	26
Hendren, E., b Reay	41	c Sandham, b Rushby ...	5
Warner, P. F., b Rushby	79	not out	14
Mann, F. T., c and b Fender ...	12	c Peach, b Fender	22
Haig, N., b Reay	18	b Rushby	1
Stevens, G. T. S., b Fender	53	not out	21
Longman, H. K., b Fender	0		
Murrell, H. R., c Ducat, b Hitch ...	9	b Reay	0
Durston, T. J., not out	0		
Extras (b 12, lb 12, nb 3)	27	Extras (b 8, lb 4, w 1) ...	13
	268	(7 wkts. dec.) ...	316

SURREY

FIRST INNINGS		SECOND INNINGS	
Hobbs, J. B., c Mann, b Hearne ...	24	c Lee, b Haig	10
Sandham, A., not out	167	c and b Hearne	68
Howell, M., c Murrell, b Durston ...	7	st Murrell, b Stevens ...	25
Shepherd, T., c Murrell, b Durston	0	c Hendren, b Stevens ...	26
Peach, H. A., hit wicket, b Stevens ...	18	b Stevens	11
Ducat, A., st Murrell, b Lee	49	lbw, b Hearne	7
Fender, P. G. H., c Haig, b Durston	30	b Durston	1
Hitch, W., b Durston	1	b Stevens	6
Reay, G. M., c Haig, b Lee	6	b Hearne	5
Strudwick, H., b Hearne	9	b Stevens	10
Rushby, T., not out	6	not out	7
Extras (b 17, lb 5, nb 2)	24	Extras (b 11, lb 1) ...	12
(9 wkts. dec.) ...	341		188

Bowling Analysis

SURREY

	O.	M.	R.	W.			O.	M.	R.	W.
Hitch	32.1	10	66	2	...	...	20	5	71	2
Rushby	23	9	48	2	...	...	22	7	73	3
Fender	28	4	76	4	...	...	16.5	2	70	1
Reay	26	17	31	2	...	...	18	1	61	1
Ducat	3	1	10	0	...	...	3	0	12	0
Shepherd	6	3	10	0	...	...	4	0	16	0

MIDDLESEX

	O.	M.	R.	W.			O.	M.	R.	W.
Durston	30	9	97	4	...	...	14	1	42	1
Haig	10	4	25	0	...	...	8	0	19	1
Stevens	16	0	72	1	...	...	13.4	0	61	5
Hearne	24	8	57	2	...	...	11	0	37	3
Lee	15	2	66	2	...	...	4	0	17	0

Chapter Four

THE PHOTO FINISH

(DENIS COMPTON)

TO Denis Compton the match is unforgettable—and he wishes it were otherwise. It is true that we won it, the hardest-fought Test match in the saga of the game; but the playing of it was so far removed from cricket's own natural benevolent sunlight and so fraught with all the dark other-worldly portents that looking back on it even today affords no better than a morbid satisfaction. The First Test at Durban in December '48—the match which Mephistopheles might have stage-managed on a wicket property belonging to a public recreation ground, in a light that thickened till it reached the consistency of the Witches' brew on the blasted heath in *Macbeth*. That is Denis Compton's immortal memory of cricket: and it is to him no midsummer night's dream, but stark nightmare.

And yet I am glad that Denis Compton, creature of sweetness and light that he is, should have endured these torments to the end. You see, without him we should have lost that grim and fantastic Test match; but with him, and because of him, we won. This is an aspect of this particular match which Denis invariably leaves out in discussing it; for Denis is (next to Martin Donnelly) the most unfathomably modest man I know.

When Sunday brought a break in his marvellous innings of 184 at Nottingham in '48, I discussed his knock with him and found him incapable of appreciating how much he had already done to retrieve our honour, and how much more it was possible that he might do. If Keith Miller's bumper hadn't caused him to duck into his stumps (and so be given out hit-wicket without raising his bat to play a

59

stroke) it may be supposed that he must have gone on to put
the match beyond Australia's reach. But that he, and he
alone, could save English cricket from débâcle leading to loss
of morale and a whole season's debasement—that was a
thought you could not persuade Denis to appreciate. All he
knew was that he would do his best, and so would everyone
else; and one or other of them might have the good fortune
to pull the game out of the fire.

If I were laid on a psycho-analyst's couch and had to utter
instinctive responses to a string of proper nouns, the conversation would run on these lines: *Hobbs — cover-drive;
Larwood—leg theory; Mailey—googly;* and *Compton—
modesty.* It is, too, a modesty which bears fruit; a hard-
working modesty, a thing of works and not of grace alone.

It will allow his good nature to take him so far, because he
has no sense of self-importance to act as a break. I remember
how he spent his Sunday afternoon during the Manchester
Test against the New Zealanders. It was his one day off, and
a distressingly hot day at that. The sensible thing to do was
to sit in the lounge of the Midland Hotel and drink quarts
of iced ginger beer till the sun was under the yard-arm.
What Denis did was to travel out to the suburban ground
where a match was being staged to swell the proceeds of Dick
Pollard's benefit, and there spend the long, parched hours
slowly walking round the ground exhibiting a bat that was
up for raffle and submitting to be photographed, for a small
contribution to the fund, on the arm of any infatuated lady
with a taste for basking in greatness.

Modesty first—but, of course, a lot of other qualities close
behind. Looking back over the years, I relish his development
from a hearty, full-bodied young wine to a vintage character
of charm and smooth elegance. The storm-hitter at number
seven has become the generalissimo at number four. Only
a trait of Elizabethanism stops him from silvering his game
over with the classic graces of a Hobbs. He adds to a light-
hearted pugnacity the ability to subordinate his natural
game to the needs of his side: against Australia he is almost
always set for the rôle of the diligent younger son paying off
the mortgage on the old home incurred by his spendthrift

seniors. His ability to fight back after having been hit by an Australian thunderbolt fair and square between the ears revives the finest traditions of the Britain Can take It school of propaganda.

On the side he has, of course, developed a two-way popularity in the deep-field. His captain is proud to have him in the team; and the small boys over the edge of the boundary who never watch a ball bowled, but work out the batsman's average over by over, sprint confidently on to the field to demand his autograph on the least buttery edge of their sandwich paper.

Again, when 350 is on the board and Jim Sims is in a muck sweat, who does not remember that, if the wicket is a dust bowl, Denis can look like Fleetwood-Smith's twin for half a dozen overs together? This, by my profit and loss account, is no asset to English batting. Jack Hobbs was a pretty good bowler, too: he was once top of the first-class averages, but England captains were broadminded enough to overlook this breach of taste.

Denis by St. George! If there is an English renaissance it must be Denis who leads the armies with the dawn gleaming on their helmets. But he will probably fall out from this Technicolor force for a game of conkers with some inky broth of a boy on the King's highway.

When he set out with the strong, but not the strongest possible, M.C.C. team for South Africa in the autumn of '48 he probably didn't consider that he was to be involved in any conflict much more exacting than just such a game of conkers. The South Africans relied on almost the same team which had been overpowered on English wickets a season or two earlier. They had only two new assets. One was Billy Wade, brother of the old South African captain, who actually headed Denis in the Test match averages and aggregate. The other was Cuan McCarthy, a nineteen-year-old fast bowler of splendid ferocity who had been taught by his father on a backyard pitch and had only a single season of experience behind him. Otherwise the side was rich in batsmen who had been part and parcel of South African cricket for anything up to twenty years. This augured ill for them; and by the time the First Test match was reached in mid-December, there were few who supposed that England was in any serious danger of defeat.

The game began with South Africa's winning of the toss. Denis smiles as he remembers this—for he holds that if they had lost it they should have lost the game by an innings. But at the time there wasn't much smiling. This was not only the ground, this was the actual pitch (used for the first time for a twelve-month) on which that timeless Test took place, or at least began, in March, 1939. Then, ten days hadn't been long enough to bring about a result. Now, the batting wasn't much weaker and the bowling certainly was. Would there be time to finish an innings apiece in this four-day match on the Kingsmead wicket?

So ruminated the prophets as Eric Rowan and Owen Wynne faced Bedser and Gladwin on a weird wicket which set the ball rearing at one end and produced shooters at the other. As horrid a piece of turf to open a Test innings on as can be imagined—the Melbourne pitch before lunch alone excepted.

Bedser, in particular, looked wolfishly hungry for wickets from the first over. Neither batsman appeared to be in high feather, and it was no surprise to the crowd, murmurous as swarming bees between overs, when Compton brilliantly snapped up Owen Wynne—no one ever saw a more nervous opening batsman—in Bedser's leg trap. A few overs later, Jenkins, rolling down his gigantic leg-breaks, bemused Rowan into a vain dab, and the catch lodged as if magnetized in Godfrey Evans's gloves.

Two gone for 18: the England bowlers were at their throats. Another quick one and the landslide would have begun.

There wasn't to be another quick one. Bruce Mitchell, frigid and flawless, and stocky Dudley Nourse held the line against assault after assault. There is no more defiant bat in cricket than Mitchell's, but its resistance is as secret as if it were a member of the Underground. Never can one watch its owner at work, damping the fire of the attack, but one remembers his origins. One remembers Edgbaston twenty years back when, England having scored 245, Mitchell played back for seven hours to make 88 runs and save his side from the ravening Larwood. Ever since that day he has undertaken the mission of stopping any collapse—this batsman whom Halliwell, the South African wicket-keeper, predicted would play for his country before he was twenty, after bowling to him at the age of six on a road through a Johannesburg mine with a petrol can for a wicket.

And the ideal partner for this lapidary defender was Dudley Nourse, son of the great Dave, whom he once asked for instruction, to be answered with the retort that he himself had learned to bat with a paling off a fence, and his son would be well advised to do likewise. Dudley Nourse, thick-set and imperturbable, who once was chosen to be coached by the great Alec Kennedy—but finding himself the only barefoot boy in the class shyly withdrew and never took another lesson until, as a Currie Cup player, he submitted to have the bloom put on his game by Herbie Taylor.

Mitchell and Nourse might have batted the game out if it hadn't been for Watkins. When Nourse had mastered the seam bowlers, magnificently storming at the gate for a long stretch of overs, George Mann loosed Wright at him. Up went the bat and round whirled the thick forearms. There went the ball, travelling so fast the eye could barely pick it up. And there went Alan Watkins, like the rubbery little Plymouth Argyle footballer that he is, spreadeagled across the grass at mid-on, the catch between his tingling finger-tips. Three for 69, the great stand broken, and the side in rout.

From this moment the faster bowlers took over. Gladwin beat down Dawson's wicket, and Bedser forced Mitchell to give Evans one of the three elegant catches with which he embellished his day. But even so the day's honours didn't go to the bowlers. The fieldsmen earned them. Not for many a lustre had English fielding reached such heights. Watkins, Compton and Evans were outstandingly brilliant and won as much applause as any batsmen or bowlers on show.

The day's play ended, after South Africa had been put out, with an over by Cuan McCarthy. While the fast bowler was still pawing the ground, light was thickening over Durban. It wasn't a light to play football in, let alone face a young fast bowler in a mood to snort flames out of his nostrils as soon as look at you. His first ball almost brought about catastrophe. Hutton groped forward to it, found it amid the encircling gloom and popped it up almost within reach of forward short-leg.

There was a run; and the rest of the over Washbrook watched suspiciously from under the peak of that Lancashire cap pulled, tight fitting as a glove, over his skull and slightly tilted above the sardonic left eye. After that an appeal against the light was granted without hesitation, and not long afterwards a long, sad rainstorm rubbed in the evening's unsuitability for cricket.

The second day's play also ended before its time; a heavy rainstorm and darkling skies causing stumps to be uprooted nearly an hour before the tea interval. In the three hours of cricket England brought their score to 144 for the loss of two wickets, a foot-slogging advance which, when it is remembered that the first 50 were whisked up in as many minutes, tells its own sombre story.

You wouldn't attribute the diehard attitude of the English team to imperfections of the wicket. Hutton and Washbrook began in buoyant mood. They took the steam out of Lindsay Tuckett and played McCarthy with calm assurance. Even the spinners didn't daunt them, though there was an altogether more thoughtful attitude in facing the off-breaks which Athol Rowan sent down on an impeccable wavelength and the tempting slows from left-handed "Tufty" Mann. There wasn't any particular reason to suppose either of them would ever be got out, however, and when at last Wade threw up his head to demand recognition of his handiwork the incident was as startling in its way as the death-knell of a dynasty.

And now the freeze-up took possession of the game. The Australians had named R. T. Simpson, the ex-Nottingham policeman, as the best player of slow bowling they had seen in England during the previous summer; but this was not his day. Mann's bowling seemed to force him on to the retreat, and soon enough there was a howl of acclamation as Begbie affixed himself to a catch at silly mid-on.

The loss of Simpson was an achievement. Even more exciting was the fact that the dashing Hutton was driven back to defence. No more threshing cover-drives. No more sparkling cuts that turned the slips inside out to get a back view of the ball racing for the boundary. Nothing but a desperate struggle to keep the ball out of the wicket and out of the clutches of those silly-points and mid-on creeping up closer and closer, like children playing Grandmother's Steps.

After reaching his 50 briskly enough it had taken Hutton an hour to crawl forward to 80. The main reason was the fine bowling of Tufty Mann. During the day he sent down fifteen overs and only had 13 runs hit off him; moreover, he had taken (and earned) the very valuable wickets of Washbrook and Simpson. Of course, we had known about his steadiness before: had he not once bowled thirty-nine maidens in an unchanged spell of sixty overs in a Currie Cup game? Why, oh, why, had Cambridge allowed him to depart with a mere golf Blue as a sporting diploma? What do you have to *do* to win a cricket Blue at Cambridge?

Not the least of Tufty Mann's achievements was that he was able to put the brake on Compton at the very time when Denis would have liked to bustle for the runs. He had fifty-five minutes' batting after Simpson fell on the second afternoon, and they yielded him a paltry 17. To render Denis unrecognizable in a time of crisis is a solid achievement for any bowler.

The third day's play left the general pattern of the game unchanged. Once again villainous light stopped play, with rain around the corner. Once again batsmen found themselves forced to defend for dear life. The only change in the pattern was that for the first time it appeared that the game was shaping to a definite end. When stumps were drawn, South Africa were still 2 runs behind England's first innings total with four of the second innings wickets gone, including both Nourse and Mitchell, the star-destined redeemers of a side in trouble.

The play began with a shock from which the English

innings never recovered. Hutton was out in the third over of the morning. Critics watched him go with a sapient shake of the head. While he and Compton were together anything might happen. Once one of them left England were forced on to the defensive. They might build up a solid lead, but they would have to fight every yard of the way. And so it proved. In no time, Denis was back where he had spent the summer before: at Nottingham, at Leeds, at Old Trafford; grimly defiant, paying off the mortgage by thrift and hard work. It was a miserable destiny for the young cavalier.

Yet he stuck to the task forced on him. Never before or since in the length of the tour was he called upon to face better bowling than Athol Rowan and Tufty Mann subjected him to that day. They were at his throat, hour after hour; never letting up, never throwing their hand in. Denis countered their efforts with every trick his long experience of the game had taught him. Down the pitch he advanced, bat swung high, determined to counter-attack until they broke like the French cavalry against the reckless infantrymen of Minden. But the opening was never there. Each sortie was met by a brilliantly conceived change of pace which forced the batsman to skip or flounder home to safety, his wicket preserved, but the enemy inching his way ever nearer to the citadel.

For three and a half hours Denis stood at bay to the spin bowlers. He never dominated them, but he kept them out. His long and splendid defiance had few moments of exultant triumph. Only four times was he able to work the ball to the boundary through the cordon of fieldsmen shadowing his every movement at the pitch's edge.

One remembers so many Compton innings, not only with ecstatic relish, but also with gratitude. The backs-to-the-wall effort of pugnacious endurance at Nottingham. The innings at Manchester in which the wounded hero returned to the battlefield and lived on to rout the enemy, foot, horse and quick-firing guns. (Neither of them was, by the way, his own favourite—that was his 168 against Kent in '47, another mighty but unavailing effort from behind.)

But for sheer value to a stricken side none of these great

innings surpassed his contribution in the first innings at Durban. He made victory possible; and without him defeat would have been inevitable.

None of his partners offered much more than a token resistance. F. G. Mann's innings suggested a courage beyond his technical accomplishment. The spinners, on a wicket which at last was frankly malevolent, held the other batsmen's destinies firmly between their cunning fingers.

When South Africa went in to bat, spin remained paramount. There had been, before the sides were at grips in a Test, a certain amount of frank dressing-room criticism of Roley Jenkins as a leg-spinner. One confident South African voice rubbed him out as the sort of bowler who had a right to hope to get schoolboys' wickets, but nobody else's. But there was Eric Rowan marching back to the pavilion, for the second time in the match a victim of the under-rated bowler.

The crisis of the South African innings (regarding it, not improperly, as the case-history of a brave struggle for survival) was when Nourse and Mitchell again found themselves fending off collapse. Once again it was the spin bowlers who were threatening to break down the patient's constitution; once again the dour South African pair staved off the peril, symptom by symptom. In a long, embattled stand they brought their side within sight of convalescence—and then Bedser caught Nourse off a mishit against a rising ball, and South Africa's vitality sank helplessly.

Bruce Mitchell struggled on, cold and cagey, ready to bat if necessary till the pitch wore away and the bowlers struck a vein of gold in the lower strata of the subsoil. But before the dusk closed down on the day's play, Wright, reformed of run and bowling with magnificent pugnacity, crashed past that rampart of a bat to destroy his wicket with the finest googly of the innings.

One run later play ended for the day. In the half-light rain could be smelled rolling up from the horizon. The thought in most minds was not whether South Africa could stave off defeat on the morrow, but whether, in the cricketing sense, tomorrow would be another day at all. Before stumps were drawn the English captain, watchful for his side's benefit, was to show the firmness of his genial character. The authorities improperly announced that play was finished for the day at 5.30. Mann would have none of that; he insisted on a final visit to the wicket by the umpires at five minutes to six. They found their way there all right, but saw no reason to expect others to follow their example. So night fell in earnest and the rain-storms broke upon Durban.

On the last day the Kingsmead ground was bathed in a light that gave a positively Götterdämmerung setting for the most exciting—not to say the most hellishly unnerving—cricket ever known in the long saga of Test matches. If the sky had forked flames from its dusky cloud-wrack it would hardly have added to the Wagnerian awfulness of the scene.

On such a day South Africa had, to hand, if she liked to take it, a simple means of staving off defeat. Appeals against the light must have saved the day for her: again it would have been easy enough to have closed the game up by negative batting followed by the placing of a purely defensive field. But—all honour to the side—it eschewed any such tactic.

The wicket when play began was gruesome. The ball lifted awkwardly, and Wright and Bedser attacked with zeal. You would have thought that on such a day wickets would rattle like musketry; but Begbie and Wade played the splendid bowling almost with enthusiasm. There was one nerve-freezing moment when Simpson at deep-point put a very hard chance from Begbie on the floor.

The hard-hitting batsman had scored 13. When Bedser arrived with the new ball he celebrated his escape by promptly hitting him for 6. Not a statistician in the Press box could be quite sure when this had last happened in either hemisphere. But in the end Bedser got his revenge. Out went Begbie, caught and bowled, with the score at 174 and the one remaining partnership that might have thwarted England blighted in its prime.

Wade stayed on, and while he stayed there was still a smell of defiance about the South African innings. When, at last, Jenkins bowled him behind his legs, the tail settled down to fight a series of rearguard actions to the bitter end of the innings, and a heroic job they made of it. But Wright and Denis himself carried too many guns for them.

In came England. The task ahead of them was to get 128 runs in two and a quarter hours. Would they accept the challenge, or was it better to live to fight another day?

From the first the answer was easy to read. Hutton and Washbrook went for the bowling as if a draw was one degree more undesirable than defeat. It was, of course, the right, the chivalric attitude in the high hour of crisis.

The first ball of McCarthy's first over cost the run-chasers five minutes. Hutton slashed it into the gully, almost hard enough to embed it in Dudley Nourse's knee.

But at last the game went on; and as soon as it restarted the thrills began to pile up. Sane, planned cricket went to the wall; the situations of melodrama sprang up from a dozen trapdoors on the Kingsmead ground. The first ball of Lindsay Tuckett's first over was short. Washbrook, lashing out at it, was a little hasty in his stroke. On the boundary, Owen Wynne stood with cupped hands. Into and out of them the ball dropped: impossibly—irrevocably—on to the ground that somehow did not open up to receive the fieldsman. A close-up of Owen Wynne's face at that moment would have conveyed human despair to future generations unacquainted with such an emotion, more adequately than Marlowe's description of stricken Niobe. All the world immediately exclaimed upon the simplicity of the catch, and all the world forgot to remark on the wetness of the ball that slipped through those unnerved fingers.

Shortly afterwards, Wynne had a chance of hiding his unhappy face from public gaze, and the English team an opportunity of gnashing in the pavilion those thwarted teeth that they longed to get into the situation and the enemy. The rain fell for ten endless, vital minutes. Then the players bustled back to the pitch, and Hutton popped a rising ball from Tuckett into the hands of silly mid-on.

Next man in was the captain. He set an example by doubling out to the wicket. Before Tufty Mann, bowling like a robot, hit Washbrook's pad in front of the wicket there had been a productive flurry of tip-and-run. Even after this catastrophe the game was resumed in the same spirit. Mann, clearly in the mood to win the match with whole minutes to spare, carted a long hop into the deep-field, was dropped, and took his escape so little to heart that immediately after he was elegantly caught by Bruce Mitchell at slip.

And then, sudden and brilliant as lightning flash, the South African counter-attack poured in. It took the form of McCarthy the Terrible on the rampage. In a few overs McCarthy became a name to frighten shrieking children into strangulated silence. The balls sprang up from that recreation ground wicket like the dragon's teeth sown by Jason. The destroyer McCarthy, who crashed down the wickets of Watkins and Evans, and who baffled and beat Simpson, in a few overs switched the game South Africa's way for the first time, the very first time, since the opening over aeons ago—four days ago.

One hour left. Fifty-eight runs wanted. Four wickets to fall. That was the position—the lightning-lashed, meteor-pelted position—when Denis Compton and Roley Jenkins came together in the stand upon which English hopes stood or fell. They came together in a dusk-daunted hour; it might have been the last hour before the world sank like a bubble, to be lost in the depths of the solar system. And if that is over-fanciful there is no doubt at all that it was no hour in which batsmen could be expected to face fast bowlers in an important cricket match. Unless you had the eyes of a hawk, any glimpse you might have of the ball whizzing from bowler's hand to the twilit stumps was purely coincidental. You hadn't much less chance of spotting a V2 on the wing.

But Compton and Jenkins had the eyes of hawks, and the level nerve for just such a situation. At a run a minute they plodded on towards victory. A snip through the gully off McCarthy; a whisk wide of long-leg off Tuckett. After half an hour the game was almost on an even keel again.

And then the insatiable McCarthy crashed through. He hit Denis's wicket—and two runs later beat Jenkins with a ball that went from his bat to Wade, who gave tongue in a great appeal almost before his gloves had closed round the catch.

Everything was now set for the final scene. This climax to

the long, tense drama was shot through with moments of sheer harlequinade. But there was a fierce poetry in the air as well.

As Gladwin, tenth man in, walked to the wicket, he uttered immortal defiance to Dudley Nourse, South Africa's captain: "Coometh the hour—coometh the man!" He then proceeded to take guard and send up a catch which Lindsay Tuckett dropped at mid-on, before he had scored.

Poor Tuckett—to drop his vital catch, and then to be called on to bowl the final agonizing over! Opposite him is Bedser, white as a sheet. Eight runs are wanted. Eight! A huge total to prise out of a single over. The first ball is wide; it goes off Bedser's pads for a single. Probably in the whole history of cricket no man ever escaped from the business end of the pitch with greater relief.

The next ball goes to Gladwin's bat—and goes from it like sling-shot out of David's catapult. Four gilt-edged, twenty-two carat runs. The big and burly Gladwin rollicks down the pitch wagging his bat happily. This crisis holds no terrors for him—he ought to be in the Cabinet. Then come two more leg-byes. The match is tied.

And now the very pinnacle of the climax: the last ball of the game. Up runs Lindsay Tuckett, his arm swinging, his nice stride beautifully balanced. Down goes the fair head and over swings the arm. Time stands still. Then suddenly a crash of thunder from the crowd. Cliff Gladwin has jumped down the wicket, swinging his bat like a Fury. He misses—the ball hits his pad and bounds away. Alec Bedser is pounding up the pitch. The wicket-keeper is standing back—imagine it, standing back to this of all balls! There is a scramble, a flashing throw—and the wicket is broken. But the batsman is in—by inches. England has won!

England has won by two wickets, off the last ball of the match. Now, you writers of overdrawn thrillers in boys' magazines, what have you got to put against this bit of history? When did the best of you conceive a marrow-chiller to approach that final hour of real life?

As the game ends the South African team races and tussles for the souvenirs: the stumps, the ball, every precious bail. How long will it be before, in such circumstances, the fielding side considers the very pad off which the winning run is scored a legitimate perquisite?

But Cliff Gladwin wouldn't care if they did. He views the souvenir hunters with pitying disdain. "Aye," he says, mopping his brow. "You can have stoomps. We've got bloody match."

So ends Test cricket's most unforgettable day. The final minutes have been fraught with tragi-comedy as well as drama. C. H. Palmer, that exquisite batsman who is unlucky not to get a taste of a Test match during the tour, is the candid cameraman of the side. He has taken photographs of everybody and everything throughout the great crescendo of the game. Only—only in the ultimate fateful minutes, he runs out of film!

In the English dressing-room the strain has been almost unendurable. The door has been locked. The players sit silent, taut as fiddle strings.

And where is Denis Compton, the man who made victory possible with his superb first innings and his brave partnership with Jenkins which brought us within sight of the haven? Well, if you want to know, he couldn't bear to see the end—this modest hero blames himself for not having stayed on to make the winning hit. He's locked himself into the lavatory. It's some little time before he ventures out—to read the result in the faces of his team mates.

That was the Test match Denis will never forget. He still has nightmares about it sometimes.

The Photo Finish

(DECEMBER 16—20, 1948)

SOUTH AFRICA

FIRST INNINGS			SECOND INNINGS		
Rowan, E. A. B., c Evans, b Jenkins	7		c Compton, b Jenkins	...	16
Wynne, O., c Compton, b Bedser ...	5		c Watkins, b Wright	...	4
Mitchell, B., c Evans, b Bedser ...	27		b Wright	...	19
Nourse, A. D., c Watkins, b Wright	37		c and b Bedser ...	...	32
Wade, W. W., run out	8		b Jenkins	...	63
Begbie, D., c Compton, b Bedser ...	37		c Mann, b Bedser ...	...	48
Dawson, O. C., b Gladwin	24		c Compton, b Wright	...	3
Rowan, A. M., not out	5		b Wright	...	15
Tuckett, L., lbw, b Gladwin ...	1		not out	...	3
Mann, N., c Evans, b Gladwin ...	4		c Mann, b Compton	...	10
McCarthy, C., b Bedser	0		b Jenkins	...	0
Extras (b 3, lb 2, nb 1)	6		Extras (lb 5, b 1)	...	6
	161				219

ENGLAND

FIRST INNINGS			SECOND INNINGS		
Hutton, L., c McCarthy, b Rowan, A.	83		c Dawson, b Tuckett	...	5
Washbrook, C., c Wade, b Mann ...	35		lbw, b Mann	...	25
Simpson, R. T., c Begbie, b Mann	5		c Rowan, E., b McCarthy...	...	0
Compton, D., c Wade, b Mann ...	72		b McCarthy	...	28
Watkins, A., c Nourse, b Rowan, A.	9		b McCarthy	...	4
Mann, F. G., c E. Ryan, b Rowan, A.	19		c Mitchell, b McCarthy ...	...	13
Evans, T. G., c Wynne, b Rowan, A.	0		b McCarthy	...	4
Jenkins, R., c Mitchell, b Mann ...	5		c Wade, b McCarthy ...	...	22
Bedser, A. V., c Tuckett, b Mann ...	11		not out	...	1
Gladwin, C., not out	0		not out	...	7
Wright, D. V. P., c Tuckett, b Mann	0				
Extras (b 2, lb 12)	14		Extras (b 9, lb 10)	...	19
	253		(8 wkts.)	...	128

Bowling Analysis

ENGLAND

	O.	M.	R.	W.			O.	M.	R.	W.
Bedser	...	13.5	2	39	4	...	...	18	5	51	2
Gladwin	...	12	3	21	3	...	...	7	3	15	0
Jenkins	...	14	3	50	1	...	...	22.3	6	64	3
Wright	...	9	3	29	1	...	...	26	3	72	4
Compton	...	2	0	5	0	...	...	16	11	11	1
Watkins	...	3	0	11	0						

SOUTH AFRICA

	O.	M.	R.	W.			O.	M.	R.	W.
McCarthy	...	9	2	20	0	...	...	12	2	43	6
Dawson	...	3	0	16	0						
Tuckett	...	6	0	36	0	...	...	10	0	38	1
Rowan, A.	...	44	8	108	4	...	...	4	0	15	0
Mann	...	37.4	14	59	6	...	...	2	0	13	1

Chapter Five

THE PERFECT GAME

(M. P. DONNELLY)

OUTSTANDING athletes, like eminent portrait painters and uppity architects of mousetraps, are divisible into the usual three classes: they over-rate, appreciate, and under-rate their own importance. Neither you nor I are likely to know any of the first class; we came, for instance, too late on the scene to indulge in part-song about the hand which shook the hand of John L. Sullivan. The former member belonged to the Prince of Wales; the latter was accustomed to banging itself forcibly but not injuriously against the right thigh as a sign that it was now prepared to deliver what I am sure it would have described (if hands could speak) as the *quietus* to its privileged opponent.

We have, however, known one or two champions with their feet firmly planted in class two: the category which does not minimize its worth. I once, for example, met Jimmy Wilde having breakfast in a Glasgow hotel. He explained that he was up in Scotland managing a young contender for the nation's flyweight championship. I thoughtlessly remarked: "I hope he turns out to be as good as you were, Jimmy"; an observation which quite properly caused his eyes to protrude with astonishment and his tongue to retort with withering realism: "Well, I'm afraid that's hardly to be expected."

Among all the athletes I have known in my time, none is more remarkably self-effacing than Martin Donnelly. He reached his peak of self-depreciation as a rugby footballer. In the Varsity match of '46 he played a game which swung the match and gave him a moral right to an international

74

cap before the season was out. He was the automatic choice
for the stand-off half position in the Final Trial; and there,
as you might have been sure, his gifts for self-depreciation
worked a powerful spell against his self-determination. He
played an unimaginative game, a clockwork game, simply
because he could not believe that he had the right to dazzle
these outsize heroes with science.

After the match I diagnosed (and correctly) the mind of
the selectors into supposing that they were sure to drop him
from the order of battle. I wrote to him at once urging him
not to give up rugby, because I was sure he had it in him
to be an international player at two games, and I wanted the
happiness of basking in the friendship of such an immortal.
He replied that he wasn't thinking of doing any such thing.
He was going to continue to play football, not, it was true,
for the University side, which would certainly be a shade
presumptuous, but for the college. Almost before I had
digested this maddening missive the news came through
that England had reshuffled her backs against Ireland, and
Donnelly was in.

I did my best to forgive him his modesty about his football. After all, he would admit that he was familiar with
the elements of batsmanship, and it was always possible he
was frightened out of realizing his footballing proficiency by
a respect for the gigantic tribal gods of his race, such as
Porter and Gallagher. What would they say among the
penguin-dotted islands of the south, or under the volcanic
rocks of Taupo, if it was imagined that he was setting himself in rivalry to these Olympians?

I warmed my hands at the hope that he really appreciated
his own cricket. Quite soon I found myself vigorously clapping those hands as much to get them warm again as to
express appreciation of his achievements.

It fell to me to broadcast to New Zealand a little breezy
double talk with Martin the night after he had scored a
century in the Varsity match which had set old-timers
resuscitating Tip Foster for purposes of reverent comparison. It had taken him less than three hours to score 142 runs;
but before we went on the air he privately asked me not to

mouth inflated praise of his little effort, which he thought a rather poor performance. The trouble was, it seemed, that he had foolishly got himself out just when he was getting his eye in (he had scored his last 113 runs in an hour and three-quarters). And, above all, would I please refrain from drawing attention to his own low estimate of his achievement. As he had been lucky enough to get some runs, it might look rather conceited. At the risk of never hearing him run himself down to me again, I have decided to break this oath of secrecy after several years.

Small, well-knit, almost dormouse-like in his somnolent attitude to anything in sport that doesn't call for personal effort from him, Martin Donnelly has added since that summer a good deal to the history of the game he loves best. The very next year I heard two tributes paid to him which I suppose I might have used to bring on a bout of bashfulness sufficiently serious to cause him to give up cricket and go to earth in New Zealand. P. G. H. Fender said to me at Lord's (his hand carefully shielding the microphone) that he would rather watch Donnelly field at cover than so-and-so bat for England. And in Charles Fry's box I heard *The Times* correspondent pontificate: "The best bat in England is Martin Donnelly. The second-best bat in England is Walter Hammond."

Well, the golden opinions have been backed in the fulness of time by historic deeds. There were, as, of course, you know, centuries in the Gentlemen and Players match and the New Zealand Test at Lord's, as well as that famous inter-Varsity game. The sober defence combined with the hurricane driving have given us, in spite of the fact that most critics have developed writers' cramp in stating it, the nearest thing to Clem Hill since that half-pint maestro was hitting Barnes and Foster into the hawthorn hedges ringing the Adelaide ground.

Even so, there were moments when the critics wondered whether they hadn't overstated the case. Early last summer, for instance, one of the pleasantest of the writers for the London daily papers committed himself to the categorical statement that Donnelly was not the player he had been a year or two back. Punctually came the retort. A match-saving 64 at Headingley; a double century in the Lord's Test; and two match-saving innings at Manchester—nearly all completed after his side had lost four wickets for dangerously few runs, and seemed an odds-on chance to lose the match.

Not surprisingly, Martin Donnelly's match of a lifetime belongs to Lord's. It is no accident that it does, for the ground is to Martin a place apart, a mirage-glimpse of Xanadu in a dusty world. To him the ground, like none other in the world, has always been a challenge and an inspiration. A day of blazing sunshine, a huge crowd on its toes, and a tight match at Lord's: that, I am sure, is the background Martin would choose if, a hundred years hence, he could come back from the dead for a single midsummer day.

But the match of his lifetime, the game he remembers, had even more to it than that. It came at the end of golden weeks of summer with the years of the Second World War just over and thankfully cast aside. Martin had fought with the New Zealand Division, and it was good to replace Middle Eastern sandstorms and Italian icicles with fair and floral English August weather. Again the game came right on top of another match at Lord's in which he'd also been playing: a lovely tense struggle in which his team, Central Mediterranean Forces, had beaten a Lord's XI by a single wicket after two days of perfectly balanced struggle. Five days of Lord's! Five days of perfect weather decked out with hard-fought cricket enjoyed by vast, happy crowds with a new light of hope in their eyes.

And the match itself, England v. Dominions, was worthy of the occasion. Wisden was to call it "one of the finest games ever seen." A *Times* critic with more than sixty years' experience of Lord's was to write that never before had the great ground known such whirlwind hitting as this match produced—from first to last there were sixteen 6's in it. Again, not only was it thrilling cricket; it was a close and equal struggle.

Never in the three days did one side draw out of sight of the other; and by five-thirty on the last afternoon the game was so perfectly balanced that either side might win or lose it.

To Martin Donnelly this perfect match offered other advantages. It was—incredibly enough—his first sight of Learie Constantine in action. It was also the very first time in his life that he was to see Walter Hammond at the top of his form. This was strange. As a tot of 19, Martin was a member of the New Zealand team of 1937 against whom Hammond had hit three centuries. They weren't, however, imperishable memories. They were quite easily forgotten: even the century at Lord's was hardly more memorable than the fact that Len Hutton made his Test match début in this game, scoring 0 and 1. Indeed, looking back on that not very important or fiercely contested series, it is hard to remember much more than that the infant Donnelly was the only man to make any serious attempt to hold the side together when Goddard got amongst them at Manchester. Then their last six batsmen scored 7 runs between them, and Donnelly left the field unbeaten with 37 runs to his name.

The great match of 1945—the perfect game—began with a disappointment. Lindsay Hassett, the senior Australian in England, was ill just before the game began. The Dominions players met in the dressing-room and chose their own captain. They chose wisely in that they chose Constantine. He showed his appreciation of the compliment by winning the toss with consummate ease. What is more, he kept up this high standard of leadership throughout the game: his use of his two leg-breakers, Pepper and Cristofani, pulled the game out of the fire in the final hour.

He opened his batting with two left-handers: Craig, a hard-hitting South Australian, and Fell, of South Africa, fresh from having hit the New Zealand Services team for the best century scored on the Hove ground since prewar days. After several brisk overs of run-getting, Wright came on at the Nursery end and at once tricked Fell into giving Griffith what must have seemed an easy chance after the regular paratrooping catches he had been earning immortality by holding in the Fifth Victory Match with Australia at Old Trafford.

The Perfect Game

Then came J. Pettiford, an all-rounder of parts. The bowling of Jack Davies, dreamy stuff that floated about among the lower cloud wrack, looked innocent enough to him. He pivoted and swung into his hook: then walked gloomily home as the ball, all snakish scurry from the pitch, glanced off the edge of his bat into his wicket.

Meanwhile, Craig was playing as lightheartedly as if all was for the best in cloudcuckooland. He had cut Phillipson and Edrich with wristy zeal on the well-behaved wicket. He went out like a punctual automaton to smother the break against Wright, Davies and little blond Hollies, wheeling up and over to search the best-laid defences. In the end he lost his wicket when slashing Phillipson to cover.

It wasn't long afterwards that Hollies got Miller out for the third time in recent innings, while Constantine fell to Wright, who was bowling with that urgent hostility that has so often characterized his form in shorter matches of high-power intensity. Five of the best of them out for 109. Really there was only Martin Donnelly left of the front-line batsmen. No wonder Jim Langridge and Harold Gimblett, Jack Davies and Laurie Fishlock enjoyed a quiet, frisky game of catch before the next man came in.

This was the burly Cecil Pepper, Arthur Mailey's four-star special. Arthur always declared he once spent an entire blistering afternoon in Sydney watching Pepper bowl at nets; when, at the end of a display warranted to fillet a superman, Pepper still had enough energy left to knock the stumps down at the next net but two.

For a few overs Wright and Hollies forced Donnelly to play watchful, unadventurous cricket; but then, as it seemed, between one over and the next he found touch and began to let fly with a lighthearted disregard of the consequences which brought the game to glorious life. While Pepper flung his left foot forward and punched at the pitch of the ball, Donnelly started to drive Hollies as unconcernedly as if he was thrashing golf balls down the fairway of the shorter holes with a number two iron. When Phillipson bowled short, he leaned back towards his wicket and hewed him spurning away south of deep point or north of square-leg.

79

The two of them were bustling for runs. They twinkled
between wickets; they made forays down the pitch as if
sharp-set for boundaries. Then, when they'd been in command for a little more than an hour and a half and put on
120 between them, Pepper resolutely cut a ball into the
slips which was unemotionally pulled down out of very
thin air by Hammond.

I think it must have been about this time that I stood
respectfully by while Hendren and Sandham discussed who
was the best slip-field they'd ever come across during a joint
half-century of cricket in half-a-dozen countries. Or rather,
they didn't discuss: they proposed and seconded Hammond. At that point I interjected a demurrer on behalf of
Constantine; where did *he* come in? As if explaining the
obvious to a child, Hendren said patiently: "Constantine
is the best field in *any* position."

With Pepper gone, it was Donnelly against All England.
True, less than a week ago, Cristofani had staggered
humanity by lambasting the England bowling for the
season's most fantastic century at Old Trafford; but all one
could say now was that he appeared to have left the magic
bat behind in Manchester. He and Williams did their best
to sprint the punctual single off the last ball of every over,
to ensure that Donnelly batted non-stop. And for a last
flamboyant hour Donnelly darted and drove, drew back
and hooked, curved over the stumps and cut with the
wrists of a swordsman. Off one almost irreproachable over
from Hollies he hit 19 melodramatic runs; and was cool
enough to put the single just where it was needed to bring
him face to face with the bowler at the other end for the
next over. At last he went to his old rival, Hollies: last
man out and caught by the bowler running back to gather
in a drive aimed at the heart of Hendon. If you measure
these things by statistics (and there are scientists who subject the rainbow to the spectroscope), you recorded the facts
that in three hours of dominance Donnelly had hit twenty
boundaries: two of them steepling 6's. But if your motive
in going to watch a cricket match had some connection with
the aesthetic or the dramatic, you sat and rejoiced, hugging

your memories to your heart and gradually letting the dazzle fade out of your eyes.

The day ended, inevitably enough, on a piano note. Harold Gimblett was suffering from a strain and was therefore switched from his traditional place to a lower rank in the batting order. (And, incidentally, this grand hitter must have made his mark as an England fourth wicket if he had played for any other side but Somerset, where, unless he went in first, there was every chance that his usefulness would not be exploited.) Even without Gimblett, the opening bats were solid enough to daunt most bowlers; but in no time at all Constantine beat Jack Robertson, that perennial twelfth man for Test teams, with his slower ball, while Fishlock was caught off an off-break from the slow left-hander Ellis, bowling over the wicket. Phillipson, good enough to rank as an all-rounder, failed as a stop-gap, and England finished the day with three wickets down for 28.

Next morning the initiative remained with the Dominions. Billy Griffith had been sent in above his rank as fort-holder, and he gave enough evidence of his powers in this direction to prepare the thoughtful for his century as an opening bat when at last the finest practising wicket-keeper in the game was given a chance in a Test match against the West Indies. But re-slanting the game was beyond him or Gimblett, caught at deep mid-off when attempting to divest Cristofani's googlies of their claims to respect. And as for poor James Langridge, he suffered the humiliation of losing his wicket to a full toss which at nets he would have hit whistlingly beyond the outfield.

Six wickets for 96 didn't suggest that England was going to make a game of it. Still there were always Hammond and Edrich, known to be in touch from recent imposing achievements at Old Trafford.

Hammond gave the customers one dreadful moment when he flicked an outswinger from the fast bowler, R. G. Williams, through a thicket of slips, all of them apparently turned to stone, for the essential fifth of a second and no more. As soon as he had given this evidence of human frailty, Hammond settled down to dominate the game in the grand manner. Those who watched him at work in this match saw him at his immemorial best. He was an emperor in aspect. His batting was cast to type; and that is an advantage if you seek to be remembered as a portent of your generation. You may have the soul and the mind for the part, but the world will not recall you as the incarnation of Lady Macbeth if your person resembles a Max Beerbohm caricature of Queen Victoria.

Hammond was cast by nature to play the part of the king of batsmen. There was power in every unhurried movement. There was a nobleness about the execution of each act. He stood upright as if he disdained attack. He struck out like a captain among men; fearlessly and unhesitatingly. The ringing sound of his bat commanding boundaries past extra-cover or behind the bowler would have been enough to tell any blind man on the ground that he was in the presence of a magnifico.

He treated the new ball in a frankly cavalier spirit, and he did not forget to be particularly severe on the most dangerous bowler Cristofani, using his feet to him in a way which suggested that his cricket was an expression of sheer inner gaiety. One remembered Hammond at Adelaide, when Allen's team lost what was in effect its final chance of winning the Ashes in the last pre-war tour. One recalled the laborious measuring of swords with Fleetwood-Smith. The pensive preoccupation with O'Reilly's flight and spin. The small score he set up, as it were spillikin by spillikin, doubtless infused gloom and helplessness among his comrades: not so much by reason of its smallness, but because the manner of its making stamped on the least impressionable of cricketers the Herculean nature of the task in hand. And now here was a memory of Hammond to dissipate with rays of sunlight that grey fog of an innings.

Edrich backed him up as Sancho Panza backed up Quixote. He was missed in the slips off the fast bowler at 17, but later he played some vigorous strokes in the wide arc between long-on and square-leg. He was finally caught at slip off a drive with block-busting intentions.

England were 20 runs behind, and finished the day by

getting the first three Dominion wickets at a cost of 145. As we left the ground we told ourselves that the position was good for Constantine's side—and good for the spectators. The batsmen were well placed to force the game on the last day; and the batsmen concerned happened to be Keith Miller and Martin Donnelly.

And on the Tuesday morning the mood of the Dominions soon declared itself. Miller sprang at the bowling and shook the life out of it from the first over. Wright made him spar and back off more than once, but he released all his pent-up aggression at Hollies. Twice in an over he hit soaring sixers off booming straight drives. His score had stood at 61 when stumps were drawn on the previous night. Within ninety minutes he had raised it to 185. After Donnelly had been yorked by Wright, Constantine arrived to help Miller cram on the pace. It was a schoolboy's dream.

The two men went for the bowling not only with Rabelaisian appetites, but also with Rabelaisian wit. Hammond was forced to set a field for Jack Davies which contained no slip or gully; indeed, the nearest fieldsman seemed to be in Mesopotamia, while the farther bodies were pretty well astral. And there went Constantine, bestowing on the ball a pat which set the wicket-keeper twinkling to third man—and then having to shy it to the bowler who was backing up at the wicket-keeper's end.

With the game slipping from underfoot in flashing landslide, I should have decided to give the ball to James Langridge. So, too, did Hammond decide. If anyone could call the game to order it must be that experienced, hard-working master of his craft. Surely no one would dare subject solid James Langridge to the sort of treatment that had been going the rounds? It would be like asking Sir Alfred Munnings to participate in some surrealist romp.

Well, James Langridge's first over yielded three stratospheric sixers: two from Miller, shaking his bronzed mane back from his gleaming eyes, and one from the unemotional Constantine. In three-quarters of an hour the pair had added 117 between them: and this against pretty well the best bowling in England.

Before cracking Wright's faster ball into Langridge's palms at cover, Miller had hit seven sixers in his third century in four matches at Lord's during the summer. The biggest of them will be talked of almost as long as Albert Trott's classic stroke. It came off an inoffensive, indeed, well-behaved ball from Hollies—which found itself whirled away to seek shelter on the roof of the broadcasting hut above the England dressing-room. This was the innings which provoked *The Times* correspondent uncontrollably to admit that he had never seen hitting like this in sixty years' experience of Lord's.

But not only great batting had been seen. Less dazzling but shining with a steady radiance had been the bowling of Douglas Wright. How often in a decade one had wondered that he was not the most successful bowler of his day—how often one had attributed failure to his readiness to bowl just a shade faster than his break would warrant. Well, this day was his. On it his potential skill was splendidly manifest at last.

And still the sun shone and the game blazed up. There was to be another four and a half hours of it: each minute on tiptoe with excitement, each over electrically thrilling. Indeed, the beginning of England's innings contained a thrill that was three-parts shock. This paralysing misfortune was the loss of Fishlock who allowed himself to be run out off a no-ball. He of all batsmen had a right to expect that this eleventh hour might be his. He was sent to earth to lead counter-attacks in exactly this sort of crisis.

Meanwhile, the slow bowlers sustained the assault, pressed home the advantage. Gimblett began by boxing the compass. All round the ground spectators welcomed the arrival of brisk hits. He was exhibiting a form which promised rich rewards in the fullness of time.

But before his innings matured Pepper pushed back his stumps with a massive googly. Not for the first time in the game one had the feeling that Pepper is constitutionally designed for this class of cricket. He abounds in nerve; he is at a little better than his best when only the heroic will serve. His fine first innings was to be eclipsed before the game was out by his own efforts as a bowler who never lost his hostility in a match in which nearly every other was driven by something like *force majeure* into chancing his arm and hoping for the best—or at least crossing his fingers against the worst.

The robustness and coolness of Pepper are great assets. One look at him and you have made up your mind that this is the man for your money if the game is to finish in a very tight over on which victory and defeat depend. He gives you the same confidence you feel in a full-back who sniffs with unconcern at the spectacle of a ravening pack with the ball at their feet. Why Australia allows a player of these majestic proportions to be lured out of its Test cricket by the blandishments of the Lancashire League, passes comprehension. If English cricket had been mulcted by Australian money of two such cricketers as George Tribe and Cecil Pepper there would have been a howl in Old Trafford and Fog Lane demanding the nationalization of cricketers that could be heard in Lundy Island.

And now, once again, it was up to Hammond and Edrich. There was no mistaking Hammond's mood. This match had flashed, gleamed, glowed and sparkled with great innings from its first day to its last. You had only to spend three August days there to have seen Donnelly looking a better and more belligerent left-hander than Bardsley himself; and Miller vault on to the whirlwind where it had bucked Jessop; and Hammond himself step from his niche in the Parthenon to defy the lightnings. Now the hour had struck to eclipse all these deathless memories. Now the time was come to win the perfect match for his side.

His grandeur was undiminished by the accidents of his innings' beginning. He swept his lovely arc of a mashie-shot into the deep, and the red-hot ball fell through the nerveless fingers of some hapless fieldsman. Again the towering straight drive rose, faltered on its run up the sky, fell, and was fumbled, and dented the turf before the most unhappy feet in all the world. These things happened before the maestro had reached 50.

The picayune innings put on weight; it grew up like a god.

There went a long, low-hit, screaming straight drive off Cristofani; two hops, and it hit the pavilion rails, to bounce back so near the bowler that neither mid-on nor mid-off stirred to retrieve it for him. Here, off Pepper's rare long-hop, came the queer scything shot to long-leg—one of the very few strokes to the on with which the Master of the Off-side indulged the groundlings. And anon the consummation of batsmanship—the cover-drive with the left foot flung challengingly across the pitch, the arms in furious upward sweep—the stroke of Hector. Two hours of him; and for the seventh time in his life two centuries in a match, before his radar misjudged Cristofani and Bremner skimmed the bails while his heel was in no man's land.

The valiant Edrich again supported him bravely until the elfin cross-bat that lurks behind his gravest demeanour poked its head out and brought about his undoing.

And even after that England sent out foray after foray, counter-attack upon counter-attack; humble camp followers who swung the fortunes of Bannockburn were as nothing to the Forlorn Hope who breasted the rampart in the last hour of this game. Griffith and Davies—who had ever thought of them as batsmen dominating a game in which the attack showed greater skill and determination than we see at Lord's in a score of Test matches?

There was always a chance, while these two defied the bowling, with stout forward strokes and an occasional late cut off Ellis to show to which end of the batting order you should look for elegant craftsmanship. The runs bustled up. In half an hour more than 40 had been made; if only the partnership could survive for an hour the tide would have turned. Well, it lasted for just two minutes short of that time, and when, having helped to add 83 runs, Billy Griffith fell gloriously to a catch nonchalantly pouched by Pepper, we knew at last that the chance of victory had vanished. Three-quarters of an hour left, and 74 runs to get; England could no longer win, though she might still save the game.

But the field was attacking now. It advanced like Birnam Wood on the foe. A whisk and a flash of white shirt—and Phillipson's wicket blew up from Constantine's clean throw from cover. And then Pepper strode down to the wicket in his seven-league boots, ducked, and flung up his heavily muscled right arm. Watch that flight, Jack Davies, king of army psychologists though you are! His wrist is innocently assuring you that the ball will spin from leg to off; knowing his dark mind, you expect it to do the exact opposite. And while your hesitant bat reaches forward, your bails are airborne by the double bluff after all.

Fifteen minutes now, and only Hollies and Wright to save England. An over from Ellis: blocked and padded-up against every perilous ball of it. An over from Pepper, kept at bay with the centre of the bat, or the edge of the bat, or (adopting the technique of the young Dutch hero against the hardly more hostile waters beyond the dyke) with the width of the thumb.

And then, while silly-point and silly mid-on crouch as avid as begging puppies, Constantine gives the ball to Cristofani. The first and second balls are survived; the third breaks through, and Wright's wicket and the hopes of England are scattered on the grass.

Beaten by 45—with eight minutes to go! So ends the great game played between an eleven which might have been picked to represent All England, and a team containing seven youngsters who never played first-class cricket before the war, and whose names have now pretty well been forgotten by the first-class game. The moral? Well, they were all Australians; of the race that says: "Cricket? I've had a game or two in my time; perhaps only two, but give me a pair of flannels and a bat, and I'll play for you at Lord's."

Half an hour after the game ended, several friends of Martin Donnelly (from whom I culled this footnote) were refreshing themselves in a pub near the ground. There entered a pink-faced, happy old gentleman, fanning himself with his panama hat. They hadn't, he supposed, any whisky? Yes, they had. Not a *double* whisky? Certainly; and he could have iced soda-water if he preferred it.

He raised the glorious draught to his lips. "I've just seen," he said to no one in particular and to the saloon bar in general, "the perfect cricket match. There were four cen-

turies—marvels, all of them. There were lots and lots of
sixers. Douglas Wright was bowling. Constantine was fielding.
It was Lord's and the sun shone all the time, and the war's
over." Then he drank his whisky and soda, put the glass
down carefully on the counter—and fell dead.

There was one old gentleman who knew the perfect
moment to return to the Pavilion.

The Perfect Game

(AUGUST 25—28, 1945)

THE DOMINIONS

FIRST INNINGS		SECOND INNINGS	
Fell, D. R., c Griffith, b Wright ...	12	b Davies	28
Craig, H. S., c Davies, b Phillipson	56	c Hammond, b Davies ...	32
Pettiford, J., b Davies	1	b Wright	6
Miller, K. R., lbw, b Hollies ...	26	c Langridge, b Wright ...	185
Donnelly, M. P., c and b Hollies ...	133	b Wright	29
Constantine, L. N., c Hollies, b Wright	5	c Fishlock, b Hollies ...	40
Pepper, C. G., c Hammond, b Wright	51	c Robertson, b Hollies ...	1
Cristofani, D. R., lbw, b Edrich ...	6	b Wright	5
Williams, R. G., lbw, b Wright ...	11	c Hammond, b Wright ...	0
Ellis, R. S., b Wright	0	st Griffith, b Hollies ...	0
Bremner, C. D., not out	1	not out	0
Extras (lb 3, w 2)	5	Extras (b 1, lb 8, nb 1) ...	10
	307		336

ENGLAND

FIRST INNINGS		SECOND INNINGS	
Fishlock, L. B., c Pettiford, b Ellis	4	run out	7
Robertson, J. D., lbw, b Constantine	4	c Fell, b Pettiford	5
Langridge, J., lbw, b Cristofani ...	28	b Pepper	15
Phillipson, W. E., b Pepper	0	run out	14
Griffith, S. C., c Bremner, b Williams	15	c Pepper, b Pettiford ...	36
Hammond, W. R., st Bremner, b Pepper	121	st Bremner, b Cristofani ...	102
Gimblett, H., c Pettiford, b Cristofani	11	b Pepper	30
Edrich, W. J., c Pepper, b Cristofani	78	c Pepper, b Ellis	31
Davies, J. G. W., lbw, b Pepper ...	1	b Pepper	56
Wright, D. V. P., lbw, b Pepper ...	0	b Cristofani	0
Hollies, E., not out	0	not out	0
Extras (b 7, lb 6, w 2, nb 2) ...	17	Extras (b 6, lb 5, nb 4) ...	15
	287		311

Bowling Analysis

ENGLAND

	O.	M.	R.	W.		O.	M.	R.	W.
Phillipson ...	16	2	40	1	...	2	1	1	0
Edrich ...	9	1	19	1	...	3	0	13	0
Wright ...	30	2	90	5	...	30.1	6	105	5
Davies ...	22	9	43	1	...	13	3	35	2
Hollies ...	20.2	3	86	2	...	29	8	115	3
Langridge ...	6	1	24	0	...	8	0	57	0

THE DOMINIONS

	O.	M.	R.	W.		O.	M.	R.	W.
Miller ...	1	0	2	0	...	5	0	28	0
Williams ...	22	4	49	1	...	2	0	11	0
Constantine ...	15	2	53	1	...	6	0	27	0
Pepper ...	18	3	57	4	...	33	13	67	3
Ellis ...	4	3	4	1	...	20	4	54	1
Cristofani ...	23.3	4	82	3	...	21.3	1	64	2
Pettiford ...	5	0	23	0	...	14	3	45	2

Chapter Six

TO THE LAST BALL

(L. E. G. AMES)

IN a quiet way Leslie Ames, bronzed of skin and with the most melting brown velvet eyes ever seen off the face of a young stag, has achieved most of the baubles of a cricketing career that all boys dream of and one old man in a million can look back upon. He has hit up his 35,000 runs; has topped 3,000 in a single season; has scored a double century in Gentlemen and Players; has hit a 100 against Australia at Lord's; and is the only man who twice won the Lawrence Trophy for the fastest 100 of the season.

But even these fabulous deeds barely touch the fringe of the massive fabric of his achievement. Of recent years the violoncello of his driving (outbooming even Hammond's lowest register) has bewitched us to such an extent that we are apt to forget that he had the fingers of a surgeon—a foot long and with an eye at the end of each—in ancient days when he performed primarily as a wicket-keeper. Indeed, last season at Canterbury I met one excited schoolboy who stopped purring over his autograph to point out to a contemporary bent on exchange and barter that Ames was a collector's piece "because years ago, before we were born, this chap's father put up the record for the number of chaps got out by a wicket-keeper in a single season." Except for a natural confusion over the generations (this man's father was his father's son, to be precise), that schoolboy was dead right. In 1928 Leslie Ames beat by a huge margin the long-standing record of the number of wicket-keepers' wickets, and in the next season he licked his own record.

While he was doing this sort of thing he was also making runs in quantities no wicket-keeper had approached since the history of cricket began. In 1928, for instance, the year of his first record, he added another to the roll of honour by establishing himself as the first to do the wicket-keeper's double of 1,000 runs and a hundred wickets. And he did the deed so emphatically that he did not lay down his bat that season till he had scored more than 1,900 runs. To make sure you appreciate just how good he was, the point must be made that he got his runs never less than magnificently and very often when his side was crying out for succour. For instance, one of his eight Test centuries was gloriously achieved against the West Indies after he had come to the wicket with the scoreboard showing four men out for 26.

No batsman in the game, not even Badcock on a fast Australian wicket or Bradman at Lord's, ever appeared to carry a heavier bat into battle, and then to flay the bowling with it as if it weighed nothing at all. His wrists were true and he cut with the flourish and the cleanness of an amateur at the time of the Boer War, but it was as a hitter into the deep with a bat with a lofted face that he will be remembered.

And wrongly, I think. The essence of the man in his prime was that he was non-stop. He batted and made 141; then he kept wicket and caught two and stumped one; then he batted again and made 68; then he finished the game by stumping one and catching two. That would be a typical Ames' match. An all-rounder? Something more than that. An all-rounder when he has finished batting is only asked to be active—to bowl—at one end at a time. But for Leslie Ames the game went on at its most concentrated for every ball of the enemy's innings.

Since he played his first cricket at Folkestone for Harvey Grammar School, to the September of 1939 when he gave up the game to join the R.A.F., emerging six years later as a Squadron Leader, he took part in a score of undying matches on which he imprinted his hallmark, any one of which might have been the game of his choice. You might have expected him to name the Second Test, fifteen years ago, when he and Leyland stemmed an avalanching collapse against the bowling of Chipperfield. Or the Old Trafford Test in the same season, when much the same thing happened against other attackers in that fine Australian team. Or the final Test at the Oval when he collapsed in agony at the wicket when at last an Englishman had been found to face—indeed to outface—the Australian bowling. Or it might have been the Lord's Test of 1938, when he and Hammond established a new sixth-wicket record. Or perhaps you would have backed the Durban Test that winter, when he set up another record with Hammond's assistance.

But his choice falls on none of these games. It belongs to a later chapter of the epic of his career: to the summer of 1949, when in his forty-fifth year the old champion played the dominating part in a game which for the sheer, exquisite agony of excitement matches the Durban Test match of the winter before. In a word, it was the match between Kent and Warwickshire in last summer's blazing July at Maidstone. The final over of that game was as fantastic and as marrow-freezing as the final over of Cobden's match, but though the latter is quoted in the Long Room at Lord's every time a game works its way towards a moderately tight finish, nothing more than the bare bones of the former result found its way into the daily papers.

Both Kent and Warwickshire were captained by professionals in this great game. Kent's regular skipper was down with influenza, and Ames took over from him, while "Tom" Dollery, a solid, calm and majestic replica of John Bull himself, led Warwickshire as usual. The two men were to play by far the largest part in their sides' fortunes, and superbly as they were to perform with the bat, their captaincy was not the least of their contributions to the unyielding three-day battle.

The game began with a sensation. Ames having won the toss, red-haired L. Todd, for long so nearly an England all-rounder, faced Warwickshire's fast bowler, Pritchard. But not for long. The ball flicked from the pitch with whiplash speed, flashed beneath the gliding white blade, and rocked the leg stump back on its heels.

0—1—0. It was the hand-tailored moment for the entry of L. E. G. Ames. An accident now, and Maidstone Week must have hurried to a tragic ending. But those brown velvet eyes in the mahogany oval of face showed no sign of trepidation. Pritchard and Grove continued to bowl vehemently, but that aristocratic bat, Arthur Fagg, and Ames the grandee continued on their imperturbable way. Fagg was particularly disdainful of Pritchard's claims to respect. Four times before the score had reached 30 he hit him to the leg boundary.

An over or two later, after an hour's play, there came a double change. Townsend bowled in Pritchard's place, and Abdul Hafeez Kardar sent down his flighted off-spinners instead of Grove. The new bowlers made not the slightest impression. The batsmen defended coolly for five balls of an over, and unemotionally cracked the sixth to the boundary. Ames off-drove Kardar with luxuriating ease, pulled a full toss to the wide open spaces, and, with riving wrists, cleft the populated gulley. Four runs each time.

By lunch the pair were on terms with the clock, and the one remaining point of interest in the morning's attack was the amount of swerve the seam bowlers were able to impart to the ball. Emmott Robinson, umpiring, deposed that he remembered noting the same phenomenon in his playing days: he attributed it to the thick ring of trees surrounding the lovely field.

After lunch the partnership appeared likely to become as rooted a feature of the landscape as the trees themselves, or the winking white tents with their brilliant banners limp against the breathless skyline. Ames and Fagg! They were a sempiternal part of the scene, like the sunlight and the line of the Downs behind the scoreboard. And then, unimaginably, Ames reached toward Kardar, touched the ball, and heard the rattle of shaken stumps in the parched earth.

Once things start happening, out there in the middle, we never seem able to doze off again. The game *will* keep breaking in. There, for instance, goes Arthur Fagg, surely not due to shed his wicket till the trees shed their leaves in the autumn, flicking away at Kardar, to see Tom Dollery's yawning left hand engulf the ball with the finality of a landslide.

After that the spectacle became inevitably less distinguished. Edrich exhibited a toughness wasted on mere cricket. When he had made 19 he hooked a ball from Pritchard on to his own head—a contortionist's skill which would have earned him a curtain at a command performance. Then he was smitten over the knuckles. Then, to prove that this assault and battery was a two-way traffic, he airily cut Pritchard to the boundary—airily indeed, for not the tallest slip of them all could get his fingertips to the ball.

But just before the 200 came up Edrich was bowled, and though Hearn, dropped in the slips at 40, lived long enough to reach his 50, there was not much body to the rest of the innings. The wicket-keeper, six feet tall and a left-handed bat, playing in his first match for the country, was about the best of a modest troupe. A fine performer, this Derek Ufton! At twenty-one, he is a Dartford boy and not so long ago was a star in his grammar school team.

Both Grove and Pritchard had on this sultry day at least the ninety-nine per cent of perspiration called for by the recipe for genius, while Kardar, as all through the season, seemed to old-timers to have a reserve of subtlety as bottomless as Percy Fender's in days gone by.

When shortly before six o'clock the Warwickshire innings began, it was hardly behind Kent's own opening act in melodramatic quality. In Martin's first storming over, Gardner flashed at an outswinger and peppered the embattled Edrich about the shoulder as he stood brooding inoffensively in the gulley. An hour later Edrich himself put his little matter right. He bowled a ball with which Gardner again threatened the gulley, and this time Hearn picked off the catch. Before the day ended with Warwickshire 201 runs behind and eight wickets in hand, Townsend had been caught in Wright's posse on the leg side.

The first day's play had been close and interesting, but the play on the second day was downright absorbing, assuming always that you had room for any interests above self-pity in a heat wave that would have daunted a fugitive from the Foreign Legion. It began with a little foray promoted by Ord against the person of Douglas Wright. First

he cut him shrewdly to the tent-fringed boundary. Then he
cast him round to leg with equal assurance and success.
Then he feathered him daintily to the leg side, and, as all
the groundlings were parting their hands for a good smack
of applause for his third fine boundary, Ufton skimmed out
at full length to take the catch just about where the dew
had evaporated above the grass.

Now came the stand of the innings, between the cautious,
well-groomed Taylor and Tom Dollery playing as if life was
real, life was earnest, but also as if it were, almost against the
grain, worth having got oneself entangled in. There was no
playing fast and loose when Douglas Wright came bouncing
up on the crest of that run that might have won a hop,
skip and jump title at the White City. Down the line of the
break, if you please, and give the golden-hearted wicket a
pat on the head between overs. The time will come when
Wright is rested, and you will no longer have to find a
way to hit a googly humming like a peg-top through a
ravenous field.

But even when Edrich and Dovey come to bowl there is
no occasion to go gay, though a discreet cut off the latter
helps Taylor on his way to that half-century against this
determined attack that is taking about as long to consummate
as most centuries. But Taylor is there at last with a 2 to leg
off Edrich, and when Dollery (a little more sedate) follows
him by means of a pull to the boundary off Wright, the pair
have added a 100 runs in a couple of not quite interminable hours.

They plod along till lunch and beyond. And then—can
someone have been infiltrating underdone beef behind that
John Bull façade?—for after lunch, Tom Dollery begins to
thwack out to left and right with a zeal that would have
satisfied Lord Palmerston. Wright is wheedled past fine-leg,
and then massively hit, under an umpire skipping like a little
hill, in a mood that Alfred Mynn would have appreciated.
The score is whisking ahead at the rate of nearly a run a
minute. Sparkling stuff this, of which grandfathers will
remind helpless tots when batting has been nationalized and
the defensive game has an Act of Parliament to authorize it

during the interval between service in the mines and compulsory cremation.

You would have said that Taylor and Dollery were two cricketing certainties for centuries. And you would have been dead wrong. The tireless hostility of Douglas Wright was to take toll of both of them. Taylor at least had never dominated the most persistent and dangerous bowler Kent had sent into action since Tich Freeman packed his cricket bag and put up the latch in the house called "Dunbolin." There had been not many confident boundary strokes by which this steady batsman had enriched himself off those fast-medium leg-breaks and clueless googlies. When Wright forced him back and hit his pads in front of the wicket, Taylor had given four hours of patient service to his side. Without him they might as well have gone back to Birmingham.

Half an hour later Dollery died a hero's death. He unleashed a statuesque leg-sweep, and Crush, on the perimeter, made a mouthful of a fine catch. This mortal blow descended upon Warwickshire at three o'clock. Not only was half the side gone, but the remaining half promised very little indeed. That promise was amply fulfilled. In less than an hour's time the team was out for an addition of 32 runs. Kardar was absent: wasting his finger-spin on a pen to bamboozle the omniscience of the Oxford examiners.

The main lesson of the innings was that Douglas Wright remained about the most dangerous bowler you could *not* wish to meet in a three-day match. If you wanted to score fast enough to make runs off him to meet the exigencies of the game, you must take more risks than any serious margin of error would allow. Observe how, when conflict was joined in a match of this kind, he reserved himself to do his magnificent best against the top-class batsmen. Dovey could collect a whole game-bagful of the minimus.

In the final hours of the second day Kent crammed on full sail. If they were to win now, the enemy was not so much Warwickshire as the clock. While Todd, reaching down the pitch, was bowled by a superb ball, and Fagg was avidly snapped up at the wicket, Ames was on the hunt for runs from the moment he off-drove a flawless ball from Grove for the first boundary of his innings. And while Hearn made classical defensive strokes that might have come out of a blue-print for batsmanship, Leslie was dipping his left shoulder to propel the ball wherever there was room to swing a cat in the deep field. He took boundaries off Grove behind the covers and past the nose of deep mid-wicket. In the seventies he hooked the same bowler for his first sixer, and before the day ended swept Pritchard billowingly to long-leg as if a strong wind had broken out to fill the Kentish spin-naker. In two and a quarter hours before Emmott Robinson grudgingly pocketed the bails, he scored 99 runs, giving his side a lead of 163 with seven wickets to fall. An impregnable position, of course; but how to turn it into a winning one, remembering that this was but a three-day match?

You could be sure of one thing—those brown velvet eyes closed calmly in sleep on the Monday evening as soon as the head that wore Kent's crown settled easily on its pillow. Without a feature of his nervous system displaced, Ames began on the Tuesday morning with the immediate task of raising his score from 99. And at that he was within measur-able distance of failing (if to score 99 may be so described). The second ball of the morning hit him squarely on the pad, turning Grove the bowler into the agonized incarnation of a question mark. For a long time the whole immemorial scene shimmered in the heat haze; then the bowler withdrew to the limits of his run to try again. Once more the red flicker, the spurring of the khaki pitch, the white flash of the bat—and once more the howl of appeal. This time the wicket-keeper tossed the ball like a Shrove Tuesday pancake, so confident was he of his catch. Again—silence. Back went Grove to the job in hand, and down came a good-length ball that Ames turned coolly to long leg, and there was the century clicking up on the scoreboard behind extra cover.

And now Ames ran amok. He hooked Pritchard to the boundary once and again, cut and pulled Grove, and then set about Kardar, bowling first fast and then slowly indeed, in the latter's place. A sixer went over one of the tents; and then came a skier to mid-off. It zoomed high enough to give Pritchard time to recollect his past life in detail; but he stood

97

his ground like a man with an unblemished conscience and fastened himself upon the catch.

Ames had scored 160. The runs had been made (and made briskly) exactly when quick runs alone could keep the close-fought battle alive. More than 90 had come from boundary hits; and the innings was the highest and the best he had hit during the summer.

Before Kent were out, there was to be another sensation. Pritchard is a fast bowler always seriously to be reckoned with in this class of cricket, though it is unlikely he would keep batsmen who cut, or perhaps lost, their milk teeth on Lindwall in any prolonged state of apprehension. He can swing the ball both ways, and he has the merit of harping on the stumps all the time he bowls. In the previous season he had been the second most successful taker of wickets in our first-class game, and he had annexed his first hat-trick. Now he achieved another. Phebey, who had shown vigour in straight-driving Kardar to the boundary, chopped late at his fastest ball, and could not parry again before the bails had fallen. Then Crush tried to pull the next ball to the on and the substitute fielding at square-leg was ready for him. Now it was Ufton's turn. It is a long way to the wicket on a boiling day with eleven men wishing you further. It is hard when you take guard to remember what some friend of the family was explaining as you buckled your pads on—that Pritchard has a knack of hat-tricks, didn't he do one against Leicester only last summer?

And then down comes the ball: a dazzling split-second in mid-air and then sharply rising to the bat. There goes the groping shot—and there is the ball snapped up in the leg-trap and tossed high against the midday sun.

His own blazing century and Pritchard's hat-trick would have been enough to make any day's play memorable, and Ames could not know when he declared Kent's innings closed at 300 that the best was yet to be. There were three hours, all but a few minutes, for Warwickshire to get the 277 they needed to win. With Douglas Wright in the lists against them, they would be a courageous side if they did not allow the game to congeal into a draw. To their credit, they went for the runs from the first ball of Martin's first over.

Dollery had changed his batting order, opening with Gardner and Ord. The latter, next to his captain and Martin Donnelly among the top-weights of the county's batting strength, was flauntingly adventurous. Almost at once he was dropped by Phebey off a flailing cut, but he did not renounce the stroke and was soon scoring boundaries with it. Again, when Wright went on (after 30 runs had been rattled off in the first twenty minutes), he regarded a leg-trap with three fieldsmen leaning forward almost within reach of the bat as just another challenge. A well-judged hook made them fall apart like skittles in an alley.

With the 50 up in little more than half an hour, that leg-trap claimed Gardner as its first victim. With the previous ball he had given Edrich, at fine-leg, the sort of chance that even the Recording Angel would hardly hold against one.

Townsend lost no time in getting to the middle, and not much in getting back again. In his eight minutes of action he both cut and hooked Wright to the boundary, and hustled 16 runs on to the board. Ord being caught and bowled off the next ball, Dollery and Kardar were at the wickets at lunchtime, and Dollery had already begun to show aggressive intentions towards Wright.

Warwickshire had made 92 runs in little over an hour. They had lost three good batsmen, but they had kept faith with the clock.

The pace was not maintained after lunch—it was increased. Martin was so unwise as to unleash a no-ball in the general direction of Dollery's leg stump. That was 6 runs less to be got. But where Dollery was concerned, they didn't have to be no-balls. He whaled boundary after boundary off Martin, and in the first half-hour after the interval, when a man could be forgiven for getting his eye in, advanced his score from 18 to 50.

The bowling was to his liking, the situation to his taste. There really seemed no reason to suppose that anyone could get him out. Doubtless he would be there when the last strawberry had been eaten in the most bulging of the marquees, majestically hammering the bowling, as if it were a defaulter on the Stock Exchange, till the final run was wrung from the attack.

Meanwhile, all Kent's work wasn't being done by the bowlers. A flashing return from Edrich to the bowler would, if fielded, have cut off Dollery in his prime. In times of crisis cricketers resemble Bourbons rather than elephants—they are apt to learn nothing and forget nothing, while their memories are less than inexhaustible. Thus, just after this awful peril had been averted, Kardar was lost in the self-same trap. Ames fielded the ball in a flash: his return to the bowler was swift and accurate, and the most dangerous partnership had shivered its timbers.

There was always danger while Dollery lived; and Wolton, his new partner, entered into the game in the same sanguine mood. He showed his teeth in hooking Dovey to the ropes, and then showed and showed again a cultured square-cut off Edrich. By this time Warwickshire, with only four men out, had 260 on the board. The match seemed almost over. Another 17 to get; with the batsmen buoyantly set and the bowlers flagging at last, there could be no other end to the game.

Ames had taken off Edrich and put Martin on to bowl his tearaway stuff. There were those in the crowd who viewed this tactic with despair—one or two were even unkind enough to attribute it to the blazing heat of the afternoon. Certainly Martin in both innings had runs scored off him freely enough, and he had not so far been fortunate enough to take a wicket. Was he *really* the man to set up against this match-winning partnership of Dollery and Wolton who had added 70 runs in half an hour? And then —crash, whizz, bang—in one minute Martin had wiped out both Dollery and Wolton. The captain grazed the ball as it flashed past wide of the off stump, and Derek Ufton flung himself over to make a catch which in importance and brilliance few men can have surpassed in their first big game. Then, one run later, Martin bowled Wolton.

What about Martin now—and what about Ames as the master strategist? The hostile critics forgot to apologize— perhaps they were too tense to be able to wag their dry tongues at all. For now the score was 263 for six wickets. Was it possible? Well, hardly. How could it be? Only 14 runs wanted; and four wickets to get them. This was first-class cricket, the real dyed-in-the-wool thing. Not a hectic boys' school story in some wish-fulfilling magazine of your youth.

And then Dovey bowled Pritchard. Two hundred and sixty-three for seven. Miracles were possible, after all. One must admit that they had become just possible.

And then Grove swung his hearty bat at Dovey and the ball soared towards the boundary. Towards it—but not to it. Aitcheson, a substitute fielding in place of Crush, who had pulled a leg muscle, was under it. His knees did not bend, nor did they knock. He was of the stuff of which the great substitutes are made—of the breed of Copley himself. His hands shut inexorably over the ball.

Out went Grove; and in came Taylor to join Spooner in the ninth-wicket stand. Martin took the ball again, and off his over Spooner hit a determined boundary on the leg side.

At last the final over (from Dovey) arrived with 5 runs wanted. Five runs, the last pair but one at the wicket—six balls to go. Miracles *must* happen now—only miracles *could* happen.

Here came the first ball! Taylor lifted it to mid-on and Martin held the catch.

In came the last man, Phillip Bromley, eighteen years old and on leave from the R.A.F. He had shown promise already in this match as an off-break bowler with a polished action, but he never had any pretensions to expertise as a batsman.

But he was not the only man on the field who was nervous. Off the second ball of the over there was a chance of stumping. None of us would have taken it, on our best days —but oh, the irony of it, to miss this little chance after you have caught Ord and Dollery in the match off chances which Godfrey Evans, away keeping wicket for his country, might have been forgiven for missing.

Off the third ball, the haplessly happy Bromley got a single. More important still, he got to the other end.

The fourth ball came down; and Spooner whisked it away to fine-leg, as if he had been Ranjitsinhji. Two more balls to come—and 3 runs wanted.

Down came the fifth ball. It hit Bromley on the pad. There was a howl for l.b.w.—met with stony silence. There was also a quick, scurried leg-bye.

The last ball now. The last ball of the match. Two runs wanted—one wicket to fall. It was straight enough. Spooner got his bat to it and played it down the line of the wicket. Dovey put his hand over it as if it might evaporate in the air.

That is that. A draw; Warwickshire needing 2 to win with the last pair in.

But what a game—what cut and thrust, what a hearty see-sawing to and fro from the first over to the last. What captaining on both sides—and what leadership! Precept and example —the strategist at the head of the commando, the man who laid the subtle plans in the vanguard of the assault.

It shouldn't, of course, have been a draw. It should have been a tie. Nothing less would have done justice to the high endeavour of both sides.

The Homeric game ends; and the champions pack their bags and depart. They speak to each other not in deathless language to mirror an immortal match, but rather with Hazlitt's self-control after Bill Neat had beaten the Gasman in the great fight of long ago. "Pretty good" about sums up such famous days to the men who stood up to the clash of arms in the heat of battle.

"Good game, Les."

"It was that, Tom—lovely game."

"Don't know when I played in a better."

The cricketers take themselves off, while there are still a couple of hours of sunlight, to catch the trains that, like time and tide, will wait for no man; not even for a definite result in the Kent v. Warwickshire match. Tomorrow Warwickshire must be in Birmingham to play Northants.

They are pulling the tents down on the Mote ground, and the swallows are wheeling where the shadow of fine-leg grew long and Gothic in yesterday evening's sunlight. The great game is but a memory; over and done with and unforgettable as Cobden's match, or the Tests of 1902, or the games played on the knoll above the beech hangers by the Hambledon men.

To the Last Ball

(JULY 23—26, 1949)

KENT

FIRST INNINGS		SECOND INNINGS	
Todd, L. J., b Pritchard	0	b Grove	10
Fagg, A. E., c Dollery, b Kardar ...	68	c Spooner, b Pritchard ...	24
Ames, L. E. G., b Kardar	69	c Pritchard, b Kardar ...	160
Hearn, P. c Spooner, b Grove ...	59	st Spooner, b Kardar ...	19
Phebey, A. H., c Townsend, b Grove	1	b Pritchard	44
Edrich, B., b Pritchard	18	lbw, b Grove	12
Ufton, D. G., not out	27	c Grove, b Pritchard ...	0
Crush, E., c Spooner, b Pritchard ...	7	c sub, b Pritchard	0
Dovey, R. R., c Spooner, b Pritchard	0	not out	3
Wright, D. V. P., b Grove	6		
Martin, J. W., c Pritchard, b Grove	0	c Walton, b Kardar ...	14
Extras (b 2, lb 6, nb 2)	10	Extras (lb 10, w 1, nb 3)	14
	265	(9 wkts. dec.) ...	**300**

WARWICKSHIRE

FIRST INNINGS		SECOND INNINGS	
Taylor, K. A., lbw, b Wright ...	89	c Martin, b Dovey	2
Gardner, F. C., c Hearn, b Edrich ...	24	c Hearn, b Wright	27
Townsend, A., c Martin, b Wright ...	1	c Phebey, b Wright ...	16
Ord, J. S., c Ufton, b Wright ...	10	c and b Wright	25
Dollery, H. E., c Crush, b Wright ...	95	c Ufton, b Martin	118
Spooner R. T., not out	37	not out	6
Wolton, A. V., b Dovey	4	b Martin	26
Bromley, P. H., c Hearn, b Wright ...	4	not out	1
Grove, C. W., b Dovey	4	c sub, b Dovey	0
Pritchard, T. L., b Dovey	0	b Dovey	1
Kardar, A. H., absent	0	run out	40
Extras (b 5, lb 15, w 1)	21	Extras (b 4, lb 7, w 1, nb 1)	13
	289	(9 wkts.) ...	**275**

Bowling Analysis

WARWICKSHIRE

	O.	M.	R.	W.		O.	M.	R.	W.
Pritchard	31	2	96	4	...	26	2	97	4
Grove	29.3	10	52	4	...	19	4	79	2
Townsend	15	3	32	0	...	8	0	32	0
Kardar	22	7	60	2	...	20.3	3	78	3
Bromley	6	2	15	0					

KENT

	O.	M.	R.	W.		O.	M.	R.	W.
Martin	26	7	59	0	...	21	4	89	2
Crush	15	2	43	0	...	4	0	16	0
Wright	38	11	96	5	...	15	0	77	3
Edrich	9	1	24	1	...	6	0	27	0
Dovey	21.4	8	46	3	...	15	1	53	3

Chapter Seven

REVENGE AT ADELAIDE

(MAURICE TATE)

IN the Press box at Test matches I like to sit next to
Maurice Tate, even if his comments rival whatever is
going on out there in the middle for sheer entertainment
and educative value. He pulls at his huge pipe, shuffles his
massive feet, and does not fail to remind me that when he
was playing it was possible (it was not only possible, it was
done) to eat a large steak at breakfast before coming out to
bowl in a Test match. Having eased his belt at the thought
of it, Maurice will gleefully comment on the perspicacity of
a famous cricket writer who dismissed him, once and for all,
as a mere seaside bowler.

And then perhaps the talk will unroll, like a ribbon of
road, through the dull country of today to the brilliant
landscapes of ten or twenty or twenty-five years back.

It's way back to the past that Maurice will look to
recapture the greatness of the game, of heroic stature to our
memories (and believe me to our champions of today), but
barely life-size to one of his own attainments. When you ask
him which for him was the greatest day of all, the pipe will
droop in the large, humorous mouth, and he will think hard
and long.

You suggest the obvious—in vain. There was the occasion
in 1924 when, with Arthur Gilligan, he shot out the South
African side for 30 runs. His own analysis was four for 12
on that occasion, when Sydney Pegler complained that he
could still read the maker's name on the ball when he went
in at number eleven. But for some uncertainty of touch on
the far side of the stumps (to say nothing of on the near),
the score would have been even smaller. Yes, Maurice will

admit, he was bowling up to his weight that day. All the same, he wasn't bowling as well, not quite as well, as in a certain match up North against Yorkshire when he blazed away with all his batteries from noon to dusk and never got a single wicket.

And there were other county occasions, too, plenty of them. As, for instance, his fourteen wickets for 58 against Glamorgan at Hove in '25, or the thirteen for 102 against Gloucester in the same season. Or if you like, there was the nine for 21 against Middlesex at Lord's next season, or the eight for 18 against Worcester, way back in '24. Or—in '27, when he also averaged over thirty-four for some 1,300 runs for the county—the thirteen for 81 against Lancashire at Eastbourne; followed next day with five for 64 against Yorkshire at Hove. Good enough, yes. But the very best game of his lifetime. Well, hardly.

The fact is that, so far, in our voyage of discovery we're in the wrong continent altogether. Great as Tate was in England, a Test match in Australia made additional demands on him to which he responded like some hothouse flower—some teak-trunked, hothouse flower. To begin with, he belonged to the tribe of bowler, fast or fast-medium with an extra snap off the pitch, which alone could carry England teams to victory since the Australians worked out the answer to the "bosie." There was Barnes, and there was Foster. There were Larwood and Voce; and, when we failed, the bowler who came nearest to turning the trick for us was Alec Bedser, whom Bradman declared, impiously in the opinion of many, to be comparable with Tate himself.

Certainly, if you took a poll among Australians as to the most formidable bowler England ever unleashed against them, Tate would win in a canter. There would be too few greybeards to remember Barnes, and far too many critics of the ethics of his tactic to proclaim Larwood. Tate is their man; to English bowling what Jack Hobbs was to English batting. And I dare say they are quite right.

The strange thing is that though Barnes and Tate were outstandingly successful on their wickets, Australians have never seriously attempted to found a school based on their specifications. They seek to produce fast bowlers—Ernest Jones, McDonald, Gregory, Wall, McCormick, Gilbert and Lindwall. They cultivate the downright googly bowler—the Hordern, the Mailey or the Grimmett. O'Reilly stands in a class apart; faster than slow, but still a worker with fingers rather than flippers, an exponent of spin rather than cut. Perhaps the reason Australia has never produced a Tate is the reason Thackeray never wrote in the high-flying sentimental vein of Dickens; for the life of him he couldn't, but for the life of him he would have given his right hand to be able to.

Tate was Tate, and not just a very fine fast-medium bowler, for three reasons. First, he never sacrificed length either to try out tricks or because he was being belaboured. Secondly, everything he bowled was intended to hit the wicket. Finally, he came off the pitch with an elastic flip, in a sudden geometrical progression of speed. There are, it is true, calculating boys of perverted genius who declare that this latter feat is a mechanical impossibility. Their logarithms may be beyond dispute; but they will never convince any batsman who played Tate in a Test match that they know what they are talking about.

Today in the Press box, Tate has a well-stropped turn of phrase and a fearless readiness to put his finger on feeble play which is rare in a professional in this connection. I remember one of his colleagues, a great left-handed bowler, who in retirement was always afraid of hurting the feelings of the next generation with their living to earn as cricketers. His ghost beside him, he sat in the Press box watching for the first time a young genius who had been spoken of as his own likely successor. The old-timer watched in silence for three respectfully received overs. Then he burst out in full spate. "Never make a bowler! Never make a bowler! Look at yon feet—wrong plaace, weight's in wrong plaace, too, run's as wrong as wrong can be. Never make a bowler —not in a thousand years."

The ghost wrote it all down greedily.

Time passed. At last the great old-timer stirred uneasily. "That stoof," he said, "that stoof I was saying about yon lad. Doan't 'ee put it down exact way I said it. You want to change it about a bit." Silence. And then at last the old-timer delivered his edited version. "Put it this way. *Say—he showed promise.*"

You would not get such lenient treatment from "Chub" Tate—so-called on the presumption that there might be a fish of that species sufficiently good-looking to pass as his stand-in. He is made of sterner stuff; not least because he comes of cricketing stock and knew the game, either at first- or second-hand, in the Golden Age.

He came into cricket, as it were, with a family injustice to expunge. If I briefly recapitulate so well known a story as Fred Tate's only Test match, it is because when I recently asked a seventeen-year-old Nottingham boy what he knew about Ranjitsinhji, he replied that he always understood he was the best of the Australian aborigine fast bowlers. Fred was a county bowler of modest excellence. In 1902 he played against Australia at Manchester. When Australia had scored 16 for three wickets in the second innings he was allowed to field in the deep, where he never fielded, and dropped an almost cosy chance from Darling, with the result that the fourth-wicket partnership survived to add an invaluable 54 runs. Then, when the game reached its climax, he left the pavilion, last man in, with 8 runs wanted. At once, the rain fell. When the game was resumed, three-quarters of an hour later, Tate straightway hit 4 of these needed 8 off the meat of his bat. Three balls later he was bowled all over his wicket by Saunders.

Maurice came into Test match cricket with this sad story haunting him on his walk from the pavilion to the popping-crease. He hadn't been in Test cricket very long before that ghost was well and truly laid. By the time his career was over, if a psycho-analyst shot the name Tate at the patient on the couch, the automatic response would have nothing to do with 1902, but would concern itself with any one of Junior's triumphs from the mid-twenties to the mid-thirties.

Of them all, Maurice Tate himself puts his finger on the Adelaide game of 1928—the Fourth Test match of Chapman's tour. It wasn't, by the way, his own outstanding triumph, but the side's. And as a game of cricket it was totally unforgettable.

That season, indeed that match, marked the beginning of the end of the most successful period of English cricket history since Warner's tour of 1911. We had begun the tour by overwhelming Australia in the First Test at Brisbane as Australia had never been overwhelmed before. That game was played to the music of the funeral march of the Old Guard.

Farewell to Jack Gregory and Kelleway, as, before the season began, farewell to Macartney, Taylor, Arthur Richardson and Mailey. Younger players arrived; new players were tried in such games as remained during that Australian summer. By the end of it the signals were out—welcome Bradman, Jackson, Fairfax, Wall and Hornibrook.

You see, this Australian era of rehabilitation was no period to compare and contrast with the state of English cricket today. Most of us can see plenty of players who would be all the better out of the England team, but none at all who should be promoted into it.

Such was far from being the case with Australia. There were whole squads of players fit and ready for international cricket; every State had one or two on ice. In Queensland there was the terrific F. C. Thompson, always capable of a double century against anybody, though purists looked down their noses at his fielding. South Australia had D. E. Pritchard, who scored a century against Chapman's team and was never heard of again. Victoria had Hartkopf; New South Wales a fine bowler in Hooker, who shared in a record last-wicket stand with Kippax. Carlton of South Australia and Alexander of Victoria were other bowlers who might have been blooded. There was plenty of talent about; it was a case of sifting the very good from the merely good.

The Second Test had been a great deal closer than the First. It had, indeed, been a well-fought match, remarkable (apart from the fact that in one innings George Geary took five wickets, without help from the field, for 35 runs) for an embattled Test century by Stork Hendry. When he was deep in the 90's, the unfortunate Hendry saw with dismay that the English team felt constrained to refresh themselves at this crucial moment of his personal fortunes from a tray full of drinks. Well, he was thirsty, too, and could do with a long, cold dry ginger ale. He had just raised one to his lips when Patsy Hendren, skimming the ground as a water-beetle skims a duck pond, arrived at the wicket to register a veto. "Whisky," he said briefly, taking the glass from the teetotal hand and hurling its contents on to the parched Bulli soil. Hendry, who told me this story, always regarded this deed as the very pink of sportsmanship. What he can have thought of the fine flower of chivalry that planned the jape he never confided to me. Perhaps he lacked an adequate vocabulary.

This Second Test has another claim to distinction in the history of international cricket. In the second innings the Australians bowled Otto Nothling and Hendry against us, generally conceded to be the weakest opening attack ever known in a Test match. At that, Stork Hendry returned the bowling analysis of two wickets for 4 runs, figures which few opening bowlers would disdain.

The Third Test brought the teams closer together than ever. Only Hobbs and Sutcliffe could have won such an impossible match for England; and at that the game was barely snatched out of the fire by the narrow margin of three wickets on the seventh day of one of the closest fought and most brilliantly interesting Test matches since the *Sporting Times* commemorated the cremation of English Cricket.

Thus to the Fourth Test at Adelaide; the game of games in Maurice Tate's long and thrill-packed career. The rubber being lost and won one would have supposed Australia would be prepared to take chances in giving every untested player of talent a chance to show his nerve and skill in a game fought out under the most onerous conditions. But in fact she chose to make only one change; Victor Richardson, less than lucky in his dealings with Larwood, being replaced by Archie Jackson, who had been born nineteen years before in Britain.

The Adelaide Test had an extra edge to it because so

many of the players had taken part in the last Test on the same ground, when Gilligan's men had been beaten by 11 runs after having to wait over the weekend to see whether their last two wickets were good for 27.

Chapman began by winning the toss, which is rather less of an achievement at Adelaide than on most grounds. The wicket there is generally sympathetic to batsmen, and it rarely changes its loyalty before the end of a match. I suppose Adelaide's annual rainfall is much the same as Melbourne's, but I somehow never remember so much as a splash of it obtruding on a cricket match; whereas in the other city I have started to cross a main street in blazing sunshine and reached the far pavement in a hailstorm. The one risk you incur with the Adelaide wicket is that it sometimes takes it into its mind to crumble from the fourth day onwards. It is always worth holding a spinner or two in reserve to cope with this contingency.

The game began in glittering weather, with Hobbs and Sutcliffe batting in a confident mood, never losing sight of the seriousness of an occasion which was none the less a Test match even though the Ashes were in the bag. The bowling was not exactly intimidating, but you could never preserve any margin of safety if you opted to take liberties against Grimmett's googlies or Blackie's spinners.

The opening batsmen left within an over or two of each other. In their hour and three-quarters at the wicket they had given no chances, but they never quite gripped the bowling by the scruff of the neck. Hobbs, for example, hit only a couple of boundaries during his stay; and no fewer than 38 of his runs came from singles. It was a suitably massive beginning, but perhaps if à Becket and Hendry had been bowling merely for Victoria (for whom they did not in fact figure as opening bowlers), the first wicket might have helped themselves to half as many carefree runs again.

The danger with which England was faced was Grimmett, bowling on his own midden better than at any other time against Chapman's team. He was gnomelike as ever, with his gutta-percha face often split with a huge grin. Now and then he would pull the great green penthouse of a cap down over his mushroom head, and, with his eyes almost hidden under this roof, would shoot forth his leg-breaks and googlies, as it were from memory.

His trajectory was low, he bowled almost round arm; and yet there was always time for him to do something occult in the air. Unlike Mailey, he did not offer a gentleman's agreement that you could enjoy a skylarking holiday at his expense so long as you paid the bill in the end. He dunned you. Every ball he dunned you. There never was such a dun as Clarrie Grimmett, whom his friends called Scarlet, for reasons which had nothing to do with Miss O'Hara. There were those who thought him, at thirty-six, a little past his best that season; but in fact he was to remain the finest bowler in the world a lustre later, and Bradman's failure to insist on his inclusion in the last pre-war Australian team probably cost his side the rubber.

Here in Adelaide's midsummer weather, which laps one in well-being rather than stews one in one's own juice, he made every member of the England side, except Hammond, look tentative or uncouth. The opening pair treated him reverently, and Jardine's gigantic reach was employed in vain —the verdict was for the dun. When it came to the fag-end of the innings he was in absolute command. Nobody could shake a bat at him.

But before this came to pass, Hammond had shown the world that one could grow up in the same game as Grimmett and live to a ripe old age. His method was uncomplicated. He played one ball at a time. If the ball was good, he stopped it with the centre of his bat, and then put his august nose in the air and surveyed Mount Lofty and the shimmering hills beyond, or the superb outline of the cathedral behind long-off. If the ball was bad, he expanded his splendid shoulders to their full width and drove authoritatively. The ball sang as it skimmed past cover, or out of reach of mid-off. If you had timed its progress with a stop-watch, you might have found it setting up records for the ground.

The leg side the great Walter in the main disdained. There lay traps and stratagems—plots to overthrow majesty and to supplant him with anarchy. The way to cope with this sort of trickery was to take one or two dance steps, such as a king takes at a Christmas party, make an off ball of the thing, and then hit it crisply to its doom.

He continued on his leonine way until, shortly before the tea interval on the second day, he found no one left to bear him company. The reason he had taken four and a half hours for his 119 runs was that far fewer bad balls than good were submitted for his inspection and sentence.

No one could say that England's 334 was anything short of a failure, in the light of the fact that the first wicket did not fall until 143 was on the board. Nevertheless, on a wicket that was still a rich grazing ground for batsmen, Australia began as if unable to believe her good fortune. Tate's fourth ball brought England her first wicket. Woodfull made an exquisitely fine glance off the leg stump which had a right to anticipate for itself respectful applause rather than a lodgment in Duckworth's gloves.

Then Hendry went pecking unwarily at Larwood swinging across the line of the stumps. Two wickets for 6 was pretty bad. The minds of all present went back a couple of months to the days when the same two destroyers, Tate and Larwood, had fatally holed the Australian side at Brisbane, leaving it to Jack White to administer the *coup de grâce*.

It looked as if this might be a sombre echo of that melancholy occasion. It looked even more likely when, after a couple more overs, White, going on for Larwood, bowled the immaculate Kippax all over his wicket. Three of the best of them gone for 16. It was a roll-over. It was duck soup. A couple more wickets now, and there'd be nearly a full week's holiday for Chapman's boys before they were due at Ballarat for a picnic game.

But there were to be no more easy wickets for England that day. The partnership of Archie Jackson and Jack Ryder was to put an end to all such airy expectations. It was a combination of all the talents known to batsmanship. On the style of the infant Jackson there glowed already the bloom of fine craftsmanship in its prime. This fledgling was of the tribe of Trumper: with a cover-drive like a shout of triumph, a straight hit that purred all the way to the boundary, and a

cut made with wrists as trim and strong as the wrists of a
fencer making the defence in tierce. He was light enough on
his feet to move across the wicket to meet Larwood on his
own terms. He played Tate, catapulting from the pitch, with
respectful caution which now and then broadened into an
exquisitely casual dominance. Jack White sloped down his
low-slung swerves in vain: the young man had a cool command of his impeccable length and his subtlety in the air.

At the other end stood the homespun Ryder. His were
the gifts of a calm spirit, a keen eye, and a pair of long arms
at the end of which he could twiddle his little toothpick of
a bat to keep the ball out of his wicket for an indefinite
period. If you dropped a short one, it was as good as a burnt-
offering to him. He bent at the knee, and by no means flowed
into his stroke; but he was good to hammer the thing to
test the quickness off the mark of the boundary patrol. By
the time White, pegging away remorselessly at the stumps
for a score of overs on end, caught Ryder with his leg in
front, the 150 was in sight, and all hopes of a collapse had
ceased to be practical politics.

After Ryder—Don Bradman. On this afternoon of
February 2, twenty-one years ago, the spectacle of Jackson and
Bradman in partnership was a design for the portrait of
Australia Irridenta. Mark well, on this day's showing the
cast is Jackson and Bradman, in that order. Bradman is the
young spark of genius, hectoring and iconoclastic; but
Jackson is Attic and sublime. You would have been little
understood if you had predicted at Adelaide, twenty-one years
ago, that last year there would be schoolboys writing to ask
Bradman for his autograph, with an urgent postscript "and
please sign Sir Don"—schoolboys to whom the very name of
the late Archie Jackson meant nothing at all.

By the time the innings had worked itself out, a slight
lead had been established: too small to wipe out the moral
advantage of not having to bat last in a Test match. The main
features of the innings (Jackson's début apart) had been the
unfaltering fielding of England, with Chapman effervescent
everywhere from silly-point to deep mid-on, and the magnificent bowling of Tate and White. Tate, in particular, had

contrived to wheedle some spark of malice out of that placid, grandmotherly wicket; and he had achieved belligerency without ever forfeiting rigid accuracy in the matter of length.

The second half of the match began sensationally. In less than half an hour, Hobbs and Sutcliffe were both back in the pavilion with the little leeway still to be made up. Hobbs, in particular, perished with melodramatic suddenness. Like Woodfull before him, he tried to feather a ball to fine-leg, and Oldfield, skimming out, low and fast as a flying-fish, clove to the difficult chance.

When Jardine came out to join Hammond, the position was grave enough. All the better—it was a position perfectly suited to a batsman of Jardine's dour gift of resistance to the death. From the first, he seemed to have complete mastery of the defensive strokes necessary to keep the ball out of his wicket. Getting the ball away was harder: the field was so skilfully placed that any attempt to riddle it with the off-drive must be fraught with danger. Both Jardine and Hammond were content to play back defensively when necessary, and when possible to force the ball away on the on side.

This technique revealed an aspect of Hammond as a master batsman unrecognizable to those acquainted with him as the off-driver dominating our county grounds from Bradford to Dover. Yet he played, with meticulous concentration, the perfect game to help his side and to suit the occasion. No bowler of them all forced him to stave off peril by keeping his back to the wall. He stood his ground and took his time; he was Barlow for five balls out of six, but for the sixth he was Bonnor. He gave no shadow of a chance and his stand with Jardine remains the greatest put together for the sixth wicket for England against Australia.

In a few minutes less than six hours the two men advanced the score by 262 runs, before Jardine, hitting vigorously at Oxenham, was neatly snapped up by Woodfull at silly mid-off. It is sad to think that this score of 98 was the nearest Douglas Jardine ever got to a Test century against Australia. He must be the best England batsman never to have achieved this distinction.

Revenge at Adelaide

Hammond was caught and bowled by Ryder in an abstracted moment after he had been at the wicket for seven hours twenty minutes, scoring less than a third of his runs from boundary hits. It was his finest innings of the tour; and one of the very finest of his whole career. Among Englishmen only Sutcliffe had preceded him in the feat of scoring a century in each innings of a Test match. Those who (like C. B. Fry) consider Hammond the most considerable of recent English batsmen can point to this match to justify their claim. For long periods he ruled passively; then in brief intervals he asserted his authority like an urbane tyrant. But all the time, he ruled. He was the master of the game. If the King had seen fit to ennoble him at the match's end for his services to sport, there would have been no complaints had he chosen as his title Lord Hammond of Adelaide as an earlier man of destiny became Lord Beatty of the North Sea.

Between Jardine's departure and Hammond's, the main stem of the innings had begun to wither. Blackie, in a fine spell, took the wickets of Hendren, Chapman and Larwood while 24 runs were being added. At this stage it did not look as if Australia would be set to make 300 to win. In spite of all the Grand Alliance had accomplished the game still seemed to be in Australia's keeping. What was wanted, of course, was some long-handled mangler of analyses to get to work on the self-possessed attack.

When Chapman was caught in Blackie's trap before his eye was in, there was only one man left in the side who might be able to undertake the job. After the tea interval on the fifth day, Maurice Tate came out to bat with a gleam in his eye, and the determination to live dangerously and die with his boots on. He lasted long enough to hit one booming sixer and five rollicking fours before Oxenham thumped his pads with the wicket behind them. The 47 runs he scored while Geary and J. C. White hung on for dear life saved England's morale for her. They meant that Australia faced the last innings in the knowledge that more and not less than three hundred had to be found, and though the margin was small enough, it made all the difference to the mental attitude of a team facing the fourth innings of a Test match. Anybody ought to be able to make two hundred and something runs in such a situation—but a score of over three hundred is a very serious undertaking indeed.

Well, the best of sides can but try. There would have been smiles instead of anxious faces in the Australian dressing-room if the players could have known that Tate and Larwood, considered to be the major dangers, were not to take a wicket between them during the final innings of the match.

And, at that, the smiles would have been misplaced. Moving a little stiffly to his place in the field is an apple-cheeked veteran with thick white hair who is to refute, in the next couple of days, the world-wide belief that his type of bowling is virtually innocuous on marble-topped Australian wickets. By the time stumps are drawn at the end of the fifth day, Jack White has had no chance of getting a cut at the enemy. Woodfull and Jackson are still there, with 24 useful runs on the board.

Next morning they plod along to 65, when the partnership is broken; and a few overs later both opening batsmen have been joined by Hendry in the pavilion. Three wickets for 74 is a score which the England team are proud to think of as providing headlines for the factory workers gulping their breakfasts in the cheerless February dawns of the Gorbals and Hull, but there is more to come before the latest score is rushed into the stop press news.

Ryder and Kippax are laying the foundations of a stand that has the look of being likely to soar to victory. They are batting with the decorum of respected citizens in church. They score their runs in whispers: a touch through the gulley off White, a muted push towards mid-on off Tate, and then a long, watchful period of quiet, as it might be when the best of men are assailed by the hard lessons of the sermon. And after that, there is very nearly a collection. Jack Ryder, generally so sure of stroke, lobs what may well be the gentlest catch in the history of Test cricket to Jack White—and White drops it. The whole incident is unbelievable; and you can read in White's face the tragic truth that he would give a year of his life to be back at home, stag-hunting in the neighbourhood of Stogumber or Combe Flory.

By the time the next chance comes, Australia has 211 on the board, and her nose a little bit in front. The position has improved to such an extent that Ryder has for some time been revealing himself as the aggressive batsman nature designed him to be. He is driving heartily all round the wicket now, and when White sends down a ball that looks surprisingly like a half-volley, he thumps it handsomely back, in the hope and expectation of seeing it bounce twice before hitting the pickets behind the bowler. But this is White's chance to redeem himself. He leaps as if he were ten years younger, shoots his left arm out and up—and the ball sticks. A captain's innings is at an end, and the game is still wide open.

Now à Beckett joins Bradman and rattles for the runs like a man who is confident his life must be charmed because his cause is just. In half an hour he is on top of the situation, and going so well that you may suppose him capable of winning the match off his own twinkling bat. Just as this view is gaining currency, à Beckett cuts hard and true at White, and Hammond keels over to hold a miraculous catch at second slip.

So the sixth day ends. Australia needs 89 runs to win, with four wickets in hand. It looks as if England is slightly ahead at the moment; but every boundary affects the thermometer of this delicately balanced crisis.

On the final morning of the game the feeling in the air is that if Bradman does not win it for Australia, it will be because Jack White has conjured it away from him. His eternal steadiness and his ability to make mischief out of pretty thin air have won the ungrudging admiration of the enemy on both sides of the picket fence.

He starts off against Bradman as full of guile and energy as ever; but the Don is in a hectoring mood that soon turns inside out those short-priced odds against Australia. He and Oxenham push the score forward, past 275, past 300, within 40 runs of squaring the game. Even at that, when White hoodwinks Oxenham into popping a ball into Chapman's protective hands, there is no cause for despair among the thousands sitting in their shirt-sleeves with handkerchiefs knotted round their heads as protection against the sunstroke invited from defying a temperature of 118 degrees.

And, for an over or two, Bradman goes confidently juggernauting along. Then, quick as the flash of an explosion, disaster startles Australia. Oldfield, who is batting with his usual trim skill, hits a ball firmly into the covers. It is a little wide of Hobbs, who, anyway, at 46 cannot be the panther he was in his youth, moreover a run is a run—and aren't the batsmen a pair of whippets with a perfect understanding between them?

But Hobbs has anticipated the direction of the stroke almost before the ball has left the bat. He springs towards it, gathers it, snaps it home as if he were pulling back a zip-fastener—with the arm hardly travelling back behind the shoulder. Duckworth's gloves gather the ball at stump height, and the bails are swept off as the loudest appeal of the match echoes across the ground. Bradman marches back to the pavilion, wondering, one supposes, how he can ever hope to live long enough to obliterate the memory of this moment. It is anybody's game now.

Grimmett arrives in the mood of the Dutch hero who is said to have plugged a breach in the dyke with his thumb. He is to hold on for half an hour. At lunch Australia are in a position where three or four full-blooded shots would give them the game—but where are the batsmen to deliver even so many mortal blows? Can Bert Oldfield and Clarrie Grimmett be expected to raise such a siege?

Against these doubts is the physical state of the English bowlers. Tate, never losing his dash and bite, and Jack White have bowled through a long tropic morning and are now weary unto death. Can you ask them to take up the assault where they left off?

You can ask them to do exactly that. Further than that, you can plan a detailed campaign of attack based on the special abilities of these two sempiternal bowlers. During the lunch interval Percy Chapman and Jack Hobbs sit apart, heads together, in solemn conclave. By the time the umpires

march forth in slow time the plan has been formulated. Tate
is to keep Oldfield, the batsman likelier to produce run-
getting strokes, tied down to inaction at his end. At the other
end, Jack White is to attack and overthrow first Grimmett,
then Blackie.

The strategy is well-founded. Moreover, it works out to
the letter; a state of affairs that must surely be unique in
modern warfare. Tate, bowling his great heart out in the
broiling sunlight, pins Oldfield to his crease for four long
overs. Not a ball can he get away, try as he will to break
the encirclement. Once a barracker gives tongue. "Hey,
Oldfield—hit old Maurice Tate for a sixer, and I guarantee
you a place in heaven." But the offer is in vain. Oldfield
will still have to work his passage.

At the other end, for a long stretch, White is as testingly
accurate in his turn. Then, suddenly, he loses his length.
A long-hop—a heaven-sent long-hop—bounces enticingly in
front of Grimmett. Only hit this one as it deserves to be hit,
and he is a third of the way to victory already. Grimmett
opens his shoulders, pirouettes, and strikes. The ball goes
with thrilling speed straight above Tate's cool head at short-
leg. Up flashes the long, unwearied arm that has bowled so
faithfully and so well all through the heat of the day. There
goes the ball, a red blur that expands with a resounding
thwack against the open palm. Up again, into the air—while
all hearts stand still. And then, the unsurpassable Maurice
has grabbed and held it at the second attempt. Surely, oh
army of ghosts who watch the well-loved game from the
balcony of Elysium, this is the catch to remember till the
end of time—not the one Joe Darling sent up to poor old
Fred so many years ago?

In comes Blackie. No man ever looked more nervous:
and, of course, no man ever had a better right to such an
expression. He takes guard rather with the air of a con-
demned man accepting a final glass, hopelessly hoping that
there may be rum in it. It is a preliminary which custom
demands of him, but it can't be expected to do much good.

Up runs Jack White. Over goes his stout left arm. *Another
long-hop!* By the living heaven, the man who has bowled

more than a hundred and twenty overs of balls of un-exceptionable length, is finishing the job with a barrage of long-hops. . . . What is more, he *is* finishing the game with them—in fact he has finished it! The ball rockets up from Blackie's hapless bat towards the leg boundary behind mid-wicket. Larwood is on his hurricane way to it, Larwood has stopped, stepped back, forward again — and claimed the catch!

The match is won by 12 runs. The great tactics have prevailed. England has wiped out the defeat, sustained by almost an identical margin, on this very ground four years earlier. Masters of prose are already hard at work, cudgelling their vocabularies for Elizabethan language to do justice to a battle which will assail the ears of the grandchildren of all who witnessed it, so long as doting tongues can wag.

And deep in the pavilion Jack White and Maurice Tate are toasting each other in the largest mugs of shandygaff either has aspired to in a lifetime of by no means negligible experience.

Revenge at Adelaide

(FEBRUARY 1—8, 1929)

ENGLAND

FIRST INNINGS		SECOND INNINGS	
Hobbs, J. B., c Ryder, b Hendry ...	74	c Oldfield, b Hendry ...	1
Sutcliffe, H., st Oldfield, b Grimmett	64	c Oldfield, b à Beckett ...	17
Hammond, W. R., not out	119	c and b Ryder	177
Jardine, D. R., lbw, b Grimmett ...	1	c Woodfull, b Oxenham ...	98
Hendren, E., b Blackie	13	c Bradman, b Blackie ...	11
Chapman, A. P. F., c à Beckett, b Ryder	39	c Woodfull, b Blackie ...	0
Duckworth, G., c Ryder, b Grimmett	5	lbw, b Oxenham	1
Larwood, H., b Hendry	3	lbw, b Oxenham	5
Geary, G., run out	3	c and b Grimmett	6
Tate, M. W., b Grimmett	2	lbw, b Oxenham	47
White, J. C., c Ryder, b Grimmett	0	not out	4
Extras (b 3, lb 7, w 1)	11	Extras (b 6, lb 10) ...	16
	334		383

AUSTRALIA

FIRST INNINGS		SECOND INNINGS	
Woodfull, W. M., c Duckworth, b Tate	1	c Geary, b White	30
Jackson, A., lbw, b White	164	c Duckworth, b Geary ...	36
Hendry, H. L., c Duckworth, b Larwood	2	c Tate, b White	5
Kippax, A. F., b White	3	c Hendren, b White ...	51
Ryder, J., lbw, b White	63	c and b White	87
Bradman, D. G., c Larwood, b Tate	40	run out	58
à Beckett, E. L., b White	36	c Hammond, b White ...	21
Oxenham, R. K., c Chapman, b White	15	c Chapman, b White ...	12
Oldfield, W. A., b Tate	32	not out	15
Grimmett, C. V., b Tate	4	c Tate, b White	9
Blackie, D. J., not out	3	c Larwood, b White ...	0
Extras (lb 5, w 1)	6	Extras (b 9, lb 3) ...	12
	369		336

AUSTRALIA

	O.	M.	R.	W.		O.	M.	R.	W.
à Beckett	31	8	44	0	...	27	9	41	1
Hendry	31	14	49	2	...	28	11	56	1
Grimmett	52.1	12	102	5	...	52	15	117	1
Oxenham	35	14	51	0	...	47.4	21	67	4
Blackie	29	6	57	1	...	39	11	70	2
Ryder	5	1	20	1	...	5	1	13	1
Kippax					...	2	0	3	0

ENGLAND

	O.	M.	R.	W.		O.	M.	R.	W.
Larwood	37	6	92	1	...	20	4	60	0
Tate	42	10	77	4	...	37	9	75	0
White	60	16	130	5	...	64.5	21	126	8
Geary	12	3	32	0	...	16	2	42	1
Hammond	9	1	32	0	...	14	3	21	0

Chapter Eight

THE MIDDLESEX MATCH

(JIM SIMS)

WHENEVER the image of Jim Sims comes to mind, one thinks instinctively of the rubbery mouth, the incarnation of that something articulately inanimate with which Edgar Bergen's Charlie MacCarthy would have been proud to enrich the slips. No man could more effectively dispose wisecracks by elongating the side of his mouth. There were those who said that, from second slip, he could carry on conversations simultaneously with first slip and third man in this way.

Jim's gifts in this direction a little tended to obscure very serious merits as a fighting cricketer. There were times when he bowled steadily enough and guilefully enough to look like a right-handed Hedley Verity. But Jim never contrived to look as profoundly immersed in research as Hedley, with forefinger laid on lip and head held slightly to one side as if scrutinizing the whole problem before him on a blackboard.

That is why one always felt Jim had reached his spiritual home when he ambled off-stage from the crease to the slips, with the world and the game well lost, for the sake of a running stream of back-chat—and side-chat, too. And then suddenly the arm, half-raised to the lips to point an aside, would shoot out, rubbery as the mouth itself, and the hand would palm a ball with the nonchalance with which a conjurer palms a shilling.

Again, there was Jim the batsman. You would not call him a fiery, attacking player, but with feet entrenched he could swing his bat as coolly as the next man, chopping square-cuts, and propping off leg-glides hour upon hour.

The Middlesex Match

If you look at the record of Middlesex's senior professional (who ranks at Lord's a little below the president and secretary of the M.C.C.), you will find occasions when you should have wondered whether that subtle, sidelong chatterbox was not the most formidable attacking bowler of his day. I saw him at work, 'way back in 1935-6, with Errol Holmes's team that toured Australasia. He played in six State games during the Australian preamble to the tour proper, and in those he took thirty-three wickets—including that of Don Bradman. Back he came to England, played his third consecutive season through, embellished with performances good enough to win him his place in G. O. Allen's side that toured Australia the following winter.

He was a superb all-rounder on this showing, but no doubt when the war was over you hardly expected to see him in action again. After all, he was forty-two; and we began our post-war cricket in the innocent belief that bowlers had finished their careers of usefulness by the time they got to forty. We did not know then that for several seasons to come the most successful bowlers in England would be J. C. Clay and Tom Goddard, the former born in the nineteenth century, and the latter only a few months out of it. We were taken by surprise when we saw Jim Sims again approach the wicket with that roll, as in a heavy swell, that counts for a gait with him, heave-to, and deliver up a cargo of assorted leg-breaks and googlies, by no means as per invoice.

In 1947, for instance, there he was, doing a hat-trick at Lord's against the South Africans. He didn't need the help of fieldsmen in this little *pièce de résistance*; two were bowled and the other was leg-before. And in the following season, at forty-four years of age, he was taking his one hundred and four wickets for 23 runs apiece; and (in mid-July, when it was too late to do much about it) proving that he was very nearly the only man in the country whose bowling left the Australians beaten and bewitched. In one over he dismissed three of their batsmen, beginning with Loxton, who had already zoomed past the milestone of his first century and was hustling cheerfully towards his second. He finished with six wickets (five of them good batsmen) for 65 runs off twenty-four overs. He was still, you see, a master at his old skill of keeping them quiet with machine-like accuracy and getting them out by an unstinted use of black magic. Not many googly bowlers have *both* these gifts.

By and large, it's a wonderful record of maturing merit. There was a time—just before the war—when, handicapped by minor injuries, he seemed not only to have reached but to have passed over the horizon of the first-class game. In 1938 he took less than fifty wickets for his county, and those at a cost of over 30 runs apiece. "Poor old Jim Sims," we all said, "you've got to make an end some time." We should have been derisive indeed if it had been suggested that ten years later he was to share the major part of the Middlesex attack with Jack Young and Laurie Gray.

And we should have been even more scornfully incredulous if told that Jim himself was to play in the game which he himself nominates as the match of his life, even after that. For this contest belongs to last summer, as ever was. It was the match in which Middlesex, outplayed in the first innings and throughout the first two days, handsomely defeated Leicester (set less than 200 to get in a high scoring match) with an hour in hand on the final afternoon.

The game began in brilliant sunshine on a wicket that was stuffed with runs. It was the benefit match of Paddy Corrall, Leicester's wicket-keeper, who was given the privilege of spinning the coin in front of the pavilion. He did not spin it effectively and George Mann whistled Middlesex in to bat.

The big Leicester crowd gave a full-lunged cheer when their little wicket-keeper led the side on to the field. It was a matter of pride to them that their hero of the occasion should have been greeted by Denis Compton as soon as he arrived on the ground to be wished a particularly thumping benefit. The two men had been close friends since they served together during the war years in the East. Later, before demobilization, Compton appeared in a touring Services football team for which Corrall acted as referee. Now they met again; and Denis had put aside his Sunday to play in a match arranged at Market Harborough for Paddy's benefit fund.

Out went Leicester into the field, and out went Robertson and Sharp, Middlesex's opening pair, to begin batting as if the ball was as big as a melon, and they themselves had an appetite for fruit. Their fine start was a notable achievement, for the Leicester attack is varied and dangerous. Jim Sperry, no juvenile, is a left-handed bowler above medium pace who can swing the new ball effectively. Young Stewart Symington, captaining the side, bowls a medium-paced outswinger which one way or another is apt to give his slips plenty of exercise. But by and large the most dangerous bowlers in the teams are the two Sydneysiders: Victor Jackson, whose medium-pace off-breaks impose on the most buoyant batsman a pensive restraint, and Jack Walsh, who is as near as makes no difference to the best left-arm bowler of leg-breaks and googlies in the land.

Yet Sharp and Robertson opened resolute shoulders to launch quite massive drives at this intimidating, attacking commando. Sharp began by slashing a flawless first ball from Sperry to the boundary behind extra-cover, and Robertson swept him away on both sides of the wicket as if his game had acquired fresh lustre from the Test century he had hit a few days back after a lifetime of sentry-go as twelfth man.

Only Symington kept the pair quiet. For over after over they watched him from within the fortress, or the prison, of the popping-crease. Now and then there was a sortie—a quick cleaving of the slips or a gentle flip out of range of Paddy Corrall's left glove—but there was no sign of a foray or a general break-out. Once, indeed, Robertson, playing late at a well-pitched fizzer, sent the ball spinning past Walsh's right hand at slip. It would have been the catch of the match; but one of those human telescopes who invariably inhabit the slips might have fastened on to the thin chance.

And then, with 70 on the board, Symington broke through both those careful defences. Robertson never moved his feet, and his back stroke had the look of a purely reflex action.

Walsh pounced across to take what seemed an impossible prey on the wing. A couple of overs later Sharp died passively enough. He made a convulsive stab at an inswinger, and the umpire's finger went up against him. Symington had bowled a dozen overs at a good pace, conceding but 20 runs for these two important wickets. On a day when the best that could be asked was the shade of a palm tree and a jug of iced lemonade this was a spirited performance.

Compton now joined Edrich and at once began to bat as if he were enjoying a light-hearted romp at the nets. He squared his shoulders to flog Walsh past point, and then sent a leg glide skimming to the boundary.

There was only to be a glimpse of Edrich. Off his right foot he lashed a whirlwind stroke at Symington; the ball clinked against the long-on boundary before the follow-through was completed. But then came disaster. Forward he played to another of Walsh's spinners: the break beat him and Corrall received the cheers due to the hero of the day claiming his own first victim.

The fourth wicket fell a few minutes later when Walsh hit Mann's off-stump with a ball which omitted the formality of a bounce. On a wicket that was almost self-consciously well-behaved, Leicester had deserved well of the gods who govern cricket. To have in the bag four of the best batsmen of the side then leading in the Championship race, was an attacking success worth gloating over. All they had to do now to screw home their advantage was to get rid of Compton.

But Compton wasn't to be got rid of. This was the sort of situation to which he had become acclimatized through a long summer devoted to Tests against Australia. If he failed now, his side would melt in the sunshine before the tea interval. Leicester would have a moral advantage before the weekend break that no side with red blood in its veins could be expected to lose.

So Compton's blue eyes gleamed with pleasure at the challenge. He flung his left leg down the pitch and swept his arms into a tremendous arc of speed as he consummated his majestic straight drive. Again, rolling away from the

ball, he administered that breezy cuff that sends it out into
the tiger country around long-leg. This is a poacher's shot,
light-hearted and immoral when administered to a well-
intentioned ball diligently plodding on towards the leg stump
as a careerist plods on towards a knighthood.

On this day Denis used the foil, the swordstick, the
bludgeon. He cut elegantly; drove like an autocrat; and
thumped away like a hawk-eyed rustic when Walsh became
erratic to the point of raining down long-hops.

Opposite him, Alex Thompson defended when necessary
with the imperturbability of the true north countryman—
he was born in Lancashire. When offered an opportunity
of enriching himself, he collected his dividends with sober
enthusiasm. Between the two of them, they thwacked and
bedevilled the Leicester bowling for a 100 in an hour,
before Compton set off on a gallop for his 100th run
from a tap towards mid-on. The crowd was standing on
tiptoe to cheer the most cavalier innings Grace Road, green
oasis among the dark Satanic mills, had seen in a summer.
But at mid-on Chapman was on tiptoe, too. He sprang at
the ball, whisked it up and in—and there was Compton,
run out for 99, walking to the pavilion with his bat flourished
high in the air and chivalric laughter on his lips.

After that the Middlesex innings soon died, and Leicester
had an hour or two of counter-assault to fill in to useful
purpose. From Leslie Berry, the previous season's captain
and Leicester's top scorer in history, came a stout 65 not out.
It was a watchful innings, in which the bad ball (and only
the bad ball) was ruthlessly punished. He was less entertain-
ing than Maurice Tompkin, who partnered him in a
gallopade which was to end early on Monday morning after
68 runs had been rushed up in forty minutes.

At the close of play on the first day Middlesex were all
out for 333; while Leicestershire had scored 134 for two—
George Lester being bowled all over his wicket by Sims
—and Frank Prentice, the most trustworthy batsman in the
team, caught by Edrich off Compton's Chinaman. The
day's honours were thus with Leicester. On the other hand, if
you had said that the game was certain to end in a draw,

you would have bought an argument with no one of common sense or experience.

But on Monday, July 4, the whole shape of the game was changed. By the time stumps were drawn as the golden evening closed over the ground, Leicester had gone far to make sure of victory. The side led Middlesex by 142 runs on the first innings, and then rubbed their superiority in by taking Robertson's invaluable wicket in the half-dozen overs left at the end of the day.

The morning's play began inauspiciously for them. Jim Sims, immaculate of length and with a wrist dripping spinners that writhed across the pitch, soon got rid of the stout-hearted Berry. The leg-break caressed the off stump so tenderly that the batsman had no idea he was out until umpire Emmott Robinson raised a pontifical forefinger.

This catastrophe might have been expected to freeze the Leicester batsmen into a shocked inaction. It did nothing of the sort. Jackson and Tompkin set about the bowling as if they were a couple of worldly wise coaches released from the stern realities of the first-class game to a rollicking net with schoolboys.

They slaughterously attacked the bowling. When Gray swung home his fast ball, a mere buzz of scarlet outside the leg stump, Tompkin sprang out to drive him. And when Sims rolled a few short 'uns out of the back of his hand, the bold Tompkin opened his shoulders and gave the fieldsman on the leg boundary plenty of healthy exercise.

George Mann wrinkled his brow and called up Jack Young from the gulley and Denis Compton from the vasty deep. It was in vain. Jackson helped the spinners through the slips with a ripple of well-sprung wrists. Tompkin continued to plaster the leg boundary with thunderous drives. He had treated all bowlers without fear or favour for two sunlit hours when the wicket-keeper, standing back, caught him off a misjudged defensive stroke against Gray's outswinger. He had enjoyed two lives—one early in his innings when he might have been caught and bowled; the other a few minutes before the end when he turned a ball from Gray into and (far harder) out of Denis Compton's hands at short-leg.

The loss of Tompkin led to a certain sedateness on the part of Jackson and Walsh. Leicester were 81 runs behind and had still six wickets in hand—but you never knew. The bowling hadn't been tamed by the onslaught of two hearty hitters with the luck running their way. Gray continued to keep an exemplary length, and to swing the ball unamiably. Sims was the Old Master to the life. He might appear to be only doodling, but masterpieces of sleight of hand kept floating in uncannily and spinning unpredictably from the flawless pitch. There were long spells of placid consolidation. Walsh was subdued; and he habitually prefers to manhandle the attack in the death-or-glory mood of a major bowler sent in not to exhaust himself just above the tail.

But when Jackson had put 50 behind him (a meticulous performance lasting nearly two hours), the game became lit up again. Walsh belaboured Sims zealously; Jackson began to employ a late cut as exquisite as a parry with the foil. Tens danced up on the scoreboard. Fieldsmen skimmed across the outfield. Jackson continued to scimitar his way through the slips, and now and then to riddle the off-side field with immaculate drives.

As the shadows lengthened Leicester began to race away. They had fought the good fight all the way down the line; resisting every assault, racing up reserves wherever the battalions were flung against the twin defences. They had held fast; and now at last the counter-attack streamed in.

The Middlesex front stood firm; then wavered; and crumpled at last. In the final hour Leicester broke through. They declared 142 runs to the good; and before they finished their stint they had the great Robertson back in the pavilion with only 6 runs on the board. You could not wonder that the few papers that troubled to take note of an occasion which coincided with Yorkshire and Surrey at Bradford and the University match at Lord's should have reported it from the standpoint of the struggle Middlesex faced to avoid an innings defeat.

Then came the last day—to eclipse everything that had gone before with its unforgettably thrilling climax. There had been rain in the night, but it was on a sunlit battlefield that the campaign was resumed. Old-timers in the crowd (and in cricket audiences such men are listened to respectfully) musingly hoped that Leicester would rise to the occasion in the mood of the Navy if challenged on Trafalgar Day. For wasn't this July 5, the anniversary of the beginning of the most brilliant match in Leicester's cricket history, their very Agincourt? Sixty-one years ago on this day Leicester had begun to overthrow the might of Australia on that very ground in Grace Road. There in the pavilion sat Mr. C. E. de Trafford, eighty-five years old and still gazing on the ageless game with a steady eye, with the silver snuffbox in his pocket presented to him to mark this famous and improbable occasion. On such a day surely the Leicester bowlers would never let sinking Middlesex come up for air.

At first, indeed, it didn't look like it. For a little while on that rain-anointed pitch the faster bowlers were rearing and starting up like so many demons from trap-doors in a harlequinade. Sperry whipped one over which popped almost perpendicularly to hit Edrich a rasping blow on the hand. When Jackson came to bowl his off-breaks the ball was skidding at almost unplayable speed off the wicket.

Yet Middlesex prospered. In no cricket match, from a Test at Sydney to a pick-up lark on a Norfolk meadow, can you prognosticate Bill Edrich's reaction to the situation, or his ability to carry out the rôle he sets himself. Pick him in a long string of Test matches and watch him waste his wicket over and over again like a spendthrift. Pick him once more, when even his best friends can hardly conscientiously defend your choice, and he hits a double century, the memory of which still makes you blink, a dozen years and one world war later.

There was no particular reason why Edrich should have chosen this day to dazzle humanity with the angelic side of his Jekyll-and-Hyde character. The rearing ball is doubly formidable to the small man; and more dangerous than ever to the small man who has a taste for undisciplined hooking from the first over onwards. On this day Edrich ravaged the leg boundary with hooks picked off the lobe of his ear

as unconcernedly as one may whisk mosquitoes to limbo with
a fly-swat. When he wasn't swinging into the hook like a
teetotum, he was frolicking into the off-drive. On the
boundary, Berry, who had injured a leg in the previous
match at Guildford, was always on patrol. Out in the deep
Tompkin stopped drives till his hands tingled as from
snowballing.

A few respectful paces to the rear of Edrich came Sharp.
There were moments when Walsh and Symington might
have adhered to putative slip catches. But there were many
more moments when the sound of the ball against his bat
was richly melodious.

The first hundred was achieved. The war dance was halfway towards the second century. There seemed no reason
why this progress should ever run itself to a standstill.
There went Edrich hurling his solid drive at Jackson's off-
spinner; and there went the ball, smaller than a flying saucer
through the stratosphere, to come to earth at last in the
heart of the happily cowering spectators behind long-on.

Then, with the suddenness with which this apparently
inevitable game does in fact change course, the game turned
itself inside out again.

Sharp had just shown a respectfully admiring world how
to play Walsh. You flung your leg out fearlessly and swung
back a bat as heavy as a trip-hammer, and the ball was
invisible until it had left mid-on in its wake. But in the
very same over this boldness was his undoing. Out he went—
and Corrall's hands swept into their uppercut; and the
square-leg umpire was unemotionally signalling the death-
warrant.

And then the ball was tossed to Jim Sperry. The score
stood at two wickets for 155, which gave Middlesex at least
a reasonable chance of wriggling away with a draw. True,
they were only 13 runs ahead, but at least they had several
sound batsmen to come: Denis Compton, George Mann and
Alec Thompson, for example.

Jim Sperry took the ball, marked off the beginning of his
run, swung his left arm tentatively, and set off on a canter to
the wicket. Eight balls later Denis Compton, George Mann

and Alec Thompson were back in the pavilion. And Middlesex were still 13 runs ahead—with only five wickets in hand now. Denis and George were finely taken at the wicket. Walsh got his fingers to the cut Thompson aimed at his first ball.

All over bar the shouting? Pretty well, one would have supposed. Of course, there was still Walter Robins to come. And Leslie Compton. But no one else—I suppose you would agree with that?

After lunch the rearguard action began in good order. Edrich set about the task of mopping-up Sperry with the sort of relish Tom Sayers might have shown for tackling Heenan. In a single over he spun thrice on his well-placed heels to wheel his hook into action, and did not drop his bat till the ball bounced over the boundary.

Surely now the pass would be held by the forlorn hope: the game saved at the eleventh hour. And then Corrall came storming into action. As soon as Jackson was brought on to bowl with the pavilion behind him, he fastened on to a catch Edrich flicked off the edge of his bat. In the next over he stumped Robins. And 5 runs later he trimmed Leslie Compton's wicket when the last substantial hope among Middlesex batsmen left his ground to attempt assault and battery upon Leicester. How many other wicket-keepers have claimed six victims in an innings in their benefit match?

Now, once again, the game is virtually over. Middlesex were but 73 runs ahead, and there were only two wickets to fall.

To the middle walked Jim Sims. I like to think that he was cracking jokes with the wicket-keeper as he took guard, as he surely was with every fieldsman within earshot, when, a few minutes later, he uppercut Sperry, the fast bowler, into the pavilion for 6. Could this indeed be Jim Sims? Couldn't Middlesex perhaps have rung in some double with a gift for vintage blacksmith's work that hadn't been seen at this end of the team's batting since Jim Smith's flat-footed drives passed out of the game? There went a boundary, mercifully out of reach of mid-wicket. There went another, the like of which cover hadn't had to chase since Compton was on the drive. And there went a gleaming late cut that Percy Holmes of old would have been proud to own; as full of colour and mystery as a flash of the Northern Lights.

At the far end Jack Young, trim and cool, looking like Gordon Richards riding out a photo-finish, held a dead bat as wide as you could want, to spin and speed alike. In fifty minutes the score rose by 107 runs—if you come to think of it, just about as many as were needed to give Middlesex a sporting chance.

By the time Walsh had bowled down the wickets of the two heroes, Leicestershire were left two and a quarter hours to get the 192 runs needed for the victory they had spent the first two days of the match consolidating.

It was too late now. Many a county has boasted batsmen who can bustle for the runs when faced with such a situation; but Leicester has not been such a one since old Mr. de Trafford's day and the eclipse of the 1888 Australians. Those of us with long and sentimental memories recall John Berry Hobbs and J. N. Crawford bustling for runs at that sort of rate while rain bedewed the fieldsmen at the Oval. And the youngest of us remember Edrich and Compton going in together to chase and capture victory at a speed which no one would reasonably anticipate as possible in first-class cricket.

But Leicester, after two days' hard battling, were not a team of such metal. There was batting there; and it made a little effort. But after Young had taken one wicket Jim Sims was brought into play with the score at 38; and from that moment onwards it was only a question of time—and not much time at that. There was the unimpassioned amble to the wicket, the gentle turning over of the arm, and the tweak of the long fingers. Then Berry's broad bat flails away in vain—the ball scuds through to thud against the pad and the sound is like the thud of a hammer on a coffin. Round turns Jim Sims, calm as a captain of the Royal Navy wondering without undue curiosity whether that entitled him to claim a direct hit on a submarine. That is the end of Berry; and an over or two later Prentice follows him, sunk amidships by the same unemphatic depth-charge.

After that, the side buckles up completely. Only Symington shows a swashbuckling defiance. He flashes out a drive and a hook, and when Laurie Gray hits him hard enough on the nose to tap the claret, he has sufficient *panache* to hit fiercely at the very next ball and run two defiant runs for the heck of it.

But then Sims has his chance at him. Down comes the low-flighted ball, swerving as skittishly as a hardly reined colt, and jigging across the pitch in an uncharted sidestep. The bails cascade from the wicket like a golden fountain foaming up in the sunlight.

After that the side perishes like a victim of hypnosis submitting to his master's voice. Chapman plays his firm, thoughtful stroke; and steps out quietly for the pavilion. Munden unbalances as he seeks to staunch the break, and Leslie Compton unzips the bails from the stumps. A little while—a very little while later, the same Compton catches Jim Sperry and starts off for the pavilion almost before the umpire has signalled his agreement that the match is over.

In less than an hour and a half Leicester have crumpled into defeat. The side that had for two days outfought mighty Middlesex at every flashpoint along the line has been routed and swept to destruction almost without firing a shot in the last action.

In sixty-three balls Jim Sims has taken seven of their wickets for a pitiful 38 runs. This, too, on top of that master-ful 61 gloriously rattled up in fifty minutes.

For two and a half days of this match Jim Sims made no real mark on it at all. Then, in the last two and a half hours, he has undone all Leicester's laborious good work, and after many have performed prodigies, he has won the match for his side, single-handed. In those final hours he has first robbed Leicester of the chance of a win by his batsman-ship—then reft from them the chance of a draw by a display of bowling not surpassed in dominance and danger since the fox on C. E. de Trafford's green cap was a milky-mouthed cub.

The Middlesex Match

And now, with the match won and Middlesex enriched by the points they are to need to share the final honours of the Championship, he rolls ashore from the quarter-deck at last; still talking out of the side of his mouth to anyone within earshot—even an umpire.

Such is the Homeric story of Corrall's benefit; of the six keeper's wickets in an innings; of the marvellous batting of Compton, of Edrich, and of Vic Jackson of Sydney. All of which adds up to—Sims's Match.

The Middlesex Match

(JULY 2—5, 1949)

MIDDLESEX

FIRST INNINGS		SECOND INNINGS	
Robertson, J. D., c Walsh, b Symington	37	c Berry, b Symington ...	3
Sharp, H., lbw, b Symington ...	31	st Corrall, b Walsh ...	56
Edrich, W. J., st Corrall, b Walsh ...	9	c Corrall, b Jackson ...	113
Compton, D., run out	99	c Corrall, b Sperry ...	8
Mann, F. G., b Walsh...	5	c Corrall, b Sperry	0
Thompson, A., c Munden b Symington	65	c Walsh, b Sperry	0
Robins, R. W. V., c Walsh, b Jackson	16	st Corrall, b Lester ...	21
Compton, L., c and b Sperry ...	36	st Corrall, b Lester ...	5
Sims, J., not out	30	b Walsh	61
Young, J. A., c Sperry, b Jackson ...	0	b Walsh	28
Gray, L. H., b Jackson	0	not out	5
Extras	5	Extras	33
	333		333

LEICESTERSHIRE

FIRST INNINGS		SECOND INNINGS	
Berry, L. G. b Sims	70	lbw, b Sims	25
Lester, G., b Sims	18	c Compton, L., b Young...	6
Prentice, F. T., c Edrich, b Compton, D.	16	lbw, b Sims	12
Tompkin, M., c Compton, L., b Gray	94	lbw, b Young	17
Jackson, V. E., b Gray	143	c Robertson, b Young ...	3
Walsh, J. E., c and b Robins ...	82	c Thompson, b Sims ...	5
Symington, S. J., lbw, b Robins ...	1	b Sims	21
Chapman, T. A., b Sims	20	b Sims	2
Munden, V., not out	12	st Compton, L., b Sims ...	0
Corrall, P.		not out	0
Sperry, J.		c Compton, L., b Sims ...	0
Extras	19	Extras	—
(8 wkts. dec.) ...	475		91

Bowling Analysis

LEICESTERSHIRE

Sperry	...	1 for 89	...	3 for 84
Symington	...	3 for 90	...	1 for 18
Walsh	...	2 for 109	...	3 for 62
Jackson	...	3 for 31	...	1 for 74
Munden	...	0 for 9	...	—
Lester	...	—	...	2 for 62

MIDDLESEX

Edrich	...	0 for 32	...	0 for 13
Gray	...	2 for 66	...	0 for 15
Sims	...	3 for 139	...	7 for 38
Compton, D.	...	1 for 130	...	0 for 3
Young	...	0 for 47	...	3 for 22
Sharp	...	0 for 16	...	
Robins	...	2 for 26	...	—

Chapter Nine

THE MEMORABLE DRAW

(I. A. R. PEEBLES)

MORE than twenty years ago Ian Peebles came to town for a few weeks' coaching at Aubrey Faulkner's cricket school. He was a tall and willowy youth, with neat curls on the top of his handsome head, a nice straight nose and the best sculpted nostrils I ever saw on a human face—indeed on any head except that of a race-horse. He was still in his teens, and his experience of first-class cricket had been confined to a few games he had seen in Scotland.

He was, as he still is, a modest person, and it must have been bewildering, not to say shy-making in the extreme, when after he had bowled four balls at the net, neither more nor less, Aubrey Faulkner came up to ask whether that fast leg-break of his was intended.

Well, yes—yes, it was. Wasn't it all right?

Aubrey Faulkner uttered a few words of praise which set Ian Alexander Ross Peebles blushing as a good boy from Glasgow Academy, where praise has rarity value, must blush when he hears words he would never allow himself to listen to in a daydream.

A little later there followed a lunch between master and pupil. Coyly fingering the pepper-pot, Ian murmured his hopes that perhaps he could be trained-on into a bowler good enough to play—er—well, if you see what I mean—er (diminuendo), *county cricket* one of these days. At which Aubrey Faulkner, not given to hyperbole, uttered the pronunciamento that with average luck the young man would play in a class of cricket a great deal more important than *that*.

137

The Match I Remember

And Aubrey Faulkner ought to have known. He had been, in his day, the natural successor or rival to F. S. Jackson or George Hirst as the world's best all-rounder and he was the finest coach who ever taught a leg-breaker how to spin them the wrong way round, out of the back of his hand.

By the time he had put the gloss on Ian Peebles, Plum Warner was ready to launch him as the finished article. He not only launched him: he kept him afloat. He had to; there was so much wind about that the prospect almost got shipwrecked at the launching. Indeed, when Ian emerged from the cloister of the cricket school to the wide open spaces of real life, he felt himself, at first, completely out of place; and the wind was the chief disturber of his peace. How could you bowl your delicate mathematical calculations with this unpredictable element allowed to roar and ramp up and down a cricket ground? Watching the new genius at work in his first game or two, there were some sour comments to be heard around the Oval (where he appeared in Gentlemen and Players) and at Folkestone (where he represented the North against the South). "It surely wasn't necessary to go as far north as *that*," growled one disgusted Yorkshireman, reading a rather dismal analysis in the morning paper.

That was the summer of '27. During the winter Ian went to South Africa, both as secretary to the captain and as one of the more successful bowlers in that adequately successful side. His better achievements never, unfortunately, coincided with the occasion of a Test match; but nevertheless his thirty-four wickets in the tour cost less than 20 runs apiece. There was one very good mark earned by his bowling even as early in the story as this. Whether or not he was expensive, you might expect wickets from him pretty frequently. One in every six or seven overs was his South African record; and that put him in Freeman's class.

Even so he had to wait a couple of seasons to justify himself before the larger public. Nineteen twenty-nine was his first real year as a member of the Middlesex side. Most people supposed that he had been but a very small flash in a very wide pan, and that there was no gold there worth digging for. But in 1929 Peebles played in every match save one for the county team, finishing as its most dangerous bowler, with more than a hundred wickets to his name.

After that the door was open to something like the triumphal march of a war chariot. Now, 1930 was a great year. Ian arrived at Oxford as a portent. He was the latest thing in Brasenose ware. They went in for great athletes at that college in those days: there was even a rumour, quite seriously circulated and believed, that Steve Donoghue's son, Pat, had won a Brasenose scholarship to put some heart into the University polo team.

In his first match for Oxford, Ian took six Kent wickets for 68 runs. No one made any show of playing him with confidence: not even Frank Woolley or A. P. F. Chapman. Later in the week he took six Yorkshire wickets. A pretty encouraging week for Oxford cricket, when your new boy bowler gets rid of Hardinge, Woolley, Ames, Chapman, Percy Holmes, Oldroyd, Leyland, Mitchell, old Uncle Emmott Robinson and all, in just over sixty overs.

And he kept it up. In the next match there were six Leicester wickets for 37 in the first innings; and six more in the second. So it went on all through the term.

At last the team came to Lord's. In the M.C.C. match Ian was put on for a second spell, at the pavilion end, with the score at 167 for five. In six overs and one ball he had wiped the side out, with five wickets for 13 runs. In the second innings he did even better. Again with the pavilion behind him, he bowled invincibly. In two overs he clean bowled four batsmen for 1 run. For the first time for years Oxford reached the University match with hopes magnificently high.

And it is that University match which one would have expected to be the unforgettable game in Ian's dozen years' experience of first-class cricket, which ended when perpetual googly-bowling made it impossible for him any longer to writhe his wrist into the contortions necessary for an ordinary leg-break. Certainly, in it, he did as much to offer Oxford the game, cellophane-wrapped on a silver salver, as any bowler has done since Reg Bettington rumbled through the Cambridge team in two hops, a skip and a googly in 1923. He took thirteen wickets in the match (seven for 75 in the first innings and six for 162 off fifty overs in the second). Melville gave the side he captained a brilliant example with four fine catches off his bowling: but no one followed it. I have heard one of the Oxford team of that year estimate the number of catches dropped off Ian's bowling in the two innings at a dozen: I have heard one of the Cambridge batsmen tot it up to over twenty.

Anyway, he took thirteen wickets, even though, if all the catches that were dropped had been held, he would have bewildered statisticians by taking far more than there were.

I have compared his performance with Bettington's, but in fact we have to look back to 1881 to find a bowler getting so many scalps in a University match. Then the hero was A. H. Evans of Oxford, who performed the feat against a Cambridge team containing the three Studds as well as Ivo Bligh and A. G. Steel. Evans had the satisfaction of winning the match for his side. Not so poor Ian. He bowled himself to a standstill, and Cambridge won by a mile.

And at that, it wasn't, for all his efforts, the match of Ian Peebles's lifetime. This belonged to the same summer, even to the same month of July—and to Old Trafford. You will remember, perhaps, an English film in which Basil Radford and Naunton Wayne, without so much as batting an eyelid, fight their way through all the perils of a trip across a spy-infested Continent to get back to England for an Old Trafford Test. When they arrive they find that, due to rain, no one else is batting so much as an eyelid at Old Trafford either. You will not be surprised to learn that such was the ultimate fate of Ian Peebles's game-of-a-lifetime, too.

England in 1930! It wasn't a bad world, so short a while ago, and it wasn't a bad country in which to suffer the ravages of Tory misrule. There wasn't, for example, a housing shortage. You could rent a four-roomed flat in Kensington for £125 a year. If your tastes were a little grander there was a handsome old-world farmhouse in a village near Marlborough with its five bedrooms, three reception rooms, and its thirty-five acres for £1,000. But if your tastes were really sumptuous there was a mansion in Devon with twelve bedrooms, three reception rooms, one billiard room, two bathrooms, two cottages, stables, a peach-house 150 feet long, and twenty-seven acres for £2,750. If that was altogether too imposing for you there was a trailer caravan, 11 h.p., furnished for two, with a fine kitchenette, for £98—and you could buy a five-inch Havana cigar for two and threepence to smoke in it, and a bottle of champagne for twelve and six; and a year-old Packard six-cylinder, seven-seater saloon, fully taxed, for £300.

That was England in 1930. It wasn't perhaps quite as good if you were a cook-general. You answered an advertisement that offered £48-£50 a year (oh, that differentiation, how much it tells!) for a job in a house with three in family. But on your night off you could spend your half-crown on a seat in the gallery, seeing (at the Aldwych) Lynn and Walls in *A Night Like This,* or (at Wyndham's) Charles Laughton in *On The Spot,* or Marie Tempest and Henry Ainley in *The First Mrs. Fraser,* or C. Aubrey Smith (in the flesh) in Walter Hackett's *The Way to Treat a Woman* at the Duke of Yorks. If you preferred variety, the Coliseum had, topping the bill, what was "acclaimed by the Press" as being the greatest entertainment of the century — a novelty called television. And if your brow was broad enough to have its wrinkles smoothed away by the cinema, there was Gary Cooper in *The Texan,* or Lon Chaney in *Phantom of the Opera,* or—London's longest run—*All Quiet on the Western Front.*

The outside world throbbed and heaved and pulsed with the chemicalization of new life; but looked at through the telescope of twenty years later, that life can barely be observed—the pool seems stagnant. No one had ever heard of Hitler. Mussolini was reforming the Italian railway time-tables. In Canada a Conservative Government had swept into power, Bennett replacing Mackenzie King. In Australia, the Sydney Bridge was meeting above the finest harbour shone on by the Southern Cross. The R100 was flying slowly but triumphantly across the Atlantic. In Outer Mongolia the skeleton of a shovel-toothed mastodon had been discovered. And a Congressional Committee was investigating Communist activities in the United States.

The Match I Remember

Boxing the compass, under Japanese cherry blossom, beside the rose-bushes of Rhineland cottages, in the shelter of the vineyards of Pommard sprawling down the slope from the wild strawberries growing on top of the hill, in the mean and sunless streets that look on the huge stretches of mud and brick that are the children's playing-grounds flanking Headingley, the tots were taking their first steps basking in the beaming admiration of their mothers' eyes. The tots who were to be bayoneted in the Ardennes, or drowned in mid-Atlantic, or slaughtered, as it is illegal to slaughter a pig, in Hiroshima. And we were playing cricket then as we are playing it this summer while other tots are taking their first steps.

In Manchester the mimic armies of England and Australia foregather for the fourth battle of the campaign. England have won the first at Nottingham, despite brave bowling by Grimmett and the ritual century from the Don. Australia has won at Lord's. Duleepsinhji, like Ranji before him and Pataudi after him, maintains the tradition that any Indian who plays for England makes a century in his first Test. Unfortunately Woodfull also makes a century in this Test match; and Bradman makes a double century. And even Chapman's swashbuckling hundred in the second innings cannot save us from the consequences of great bowling by the goblin Grimmett, grinning his bony grin under the mushroom of his over-spreading green cap.

At Leeds a series of rain-storms and blackouts saves England; but not before Bradman has scored the first triple century in Test history. After Duckworth has caught him off Tate for 334 (scored in six and a quarter hours, too), we have a picture of him chuckling malevolently in the dressing-room as he plays a few practice shots and observes that his innings will serve as quite good batting practice for next time.

And now we have reached *next time*. A century in the first Test; a double century in the second; and a triple in the third — what are we to expect from the superman at Manchester?

Ah, but there are changes in the England team. The old

warhorse Maurice Nichols is in instead of that disappointing fellow, Larwood. Ian Peebles and Tom Goddard (he who spans that summer and the present age) are playing in place of fat Dick Tyldesley and George Geary. There was long and anxious consideration as to whether Walter Robins shouldn't be in the side; but in the end, it being Manchester and rain being the expected order of the day, Tom Goddard is preferred.

The night before the game began the rain fell with the punctuality of some hoary music-hall gag. But the first morning was dry and the game was started without any heel-cooling or thumb-twiddling wait. Chapman lost the toss; and if ever captain were glad of not having to undertake the responsibility of sending his side in, it was he. It was all very well facing the best of googly bowlers and the renowned off-tweaker on the sodden, lifeless turf: but what about if the sun came forth to bring out the gluepot in the black heart of Manchester?

With a light breeze blowing down the ground, Nichols and Tate bowled the opening overs to Woodfull and Ponsford. It wasn't, to be frank, an attack to cause gooseflesh in the Australian dressing-room or panic on the pitch. Nichols helped the batsmen get their eye in with a whole quiverful of no-balls; and those that were not no-balls were reasonably negative. It was fairly easy to stand your ground and push them off your legs for comfortable singles.

At 13 Nichols and Tate changed ends, but the mixture remained as before. It was the sort of prescription that wasn't likely to shift anybody.

There was, however, just one little moment when the lack-lustre bowling nearly did the trick. The score stood in the becalmed twenties, and Goddard was pegging away on the fringe of the leg stump with three hungry fieldsmen clustering at short-leg. There came the restrained swing of Woodfull's bat, which appeared to have sworn an oath to keep away from back-lift as others foreswear liquor or tobacco till the age of twenty-one. The ball ascended in a gentle arc towards the group of praying mantises. Alas, for the chance! For a split of a second Chapman, the only fieldsman on the ground who could have contemplated such a miracle of a catch, stood waterlogged in the swampy ground where the rain had drained off the pitch-covers. When he moved, it was to slip; and the chance slipped with him.

On went the innings; still slow and once again sure. In an hour 32 runs had been scored. On the Sydney Hill, Yabba, king of barrackers (a rabbito by trade), would have been cheer-leader in a chorus of "Never Get 'Em Out." In Manchester they sat and suffered in silence. Shortly before lunch Ponsford hit the first boundary of the day: a grandiloquent swish to long-leg.

But meanwhile Ian Peebles had been rushed from the base area into action. The base area, in his case, was the long leg boundary. He fielded there long-sufferingly for a great many overs on end, a fact that was forcibly commented on by Lancashire's Grand Old Man, Arthur Priestley, who (lobster-red from a hot bath in which he had fallen asleep) was awakened in time to share his dinner with the new man. From *hors d'œuvre* to duckling, Arthur complained about the position they had allotted young Peebles in the field. "Why, you might have thrown your arm out, down there in the Antipodes," he grumbled.

"No, it was all right really," Ian reassured him, "you see, I had made up my mind always to lob her up underhand."

Arthur spluttered explosively. *"Lob her up underhand!* Let me tell you, sir, that by doing such a thing you outrage every convention in the game."

Ian felt mildly proud: it was something that there wasn't a single convention left unravished as the result of this single, simple act.

But at last Percy Chapman whistled him up from the deep. As the field crossed the over before he was to bowl his first ball in an Australian Test, Jack Hobbs stopped him for a smile and a heartening word. "Well, so it's your turn now to have a cut at 'em. Don't forget this is just another game of cricket. Nothing more."

"Thanks, Jack. I expect I'll be all right as soon as I really get going."

Maurice Tate in action. Note the splendid balance at the moment before delivery.

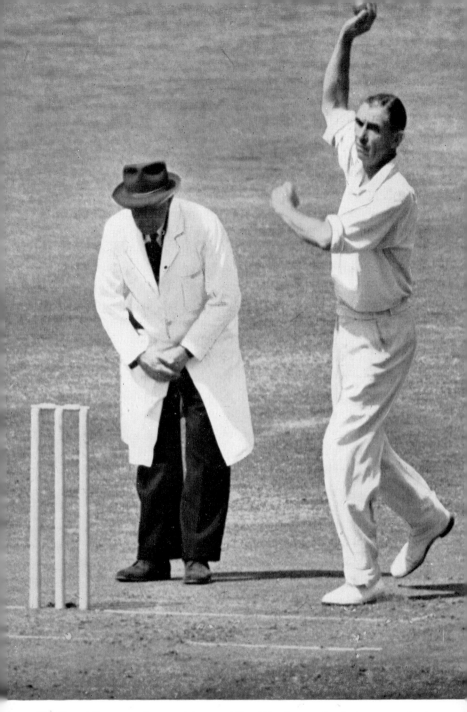

Jim Sims delivers a crafty one (the googly?) while the umpire looks reverently downwar

And a few minutes later the ball was in his hand at last. The long period of waiting was over. This was the great moment of a lifetime—come suddenly, come at last. This was the full flowering of the spring of promise Aubrey Faulkner had noted in the green days. The long-striding run began, gathering pace at the wicket. The body was flung back, the right arm was swept over in full circle. And the fastest leg-break since Barney Barnato is fizzing off the wicket at Woodfull's off stump. For the few overs before lunch the bowling pays no dividend, though those who watch through their binoculars for the least of omens note Woodfull's lips thin as he plays to the break of the ball, and Ponsford's brow furrow as he pats down the wicket at the over's end.

And Woodfull, certainly, needs to draw on his reserves of luck to survive. While Ponsford comes at last to bat with confidence, his partner is tentative, and increasingly tentative, as the overs roll by. Ian is bowling with a single slip, and twice the Australian captain flicks the ball exactly where Duleepsinhji, if he had been fielding in the place destiny ordained for him, would have pulled down the catch with an air of cool assurance. But "Smith" is not there; and the chancey strokes yield runs, not wickets.

And so to lunch. The advantage so far rests with Australia: but those who watch cricket matches while summers wane and the years wax are telling each other that Ian Peebles is bowling well enough to run through a Test team, with luck.

With luck. It still plays its part in this game, even at its highest level—as it did in the Varsity match. After lunch Woodfull goes at last. He is caught at the wicket off Tate at a quarter to three, and before he goes he has two full-blooded drives off Ian (one of them a straight hit) to set against a considerable debit account.

In comes Bradman, to one of the greatest thunderstorms of cheering even he will ever face. It is Ian's luck to bowl the first ball to him: the man with the huge crescendo of Test match centuries to his name. To that first ball Bradman hangs out his bat with complete nonchalance. The ball whips away over the wicket, missing the top of the middle stump by about the depth of the groove on a bail. The champion is morally beaten—beaten, bewitched and bewildered.

Why isn't he out? For the most tragic reason imaginable. All season through, Ian has been bowling, in county cricket and for Oxford, at the *new larger wicket,* in use for the first time that summer. But the Australians have insisted on playing with the old, smaller-sized stumps, and these are in use in the Test match. If Bradman's wicket had been the size of the wicket Ian had been bowling at the week before, and the week after, and all summer through—his innings would have ended with that first ball. As it is he stays on; by no means entrenched in his position but still there, an army in being.

Within a very few overs he has his second stroke of good fortune. Ian bowls him a wrong 'un which he attempts to lash to the boundary behind mid-off. The drive never connects. The ball skids from the bat to Hammond at slip—and Hammond, of all imaginable people on earth, fumbles the catch.

In the pavilion faces grow as long as coffee-pots. Saved by the thickness of a coat of varnish first ball: dropped at slip at 10. Conquistador cannot now fail to make at least a double century. And to show that he concurs, Bradman smashes a full pitch for 4 with the zest of a lawn-tennis ace putting one away at the net.

And then Ian Peebles delivers up to him the same ball that baffled him an over or two back. Snap goes the break off the wicket: snip goes the cut for the gap in the slips—and there is Duleepsinhji tossing her up high and handsome against the sun that has begun to gleam at last above the Manchester cloud-wrack.

And at last the wicket begins to stick out its tongue at the batsman, now and then; or at least to bestow a benevolent wink on the bowler. It is no black-hearted diabolist of wicket; but it has a little spirit in it at least.

But even before this is apparent, the sheer overwhelming hostility of Ian Peebles's bowling has made itself felt. As soon as Bradman goes, the feeling is unleashed that, far from being a luckless toiler denied his rights, he is a giant cat who has been playing with a broth of a mouse.

Anyway, the initiative is in his hands: and the test of whether he can retain it is upon him. The test is Kippax. If he can pen down the most graceful Australian stroke-player since Victor Trumper he will be the hero of his own first Test match.

In comes Kippax to be hit hard upon the pad by the first ball bowled to him. Ian and George Duckworth appeal with thunderous confidence. Hardstaff, the umpire, puts his nose in the air and makes his face empty of all emotion, as if there is a bad smell about, but he is too well-bred to notice it.

Down comes Kippax's second ball. The same helpless flashing at a stroke: far too late, and outside the straightening ball. Again the chorus-wail from bowler and wicket-keeper. Again Hardstaff stares concentratedly at the sun peeping through the chequered cloudscape as if that was the only thing in the world worth a serious man's attention.

Up to the wicket strides Ian, the spring still in every lilting footstep. Over goes the arm, while the straight body over the bent legs curves away to the left. The ball glints in the air, spurns the pitch: and beats the waving bat again. And again the cry: assured, eager, not a mere piece of salesmanship only anxious to draw attention to some *lusus naturae*. And again the freezing face of the umpire, his hands locked behind his back. *Not out. Not out. Not out!*

Three times running Kippax has been hit on the pad plumb in front of his apparently forfeit wicket: and three times running he has been given not out. To their death-beds Ian and George Duckworth will assure you that at least twice (if they are any judges of cricket) Kippax was as certainly out as if all three stumps had been laid flat on their backs; while the third time he was as nearly certainly out as for the event not to be worth betting about. Old Joe Hardstaff's deathbed is behind him now; but from those Elysian fields where he has resumed his place in the game, not as an ageing umpire but as an England batsman in the prime of his powers, I hear him retort that the smaller stumps are in use in this game and, in his judgment (since checked with the Recording Angel), the ball would have passed over the top of them every time.

Kippax lives on; and Bradman's is the only wicket Ian gets in the two and a quarter hours immediately before and directly after lunch, though impartial *Wisden* declares that during this period he bowled so superbly that he has a moral right to five or six victims.

At last Hammond breaks the firmly established partnership of Ponsford and Kippax by bowling the Victorian, who has been about his business for over four hours, with a break-back worthy of the fingertips of a magnifico. The leg-bail is just brushed, and flickers in the air.

And even though McCabe is a quick victim to a fine ball from Ian (l.b.w. at last, too late to tip the balance of the game), Kippax plays himself in to enjoy some smack of revenge for his earlier humiliation. The most exquisite late-cutter in the game shapes a couple of flawless cover-drives off Ian to the boundary: then, when a man is brought from the sightscreen to block the stroke, the next shot he discovers is a straight drive to the exact point on the boundary's brim where the changeling had been standing. In the end Chapman takes Kippax shin-high in the gulley off a cut aimed at a rising ball from Nichols with the clean wristiness of a master of fence.

Tall and angular Fairfax is as hesitant and uncertain as his seniors in the early stages of his innings. Ian whirrs over the top of his middle stump first ball, missing the wicket so narrowly that it is a wonder the draught doesn't disturb the stumps.

On the second day, bowling from the city end, he begins by nearly getting Grimmett caught off a genuine leg-glide by the airborne George Duckworth. The little gnome (who is not to take a wicket in this game) comes out with honours thick upon him as a batsman of merit before Ian forces him to play too soon at a rising ball and Sutcliffe grips the catch at short-leg. He has hit bravely at the pitch of the ball, and a large proportion of his half-century comes from determined drives.

A few balls more, and Goddard has persuaded Hornibrook

to edge an off-break within reach of Duleepsinhji; and Australia's innings is over. The outstanding feature has been none of the batting, but Ian's commanding bowling. He has taken but three wickets for 150 runs; but with ordinary luck (or even with the usual stumps) he would have had six for 60.

The rest of the match was in minor key. The bowling of Tim Wall suggested that Australia still had some hope that shock tactics would prevail. He began to fire down bouncers from the first, and soon enough Hobbs was buckled up under a sobering blow in the groin. It seemed to leave him with little relish for the game. For the most part Sutcliffe farmed the bowling; and once an over at least he lashed a bumper far away to long-leg. His eye seemed as true as ever and his wrists as finely sprung. There was, it is true, one false cut that ended up an inglorious career by bouncing out of Richardson's palm as a result of Hornibrook projecting himself across the fielder's line of vision.

But by and large Sutcliffe was in dynamic form—he flourished his hook against the fast bowling in a way that suggested that he would rather cope with savage bumpers than go gardening any day. When at last he fell it was to the great stroke which had yielded him so many boundaries. At long-leg Bradman stood poised for the catch, bent backwards to avoid stepping over the boundary, and then, with the ball in his hand, toppled into the front row of the spectators. Umpire Hardstaff waited until he held his hand up with the ball in it; whereupon Sutcliffe set off at once for the pavilion.

Only Duleepsinhji invited comparison with Sutcliffe on that day's form. He punched Grimmett and Hornibrook around the field. He unleashed a series of fine, flowing drives, which should have brought a smile to the lips of Uncle Ranjitsinhji sitting in the stand and opining, perhaps out of family modesty, that his nephew was not quite in the class of the Nawab of Pataudi.

Over and above this, there was nothing to write home about except the weather. Much of the English batting was unworthy or unlucky. Hammond tipped a genuine shooter with the outside of his bat on to his wicket. Leyland tottered but endured. By the time stumps fell England had scored 221 for five against Australia's 345.

And on the third day the rains fell. There were occasional bright intervals when a few overs of cricket could be squeezed in, but for most of the time the picture was of one heavy squall after another driving the players back under cover.

In the interval McCabe came into his own as a bowler. He was always, in my eyes, the most dangerous change bowler of his generation, when launched against a well-founded and developing partnership: his medium-pace half-volleys must have looked so commonplace to the good batsman that he disdained to reserve for himself any margin of error. But on this wicket and on this day's form, little McCabe became Napoleon's double in more than appearance. He ran through as much of the rest of the side as there was time for.

His victims included Ian, wished good luck by Fairfax as he passed him on his way to the crease for his first Test match innings. Years afterwards Ian put it to Fairfax, now his neighbour in London, that these words must almost have stuck in his throat. Remembering Ian's form as a bat (and the 6 he scored perhaps over-emphasized his abilities), you will understand from this how tense is Test cricket even when the harlequinade at the innings's end is reached.

Most of the third and all of the fourth day were sacrificed to Manchester's jealous god—rain. The only incident that sticks in the mind is a picture of Maurice Tate, pipe in mouth, sitting in the English dressing-room beside his captain, watching a cloud as black as a tar-barrel roll over the horizon. At last he plucked his pipe from his mouth and pointed the stem.

"See that cloud, Skipper?"

As if you could miss it.

"Well?"

"It flatters but to deceive," said Maurice. And put back his pipe with the air of a man who has relieved his conscience by the utterance of a great truth. To this day, nobody quite knows what he meant.

So, in rain and darkness, in washout and lack of decision,

ended Ian's first Australian Test, the match to which he gave the best bowling of a lifetime, and in which the googly was best bowled by any Englishman, admitting for the moment that the boy from Glasgow Academy has the right to qualify for such a description.

The googly. Yes, the googly. That famous ball, the most difficult in the game, leads Ian, looking back down the years, to theorize in a way that will startle you. When he first came into big cricket, Jack Hobbs could spot and cope with the googly—Jack Hobbs and one or two more. After a few years the numbers five and six bats on county sides were unmasking his conjuring trick. And just before the Second World War *everyone on the side* knew a googly when it was launched, and shaped for the appropriate stroke.

Doesn't this mean that batting (allowing for the interval forced on it by war) is a *developing* art, getting better and better all the time? After all, in almost every other sport the trend is upward; and you can't always attribute it to improvements in conditions. As Sir Donald Bradman points out, swimming records are always improving, but the water isn't getting any better.

There, at any rate, is the theory, a tribute to batting bestowed upon it by one of the great bowlers of our day. I am bound to add that it does not commend itself to certain critics who find cricket more and more delectable and its gods looming larger and larger as the landscape recedes. Neville Cardus, for example, when this particular plea is advanced, does not give any very conspicuous display of philosophic detachment or Christian charity. He becomes, to be frank, just about as hostile to the art of batting, degraded since the days of Trumper and MacLaren, as Ian Peebles himself had been on a weekend in July twenty golden years ago.

The Memorable Draw

(JULY 25—29, 1930)

AUSTRALIA

Woodfull, W. M., c Duckworth, b Tate	...	...	...	...	54
Ponsford, W. H., b Hammond	...	...	...	...	83
Bradman, D. G., c Duleepsinhji, b Peebles		...	...	...	14
Kippax, A. F., c Chapman, b Nichols	...	...	...	...	51
McCabe, S. J., lbw, b Peebles	...	...	...	...	4
Richardson, V. Y., b Hammond	...	...	...	...	1
Fairfax, A., lbw, b Goddard	...	...	...	...	49
Oldfield, W. A., b Nichols	...	...	...	...	2
Grimmett, C. V., c Sutcliffe, b Peebles	...	...	...	...	50
Hornibrook, E. M., c Duleepsinhji, b Goddard	...	...	...	3
Wall, T. W., not out	...	...	...	...	1
Extras (b 23, lb 3, nb 7)	...	...	...	...	33
					345

ENGLAND

Hobbs, J. B., c Oldfield, b Wall	...	...	...	...	31
Sutcliffe, H., c Bradman, b Wall	...	...	...	...	74
Hammond, W. R., b Wall	...	...	...	...	3
Duleepsinhji, K. S., c Hornibrook, b McCabe	...	...	...	54
Leyland, M., b McCabe	...	...	...	...	35
Chapman, A. P., c Grimmett, b Hornibrook	...	...	...	1
Tate, M. W., c Ponsford, b McCabe	...	...	...	...	15
Nichols, M. S., not out	...	...	...	...	7
Peebles, I. A. R., c Richardson, b McCabe	...	...	...	6
Duckworth, G., not out	...	...	...	...	1
Goddard, T. W., did not bat					
Extras (b 12, lb 12)	...	...	...	...	24
				(8 wkts.) ...	251

Bowling Analysis

ENGLAND

		O.	M.	R.	W.
Nichols	...	21	5	33	2
Tate	...	30	11	39	1
Goddard	...	32.1	14	49	2
Peebles	...	55	9	150	3
Leyland	...	8	2	17	0
Hammond	...	21	6	24	2

AUSTRALIA

		O.	M.	R.	W.
Wall	...	33	9	70	3
Fairfax	...	13	5	15	0
Grimmett	...	19	2	59	0
Hornibrook	...	26	9	41	1
McCabe	...	17	3	41	4

Chapter Ten

ARTHUR REMEMBERS ADELAIDE

(A. A. MAILEY)

THERE is a character in *Richard Feverel* who considers himself so insulted by any call to come indoors and attend to his homework that he has to be "dug from the earth like a root." I have no very clear picture of what he looked like, but I have the feeling that by the time he reached the age of sixty-two that cheerful, solitary, determined communer with nature would have been eligible under type-casting to play the part of Arthur Mailey in glorious Technicolor. He would have needed a sun-tanned face, wide and flat as a steppe, a long upper lip which could lift up and look almost as prehensile as an elephant's trunk, and hazel eyes often alight with laughter in a face otherwise grave.

The original of the picture earns his living in a variety of ways, to none of which is he fool enough to contribute any over-serious endeavour. He is a caricaturist of eminence, whose work has made people laugh in most continents. He is a cricket writer read by even solemn students of the game.

He also enjoyed, fairly recently, a short life and a merry one as a general reporter. His editor sent him out to cover the funeral of an ex-Lord Mayor of Melbourne. Arthur's story was weighty enough to satisfy the most gloom-laden witness of the sad occasion; but even so his editor sent for him more in anger than in sorrow.

"Do you know how many names you've mentioned?" demanded the editor.

As if he would. . . .

"Three hundred and eighteen," boomed the editor.

"You've got three hundred and seventeen right. The one you've got wrong is the name of the corpse."

Pausing only to point out that few men can have attained a higher standard of accuracy in their work, Mailey passed resignedly (and the word is chosen with care) out of the office and into the street. He got on a tram which took him to the Sydney Airport.

A few days later I found him sitting on a Fleet Street doorstep, eating an apple. He'd come over to see if anybody would be playing any cricket for him to watch. As it was May, he'd a suspicion that somebody would be. He hadn't bothered to make arrangements to see that his very valuable comments on the game should be collected for the benefit of the reading public, and incidentally of his own bank balance. He'd left one of his sons in charge of the general store on the shores of Cronulla which he owns and runs when in the mood. Between bites of his apple he gently explained that he had a son good enough to play for Australia: a better googly bowler than he himself had ever been. As a consequence of this casual mooch, he knew the strength (if that is the word) of English cricket as no other Australian writer knew it when the first post-war M.C.C. team went (and that *is* the word) Down Under. There never was a reconnaissance made at a strategically more important time; but Arthur drifted into it rather than planned it. If only he could have spelled that ex-Lord Mayor's name properly, he'd never have become the best informed of all Australian critics on English form.

I myself look back over a great many years of close friendship with Arthur Mailey as a lotus-eater looks out across the sunlit landscape of a land where it is always afternoon. Every memory is golden. There was the time when I had no money and wanted to cash a cheque in Tasmania. A bank manager paid up at once as soon as my companion had identified himself as being *really* Mr. Mailey by producing an incontrovertible googly with a bath bun from the office tea tray.

There was the time when Arthur and I decided to replace the somewhat hackneyed cricket number in Syd Beck's variety show in Melbourne's Bourke Street theatre with a streamlined modern act, full of a wit subtle enough to have gratified Max Beerbohm. We gave our order to the scene-painters. We delivered the script to Syd Beck. We explained how you interpreted the gags to the other stars. We gave a pep talk to the chorus. We rehearsed that show with the thoroughness of a couple of Reinhardts. Then came the night. Most of England's Test team filled two boxes: many of Australia's squeezed into another. Searchlights were directed on to Arthur and myself in boxes opposite each other, wearing the only two suits of full evening dress being worn that evening in the Commonwealth. And then—on danced the chorus. And there it was: the same corny scenery, the same corny script, the corny gags, the same corny show as had been shown in Bourke Street, Melbourne, during Test match week since Blackham was a beardless tot. Afterwards they presented us with bouquets. Mine was white roses. What was yours, Arthur?

Those were golden days; but the later days have been finer still. Last time the Australians were over here Arthur drifted round with them, marvellously interpreting the game to newspaper readers in that casual vein of which he is a pastmaster. But this was a sideline. The love of his life, the reason for his being sent to live on the earth at all, was at last made manifest to him; and it possessed him like the passion it was. He discovered, at over sixty, that he was a painter. A solemn, serious painter, painting landscapes that reflected the joy of life that surged in his veins. He painted the skies and wide fields and shallow streams of Norfolk with dedicated ecstasy. He painted beautifully; continually criticized his performance, and improved from livelong day to livelong day.

That was Arthur, the last time I saw him: the enthralled lover of an art which had displayed before him her rich seductions late in life.

Underneath, almost it seemed generations back, there was a cricketer. A cricketer who lost his zest for victory after the Australian authorities flung him out of the game for writing about it when in his prime. A cricketer who replaced the will to win with the desire to have fun. But, farther back still, a cricketer who felt the lust for victory and who knew that winning and losing were the pith and purpose of the long hours of sunlit struggle.

With Arthur Mailey, you can turn back the hands of the clock easily enough. The face of the Australian who (bowling in only four Tests, too) took more wickets in a rubber than any of his countrymen, hasn't changed at all in the twenty-nine years that have passed. The short, trim figure, catlike in its speed and economy of movement, hasn't changed at all. Nothing has changed but the hair: as thick as ever, but snowed under at last. Knowing Mailey, it's hard to resist the conclusion that he's pulled on a white wig to persuade someone in authority he has turned respectable at last.

When the thick hair was brown, at what period was Mailey at his best? He began before the First World War, and for a few overs in picnic games against club players after the Second World War he looked as dangerous as any leg-breaker England was able to call on. But I think he was at his best, because he was most full of fight, quite early in his career. There were giants abroad in those days: and Mailey wheeled up opposite them, turned his arm over as high as a mill-sail, and watched the ball skid and scud away towards the leg stump, while the batsman went through the noblest motions in the general direction of extra-cover. He bowled his googly at Trumper on the Paddington Oval in Sydney, when Trumper was Trumper and Mailey was still wearing borrowed white flannel trousers. The very first googly he bowled at him mashed and minced Trumper's wicket for him. In the second innings he bowled it again. This time Trumper hit him to the wind's four quarters. Arthur is glad to remember this: gladder than he is to remember the first innings. He reverenced Trumper—even his name had a ring and a splendour to it in his ears, then as now.

Arthur had only seven years in Test cricket, and he played in only twenty-one games. In his very first series he did what no one up to then had ever done in a rubber—he took thirty-six Test wickets. In the Fourth Test at

Melbourne he did what no other bowler has ever done in this class of cricket—he took nine wickets in an innings. The only batsman he didn't get out was Hendren. Charles Kelleway bowled him: but not before he had dropped him off Arthur Mailey's bowling. If Warwick Armstrong had bowled Arthur in that First Test when he gave seven other members of his team a chance, it seems certain that Mailey would have exceeded the bag of thirty-eight in a Test series, which, standing to Tate's credit, alone exceeds his record. For one thing, he would almost certainly have got Johnny Douglas out a couple of times. In those days a match counted as inexplicable failure if he didn't get Johnny out once at least; and it was nothing to write home about if he got him out in both innings. In the fullness of time Douglas learned to play him: that is the part of the story Arthur always likes to remember and the only part I have ever heard him tell.

But the match Arthur Mailey remembers best wasn't in '20, nor next summer when, with his help, Armstrong's team pursued its juggernaut way over England. It took place in Adelaide, and it spanned the third and fourth weeks of January, 1924. It was one of the three tightest finishes in the history of England v. Australia, and Arthur Mailey bowled the ball that finished the match.

A. E. R. Gilligan's team reached this Third Test match in desperate straits. It had proved itself an adequate rather than a brilliant side in the earlier games; its victory over a New South Wales team that was virtually of Test strength being its greatest achievement, rather more than offset by defeat at the hands of Victoria and a poor performance in the drawn game against an Australian XI in Brisbane. In the Tests the luck had been against the Englishmen, as it so often is against the weaker side. They had lost the First Test by 193 runs squarely on their merits, but M. A. Noble always insisted that only Gregory and Mailey troubled the English batsmen in the least.

In the eight-day Second Test at Melbourne, England came nearer victory. They lost by 81 runs after a match full of collapses and recoveries, glorious advances and

fantastic counter-attacks. England began by getting the first
three Australian batsmen out for 47; then let the side score
600, at that time the highest total ever hit in a Test. After
that Hobbs and Sutcliffe batted together for a whole day,
bringing the score to 283 for no wickets by the time stumps
were drawn. The game was a perfectly poised riddle; anyone might have won it.

That was the position on Saturday night. Sunday must
have seemed a long day to a lot of people; though not, I
think, to Arthur Mailey, who always snored or smiled totally
unperturbed through those terrible gaps in the action of
white-hot battle. Certain it is that he yorked Jack Hobbs
with a flighted ball that looked simple from the pavilion,
but which was good enough to swing the game once and for
all into Australia's keeping.

And so to the Third Test match at Adelaide: the very
peak of Arthur Mailey's cricketing life.

From the beginning the game was electric. For the third
time running "Horseshoe" Collins won the toss—indeed
Arthur Gilligan has since admitted to me that it was at
about this stage in the tour that he decided that tossing with
Collins was an empty formality unworthy of a great cricket
match. In blazing sunlight, Collins and Arthur Richardson
went out to bat against the bowling of Tate and Gilligan.

At first the wicket, which should have been bland and
mellow, exhibited a quirkishness such as one might expect
of Wells, or a well-sanded Bristol pitch. The experts attributed this to sweating from being covered by tarpaulins to
give protection against fieldsmen during a Sheffield Shield
game immediately before the Test. Certainly it was a
surprise packet, and an argument for a trial ball at the
beginning of an innings. Almost at once Collins held up a
disdainful bat at a good length ball from Tate that he felt
sure was meant to lure him to tickle a catch into the slips.
The ball broke back and hit the stumps.

The game was still less than an hour old when Freeman
had bowled Gregory (promoted from number nine to first
wicket down) and Tate had hit Johnny Taylor's pad in
front of the wicket. Three wickets for 22 runs had redressed

the balance of the luck of the toss, generally considered to be worth at least 100 runs.

But rearguard actions in general and fourth wicket counter-attacks in particular were to be expected of that great Australian team of a quarter-century back. At Melbourne, Ponsford and Taylor had turned a rout into a victory procession. At Adelaide it was to be the turn of Ponsford and Arthur Richardson to stem the breach. That was all that they could manage, but it was enough. It gave the innings buoyancy at least: when a favourable wind blew later, the craft was still afloat to take advantage of it. Richardson, solid and bespectacled, played strong shots off his right foot and occasionally drove redoubtedly. In the end Kilner, cap pulled down over one eye, took his first Test match wicket by hitting his stumps with a ball that spiralled in from far out on the leg side.

And then came fresh disasters. With 100 on the board, three men out and Arthur Richardson and Ponsford in majestic command, the game had seemed reasonably open. But before 120 was up, six Australian wickets were down: Collins, both Richardsons, Gregory, Taylor and Ponsford. Six for 119, and the bowlers at the batsmen's throats, and it's a situation which suggests that there will be an undue amount of clapping if the 200 ever goes up on the board.

Meanwhile the conduct of the fight passed to Tommy Andrews and Jack Ryder. The two of them were the only newcomers in the side after the second Test, brought in to replace Bardsley and Hartkopf. Andrews, square and swarthy, an undertaker by trade, was the finest silly-point or silly mid-on I remember, rolling hard drives up with his hip-bath hands before the days of Sidney Barnes. He was by nature an aggressive driver, a hammerer of short balls, and a flogger of the overpitched. Most people thought him unsuited to the war of attrition into which so many Test matches degenerate.

There were no such doubts about John Ryder. Tall, long armed, with the face of a grave goblin, John Ryder (to whom even *Wisden* gave the initial S for no valid reason whatever) was in Collins's class as a skinner of hostile bowling in a game framed not by time but by eternity. When the bowling fell to pieces, Ryder could punch it. His clockwork defence was varied with a larrup through the covers or a husky pull to leg, the body bent, the arms flailing like mill-sails. Tate was generally good enough to get through his defences, but at this time there was no Tate to hurl down the challenge.

There was no Tate—there was no Gilligan—there was no Freeman. Tate bowled on till the biggest toe of the biggest foot in cricket was a lump of red pulp. Gilligan strained his left thigh after bowling eight overs with a cutting edge to each, and never sent down another ball in the match. Freeman was off the field with a badly injured wrist during most of the Australian innings.

Chapman, captaining the side in Gilligan's absence, faced a catastrophe no Test team leader ever encountered before or since. To realize its magnitude, ask yourself what would have happened if, on the last Australian tour, Bradman had suddenly found himself deprived of the services of Lindwall, Miller, and Bill Johnston. Wouldn't even the English batting have been guaranteed to hit up a match-winning score? Yet Chapman fell back on Kilner and Woolley in a mood that did not suggest he was surrendering the initiative. Of course, Kilner and Woolley were bowlers of experience and skill, but, before this match, with the tour more than half over, Woolley had taken but three wickets and Kilner only one in first-class games with the side. As bowlers, they weren't really second-line troops in Gilligan's army—their place was in the strategic reserve. Moreover, Woolley was suffering from an injured knee; the most serious of all handicaps for a bowler, because it undermines confidence.

Between them, Woolley and Kilner bowled ninety-one overs in this innings, nearly twice as many as the other six bowlers put together. When either of them was too exhausted to struggle through an over, Chapman had to fall back on Hobbs, Whysall or Hendren—the appearance of any of whom as a bowler in a county match would have been the laugh of the season.

How well Woolley and Kilner stuck to their job can be seen by the grim nature of the Australian batting.

This was no time to gather ye rosebuds while ye may. Over after over passed by with Andrews stabbing Woolley to squirming death on the brink of the pitch, or with Roy Kilner's spinners break, break, breaking in vain on the rock of Jack Ryder's defence. The two left-handers had the wicket of all wickets they would have wished to enjoy as batsmen: a brassy, hearty wicket which all but sneered at them. Yet Kilner's high-tossed slow ball which wriggled in from the leg was accurate enough to keep the batsmen pensive: if Tate had been there, to flash and crackle at the other end, the attacking machine would have been magnificently lethal. As it was, it took Ryder six and a half hours to reach a score which equalled the highest ever hit by an Australian cricketer at home in the pre-Bradman era.

Australia's innings lasted through Friday, and nearly through Saturday. Oldfield, dapper and lightfooted, helped to add 108 runs for the ninth wicket. He drove crisply and cut cleanly, and not for the first time made the imaginative wonder whether Australia was right not to promote him to the rank of opening batsman. And Mailey, too, batted seriously and well: his share of the last-wicket stand that raised the score by 73 was contributed by fluent and determined strokes all round the wicket.

For once, in this series (in which forty-five catches were dropped), the fielding was excellent. Hobbs at extra-cover and Chapman, in the gully, at mid-off, or in the deep, each won as much applause during the day as Ryder himself. Only two catches were dropped; the more serious being a stinging drive to mid-on, from attempting to cope with which Freeman retired with a badly damaged wrist.

In the last minutes of Saturday, England opened with Whysall and Tate, preserving Hobbs and Sutcliffe for the long uphill struggle on the far side of the weekend. This escapist tactic fizzled out. Gregory pounded to the pitch, whirled his tearaway arms, and blew Whysall's wicket out of its socket. Strudwick, squat but gallant, waddled out to survive for an over or two before steering Kelleway's length ball into Jack Gregory's big palms at slip. The dauntless acting-captain came out with that seven-leagued stride of his that made it clear that he must have smacked his lips for sheer lust of battle while buckling on his pads. The sun went down on Chapman; but on a blazing Monday morning, he flourished too late at a fast full-toss and heard his off stump skip and somersault like a bewitched thing.

There were four Englishmen out for 69 before Hobbs and Sutcliffe came together with the game to make or mar. They battled from the first as if with their eyes on the last hour of the day: you had only to consolidate till then, and the bowlers, wellnigh filleted from toiling through eight-ball overs in the glaring Adelaide sunshine, would offer them the plucking of a lifetime. All you had to do was to wear them down till their legs were like lead and their arms no longer brushed their ears as they came over. That was all—except, of course, that you had to remain as fresh as a dew-washed daisy yourself.

It was too much even for Hobbs and Sutcliffe. They played the dour game unremittingly, but the hour never dawned when the last defences were ripe and the citadel lay open for sacking. Long before it could be expected Sutcliffe had tilted one from Jack Ryder, that wholesale purveyor of spoon-fed long-hops, into Oldfield's smacking gloves. Hobbs went on; sombrely, ruthlessly. Hardly ever did he show a flicker of his native quality. There were no jaunting-trips halfway up the pitch to breast the spinners as they landed. There were no ballet dancer's spins ending in leg-glides feathering Jack Gregory to the long-leg boundary. There was unblinking concentration; unwavering attention to detail. The runs accrued; as the savings of the thrifty used to accrue, once upon a time.

By the time Jack Gregory's left hand scooped a miracle of a catch off his toecap, Hobbs had achieved one or two major records. He had become the only player in history twice to score three centuries in successive Tests; with his ninth hundred he had established a lead of three Test centuries over his nearest rival; and during the innings he had become the scorer of the greatest number of runs put together in these games. His stature seemed unlikely to be approached in our time. And all the while some thousand miles to the east, a boy named Bradman was beginning to make so many runs in bush cricket in the Blue Mountains that people were saying he should spend his savings on a pair of cream flannel trousers and a one-way ticket to Sydney.

After Hobbs, the English innings was Hendren's. He too was forced by the occasion into playing an innings which was no true reflection of the batsman behind it. Most of the time he merely plodded; but at the innings' end he found himself in such a position that if he didn't get the runs they weren't got at all. Then the giant's arms telescoped out of the sawn-off shot-gun of a torso—and away scudded the ball, half cut, half drive, and wholly out of the reach of the most quicksilver fieldsman.

Freeman helped him to add 39 for the last wicket, making only 6 of them himself, and heroically contriving to provide him with the strike on all suitable occasions. And so the English innings died with its boots on. The side was 124 behind, and was overshadowed by the disadvantage of having the last innings in a marathon game on a wicket which could not endure for ever. But the side was still in the game. The side was still an army in being.

It was still unbroken even when Australia entered the fifth morning of the match 355 runs ahead and with seven second-innings' wickets to fall. What was the betting then—a thousand to one on Australia, or write your own ticket?

And then the luck that had run against England since the first morning, swung in the wind like the weathervane on top of the cathedral overshadowing the lovely Adelaide ground. The rain fell. Every bucketful changed the shape of the scoreboard as if it had swallowed some pill in Looking Glass Land. The great Ryder (86 not out), the highest scorer to date of all Australians in Test cricket, added two surprised runs and was caught and bowled off an ineptitude by Woolley. Ponsford (40 not out) tickled 3 runs out of the Fates and was beckoned to his doom by Kilner. Only Kelleway presented fortitude and the dead bat in a whirling world. England were set to get 375 runs to win.

One thing was palpable. There was no one among the Australian bowlers likely to make as much of that menacing wicket as our pair of left-handers who had in this penultimate chapter come into their own kingdom. Not even Arthur Richardson or Mailey could play upon it as seductively as Kilner or Woolley.

Again, Hobbs, Sutcliffe, Whysall and Kilner were batsmen designed by nature and training to play the sort of cricket that wins Test matches on gluepots. The opening pair settled down thoughtfully, resolutely, to bat their way through to calmer weather where a fruitful wicket would flourish like the green bay-tree. They played the skidding balls firmly enough, and often used their feet to staunch the big breaks; but before the close of play the side had suffered several major blows. Hobbs was gone. He had played his characteristic defensive game—nosing out trouble like a suspicious fox-terrier—until 63 was on the board, of which his share was a judicious 27. Then he had lashed at a downright long-hop from Arthur Richardson, and, before he had time to lean on his bat and admire its progress to the square-leg boundary, had seen it plucked up by Herby Collins with a gesture that suggested that even his gnarled palms were singed. Well, one for 63 was catastrophic news indeed; even though on much the same wicket Australia had lost seven wickets for 39.

Sutcliffe lasted out the day, but before the stumps were drawn he had seen Woolley comprehensively bowled by Kelleway, and Hendren beaten by the same bowler with a ball that might have come on skates from the pitch.

Next day was devoted to defiance by Whysall and Chapman, and afterwards to a series of dour rear-guard actions which gradually wrung a favourable position from the unbudging enemy. Chapman's approach to the crisis was ideal. He rollicked and he frolicked. He went for Mailey in the mood of a younger son using his slim patrimony to confound the bookmakers. What is more he prevailed—it took the negative Kelleway to bring about his downfall, not as Iago wrecks Othello, but as an income-tax inspector contrives the finish of some magnifico among speculators. John Ryder was positively knocked off his outsize feet by clinging on to the tremendous square-cut Chapman smashed towards him at deep-point, but he held the ball above his head, and the scoreboard credited Kelleway with a victory.

"Dodger" Whysall was less abandoned than Chapman, as a sober Nottinghamshire lad should be less cavalier than a playboy from the painted orchards of the Garden of England. His attitude was suspicion first; execution afterwards. He blocked ball after ball, until he was reasonably certain that no one was trying any confidence tricks on him: then he punished the overpitched ball with a whistling straight-drive or a crack through the covers as correct and only slightly less graceful than such strokes as extracted from Hobbs. His end was worthy of the majesty of his achievement. He cuffed Gregory violently and the bowler swooped down the longest arm outside the monkey house to hold the catch against his hocks.

From then onwards, England fought in the fine frenzy of desperation. It was backs to the wall at last—you couldn't expect the last four English wickets to muster 120 between them. But somehow they fought on. Kilner hung out a dead bat, and Tate hit as if all the Sussex sea-breezes were animating him. The two of them went, in due time—Tate, after two firework overs, to a googly from Arthur Mailey that resembled something out of a conjurer's command performance rather than a ball by a Christian bowler.

And now it seemed that the end was at hand. Arthur Gilligan—Freeman—Strudwick. You would really not have looked to them to be good for more than 20 between them against determined bowling from a race of supermen. Yes, 20 would have been a very reasonable score to insure them at, and they were set to get 63.

Arthur Gilligan and "Tich" Freeman set off as if they meant to get them. The bowlers were tired. Against that, Gilligan was handicapped by a leg that made every turning movement exquisite agony, and going for each run at least serious discomfort. While Kilner was still there, mortality was written all over his performance; but after that the limp that took him to the batsman's crease began to take on the authority of a captain's stride to the quarterdeck. Freeman, hardly taller than his bat, stood his ground on the lower-deck—Jack Gregory could pump his shells into him; Freeman wasn't going to strike his flag.

The two fought on. They had inched the score forward by some 30 runs, when again the rain fell. This time the shower was no friend to England. The bowlers were leg-weary; the batsmen sustained by the inspiration of achievement against odds into some sort of miraculous lunatic energy. They had only to keep on keeping on, whereas the bowlers had to find a second wind from somewhere. The hour's respite that night gave them that second wind. When battle was joined again on the last morning the English pair had to do something more than just keep on keeping on: they had to get going.

Of course, no game ever broke off at a more tantalizing moment. The unluckiest man who ever lived was the lover of cricket who died on the night of January 22, 1925, with the greatest riddle unsolved.

Twenty-seven runs to win: two wickets to fall. Gilligan, Freeman and Strudwick against Gregory and Mailey—and Collins. That, in essence, was the crux of the situation: a crisis held in suspense overnight.

I suppose if the two teams had played the match out from that position every day for a fortnight the result would have been a tie. But they had to do no such thing. They had to fight it out once and for all; and perhaps in those circumstances the game was won and lost in the watches of the night of the 22nd.

A dozen years afterwards I dined, on the night before a Brisbane Test match began, with the two protagonists of that duel: the two Arthurs—Mailey and Gilligan. Arthur Gilligan told me that he had been unable to sleep all night, his responsibilities as captain and as batsman-in-chief for the occasion weighed terribly upon him.

Arthur Mailey did not sleep either. He put on tails and the white tie in which he felt happiest, and set out to enjoy himself. He finished up at dawn in the flat in which Herbert Collins, the Australian captain, was staying. From the window they looked, far down, on to the scoreboard on the distant cricket ground itself. They looked at it thoughtfully, silently—that symbol of the romantic duel upon which the attention of an Empire was riveted.

At last Mailey spoke: "Well, Herbie, I suppose you'll start off with Jack Gregory and Charles Kelleway." Yes, that was certain to be it. Gregory to attack. Kelleway to shore up against possible collapse at the other end. That was bound to be the tactic.

And Herbert Collins, that great gambler, answered him in his high-pitched, cool voice: "No, Arthur, I open with Jack Gregory—and you. It's to be all duck, or no dinner."

Soon they were to be on the ground; and soon (though it seemed like waiting for ever) battle was to be joined.

Gilligan and Freeman would be struggling with their backs to the wall, against Gregory and Mailey. *All duck or no dinner.*

But Arthur Mailey didn't get out to the middle without a little adventure. In the dressing-room he decided to drink a bottle of soda-water before going on to the field. He wandered around, looking for an opener. Up bustled an attendant, feverishly longing to be helpful. "Let *me* open it, Mr. Mailey. Oh yes, let *me* open it. After all, you might cut yourself, one's heard of such things, and where would Australia be then? Why, you might cut half your thumb off. You might indeed. In the paper only yesterday——"

It seemed simplest to let the fellow do his good deed for the day.

Arthur Mailey stood around, gazing at nothing, when a sound between a coronach and the howling of the Hound of the Baskervilles brought him back to earth. The zealous attendant had done his stuff with the bottle opener. Now his thumb hung from his hand, all but severed. People were rushing out into the pavilion to ask if there was a doctor in the house who preferred treating semi-severed thumbs to watching the tightest finish in Test match history. The last thing Arthur saw before ambling on to the field was the man who had opened his soda-water for him being carried on a stretcher into the ambulance.

And then at last the game began.

All Adelaide, of course, was there to watch it. The impresarios of South Australian cricket had two possible courses open to them. They might have charged double price for admission, claiming that though the spectacle on show couldn't last more than half an hour or so, it was the most unforgettable half hour any spectator there was ever going to spend. Alternatively, they could throw the gates open and invite the public in free. With true Australian generosity they chose the latter course.

And the public responded. Every office in the city changed its lunch hour; and everyone who could walk, drive or be carried was inside the Oval to watch the end of a game which had swung from climax to climax through six long days.

They were to see five overs and two balls—forty-two balls in all.

Australia began with a stroke of dramatic misfortune, when you remembered that this was a match where every run counted. Gregory's first ball flew wide of Oldfield to the boundary. Four byes. Only 23 needed now.

The second ball was better: a great buzzing brute of a yorker which Freeman just stifled in time. The fourth ball made the crowd shriek, too—the batsman just succeeded in keeping it out of his wicket, but an extra coat of varnish might have been fatal. Off the sixth ball came the first runs of the day from the bat; 2 from a square-cut which Hobbs couldn't have improved upon.

When Collins threw the ball to Mailey for the second over of the day, there was a silence as opaque as the silence at the bottom of the sea. A blockbuster landing in the far-away world beyond the cricket field would hardly have raised a ripple. Collins and Mailey stood together, conferring, planning. They were the two men sporting (but it is the wrong word) the most mask-like faces in the world. The interval before the bowler got to grips must have been as testing for Gilligan as the agonising moments during which Carpentier kept Billy Wells waiting in the ring.

At last the bowler was ready. Andrews had been shifted

a few feet nearer the bat: then fewer feet farther back. Gregory had been moved closer in towards the wicket-keeper. Ryder had gone out a couple of yards at deep-point.

Down came the ball; a balloon drifting slowly through the tranquil air that suddenly put its nose down like a V1 shooting in to land. Arthur Gilligan tapped the leg-break safely away; and mopped his brow. And thus, the over, cooked up in black magic, was digested and survived. Gilligan on-drove the fourth for a single; and Freeman scored a run off a horrible poke to silly mid-on which went like a mashie-shot over Kelleway's head.

The third over brought the crisis to its peak. Gilligan, no professed bat at all, had endured at the wickets for an hour and three-quarters, surviving plots against his person during every minute of his stay. He had batted better than ever before in the tour—and this with a grievously injured leg. His ninth-wicket partnership with another professed non-batsman had enriched his side with 45 runs, every one of them a penny from heaven.

Now, at last, the captain's hour had struck. He shaped to drive Gregory's slower ball towards mid-off. Richardson was standing there impassable, as if his name had been not Victor but Verdun. He sprang into the air as the ball came at him, as if to take it above his head; then dropped his hands and made an easy catch of it. The experts assumed that the little jump was the instinctive gesture of a great Australian Rules footballer going in for a mark; but Richardson told me later that the plain fact was that he began by misjudging the flight of the hit.

Strudwick now—and 18 runs still needed. Nothing dire came to pass during Mailey's second over, which was featureless except that Freeman hit a majestic cover-drive to the boundary off the seventh ball.

Gregory's third over was almost entirely off the wicket— you see, even great bowlers wasted golden opportunities in the Heroic Age, whatever you may have heard to the contrary. Strudwick hit a two to the on: there was no other incident.

Then, at last, the end. Freeman stood away from Arthur

Mailey's first ball; but he covered up to the second—the break beat him—there came a click—and there was Oldfield, bending back wide of the off stump with the ball in his gloves. Every other Australian's hands were stretched high over his head; and the appeal was the crashing crescendo when the electric atmosphere breaks and the storm has come.

After that, of course, the crowd stampeded over the ground, slapping everybody's back, and by a fine dramatic instinct carrying one conqueror shoulder high to the pavilion. That was how you could have seen Arthur Mailey, a quarter of a century ago, at the pinnacle of his finest hour.

Today, if he plays cricket, he would rather his side lost than won: "Because it seems to give the others so much pleasure."

Moreover, he would probably swap you even that victory for one good canvas—one real painting he could feel proud of—which he will never allow himself to believe he has actually achieved.

Rather like Wolfe, if you remember, in front of the Heights of Abraham.

Arthur Remembers Adelaide

AUSTRALIA

FIRST INNINGS		SECOND INNINGS	
Collins, H. L., b Tate	3	b Freeman	26
Richardson, A. J., b Kilner	69	c Kilner, b Woolley ...	14
Gregory, J. M., b Freeman	6	c Hendren, b Woolley ...	2
Taylor, J. M., lbw, b Tate	0	b Freeman	34
Ponsford, W. H., c Strudwick, b Gilligan	31	c Hendren, b Kilner ...	43
Richardson, V. Y., c Whysall, b Kilner	4	c Tate, b Woolley	0
Ryder, J., not out	201	c and b Woolley	88
Andrews, T. J., b Kilner	72	c Whysall, b Kilner ...	1
Kelleway, C., c Strudwick, b Woolley	16	not out	22
Oldfield, W. A., lbw, b Kilner ...	47	b Kilner	4
Mailey, A. A., st Strudwick, b Hendren	27	c Sutcliffe, b Kilner ...	5
Extras (lb 9, nb 4)	13	Extras (b 4, lb 4, nb 3) ...	11
	489		**250**

ENGLAND

FIRST INNINGS		SECOND INNINGS	
Whysall, W. W., b Gregory	9	c and b Gregory	75
Tate, M. W., c Andrews, b Mailey ...	27	b Mailey	21
Strudwick, H., c Gregory, b Kelleway	1	not out	2
Chapman, A. P. F., b Gregory ...	26	c Ryder, b Kelleway ...	58
Hobbs, J. B., c Gregory, b Mailey ...	119	c Collins, b Richardson, A.	27
Sutcliffe, H., c Oldfield, b Ryder ...	33	c Ponsford, b Mailey ...	59
Woolley, F. E., c Andrews, b Mailey	16	b Kelleway	21
Hendren, E., c Taylor, b Gregory ...	92	lbw, b Kelleway	4
Kilner, R., lbw, b Richardson, A. J.	6	c Richardson, V. Y., b Richardson, A. J. ...	24
Gilligan, A. E., c Collins, b Richardson, A. J.	9	c Richardson, V. Y., b Gregory	31
Freeman, A. P., not out	6	c Oldfield, b Mailey ...	24
Extras (b 8, lb 10, nb 3)	21	Extras (b 5, lb 5, w 1, nb 6)	17
	365		**363**

Bowling Analysis

ENGLAND

	O.	M.	R.	W.	O.	M.	R.	W.
Tate ...	18	1	43	2	10	4	17	0
Woolley ...	43	5	135	1	19	1	77	4
Kilner ...	56	7	127	4	22.1	7	51	4
Gilligan ...	7.7	1	17	1				
Freeman ...	18	0	107	1	17	1	94	2
Hobbs ...	3	0	11	0				
Hendren ...	5.1	0	27	1				
Whysall ...	2	0	9	0				

AUSTRALIA

	O.	M.	R.	W.	O.	M.	R.	W.
Gregory ...	26.2	0	111	3	23	6	71	2
Kelleway ...	15	6	24	1	22	4	57	3
Mailey ...	44	5	133	3	30.2	5	126	3
Richardson, A. ...	21	7	42	2	25	5	62	2
Ryder ...	6	2	15	1	2	0	11	0
Collins ...	5	1	19	0	9	4	19	0

Chapter Eleven

THE BALL THAT SWUNG A TEST MATCH

(W. J. O'REILLY)

THE right people never get knighted for their services to literature. Knock off a dozen plays, and a score of ponderous novels, showing not the rise and fall but the dead level progression of the weary generations, and you can hardly side-step an accolade.

Someone has a better right. He's probably on the Sydney Hill, straining on tiptoe at this moment to get a glimpse of the wicket through the back of a well-nourished neck— a little old man who gave two hemispheres a household word when he applied the Homeric epithet to W. J. O'Reilly. "The Tiger's going on to bowl. Go it, the Tiger!" Nothing garish about it; nothing forced or fanciful. Just a nickname that is inevitable—once you have thought of it. A nickname that has brought a gleam of happiness into the eyes of a generation recognizing its aptness, its poetic quality, its imaginative perception. To have enriched the public with the only perfect nickname in a quarter-century should have been worth a knighthood.

And what was it worth to be a bowler who bore such a universally respected nickname? There is, it seems, no knighthood in that line of business. It is the batsmen who get promoted to captain teams; it is their centuries which are splashed across the headlines of the great newspapers; it is their autographs which can be swapped on level terms with those of Danny Kaye or Gordon Richards. They receive honours from their king; and doubtless after death they will be given State funerals.

But bowlers do their job with all the world against them. "What a wonderful match! Three double centuries and ten sixes!" I've heard it said plenty of times. Who ever heard crowds streaming off the ground excitedly praising the game they'd seen because the bowlers had got each side out for under a hundred in every innings? And what sub-editor ever cleared his back page headline to make room for the news that someone or other had taken six wickets in an innings?

It is only by achieving sheer sensationalism or by long unremitting service to the game that a bowler can win a permanent place in the cricket public's consciousness and memory. One such type was Larwood—because it was whispered that Australia might leave the Empire unless this man bowled slower or re-arranged his leg-field to please the batsman. There were Mailey and Grimmett and O'Reilly, and Barnes and Foster and Maurice Tate; all of whom took Test match wickets for a decade or so. *Wisden* never fails to print long lists of batsmen with Test centuries to their credit; but it omits the roll of honour of bowlers who took six wickets in an innings.

And yet sometimes, the cricket public being sagacious and judgmatic, a great bowler will win a name for himself on a single day's play, and that a day on which he has not had any very imposing success. Bill O'Reilly was one such player. He became a Test cricketer against England in Woodfull's side opposing Jardine's touring team of 1932-3. He had earned for himself a great name in bush cricket: indeed it was said that this young bowler was the only man capable of taming a Bowral boy named Bradman who was breaking records with monotonous regularity in upcountry games less than a hundred miles from Sydney.

By the time Jardine's team reached its first Test match in Sydney, he was regarded by optimistic Australians as only less likely than L. Nagel to run through the English side. Nagel was preferred, because in the match against an Australian XI at Melbourne a fortnight before the Test, he had taken eight wickets for 32 runs in ten overs: perhaps the most sensational piece of bowling against an England side between the two wars. O'Reilly had his chance in the next game, which he could not prevent New South Wales losing by an innings. Off forty-five overs he ceded only 86 runs, taking four wickets

There were great hopes after this that he would begin his Test match career with a burst of easily earned glory, but in fact it was to be an uphill grind from the first. When the weekend arrived, after two days' play, England had 252 runs on the board for the loss of one wicket—and Grimmett had taken that one. True, O'Reilly had constantly troubled Wyatt and all through the afternoon had bowled superably, well enough to be clapped all the way back to the pavilion: but to the bowler all the applause in the world has a less agreeable sound than the tinkle of one little bail.

The same thing happened throughout the third day of the match. Once again there was tireless, ferocious bowling —and not one wicket. No bowler ever had to serve a sterner apprenticeship, but by the end of the innings O'Reilly had established himself as a permanent feature of the Australian side. Not till he had bowled more than sixty overs (at less than two runs apiece) did he get his first victim. Then he took three quick wickets. Perhaps the most impressive thing about this marathon performance had been his accuracy. Almost half his overs were maidens—he bowled no less than thirty-two of these. Moreover he got these maidens without ever indulging in negative bowling. He never left the wicket alone: miss him, and you had your bails in the air almost for a certainty. When the team for the Second Test was chosen it was no surprise to find that the much publicised Nagel had had his day: but O'Reilly was there—as opening bowler with Tim Wall.

It is this Second Test match which O'Reilly picks as the unforgettable game of his own career. It was a crucial game; as crucial in its way as the Second Test against Chapman's side four years earlier, when the selectors and John Ryder had the almost hopeless task of discovering a new generation of cricketers to replace the Old Guard who had at last collapsed on duty.

Three changes had been made from the side so severely beaten at Sydney three weeks earlier.

The Ball that Swung a Test Match

Among the batsmen, Ponsford and Kippax were replaced by Bradman and O'Brien. Bradman had not been fit to play at Sydney. There was world-wide interest to see how he would face an England attack which (since Bowes replaced Verity) was expected to rely almost entirely on its battery of four fast bowlers. Bradman's admirers assured the world that of course he was certain to hit a dazzling century. His detractors scornfully proclaimed that, on the contrary, this was one time when he would settle for a duck. Both turned out to be right.

There was, of course, no argument about Bradman's place in the team: and not very much about Ponsford's exclusion from it. It would be fawning flattery to pretend that Ponsford was at home against the bowling of Larwood. I remember occasions when he turned his back on it, and then ducked. I remember others when he moved away, leaving his leg stump unprotected and then fired off strokes which sometimes looked impressive—for a while. The best batsman you could wish to have against any bowling except the very fastest, he was certainly less than his magnificent self against Jardine's special form of attack.

O'Brien had twice made runs against England, and deserved a Test match trial. He was a flashing, and sometimes a flashy, left-handed stroke-player. There wasn't a finer fieldsman at silly-point or silly mid-on: he ranked in such positions with Sidney Barnes, Tommy Andrews or A. P. F. Chapman. He was very unfortunate to be relegated to twelfth man after his failure in this match: a quite insufficient trial.

The single bowling change was to replace Nagel with "Dainty" Ironmonger, a square, grizzled war-horse who could bowl slow spinners for any given number of overs with the most complete accuracy, who was vitriolic on a rain-damaged wicket, and who was, without any shadow of doubt, the worst fieldsman who ever graced a Test match. In fact, he was not a fieldsman at all: he rarely made an attempt to stop a hit in his direction at mid-on, preferring to rotate slowly on his axis and lumber after the ball. His catching of Larwood for 98 in the last Test of this tour was one of the most melodramatic improbabilities in the history of big cricket. There are those who believe that the Australian crowd never clapped Larwood home to the pavilion at all—they just never stopped clapping Ironmonger.

Such was the team Woodfull led at Melbourne for the Second Test. It contained six batsmen, four bowlers, and a wicket-keeper. Remembering that England batted to number nine and had much the stronger bowling, you would have been forgiven for not expecting Woodfull's men to offer any very formidable opposition to a side which at this stage in the tour gave every indication of being unbeatable.

If you thought that, you were one of a minute minority in Melbourne. The game began on a Friday, but that didn't stop nearly 64,000 people from watching the first day's play. This world's record crowd for cricket, as it was at the time, was about eight per cent of the city's population: if London showed the same interest in Test matches we should get well over half-a-million queueing for the 30,000 seats at Lord's.

Woodfull began by winning the toss; never an unmixed blessing on a ground where the wicket is traditionally full of genial diabolism before lunch on the first day. But for once the Melbourne pitch behaved like a reformed character. There wasn't a sneer at humanity or a degrading dig at the pretentiousness of mankind—the wicket purred and prosed like a platitudinous bore at a prize-giving. Larwood poured his fury out on it in vain; there wasn't a spark to be struck out of the cloddish earth. In his second over, Jardine switched to the leg-field. There they went to take up position; Leyland at forward short-leg, Allen square with the wicket, Jardine bending forward like an inquisitive stork at short fine-leg; with Sutcliffe and Hammond a little deeper. But the ball did not spurt up above stump height: no uncontrolled defensive stroke appeared, as by reflex action, to offer a catch on the packed leg-side.

Indeed, the only incident was the breakdown of the ball in the third over. It had gone in the seam, and when the umpires procured a new one from the pavilion, Woodfull pointed out that the Australian batsmen should not be

Determination in person! Even in the nets "Bill" O'Reilly puts more "hate" into delivery and expression than many less wholehearted bowlers do in the field of play itself.

Manchester Test. Third Test between England and Australia, 1930.—Peebles bowling.

Ames (batting), during England v. Australia Test match at Nottingham, 1938.

asked to face two new balls in three overs, and was given permission to play a sort of French cricket to take the shine off the new arrival until its general condition was indistinguishable from that of its predecessors. After this solemn rite the game went on, and Larwood retired from the crease without a single victim in his opening and most dangerous spell of bowling.

Soon enough, however, Allen, bowling with fire and precision to a field conventionally set on the off-side, did what Larwood had failed to do. The ball that hit Woodfull's stumps was magnificent of its kind: of a length to force the batsman to shape for a defensive stroke, and with a whiplash speed off the pitch to race the putting into effect of this instantaneous reaction. The unfortunate Woodfull was the less ready to face such a humdinger because he had just previously been hit over the heart by a bumper.

One for 29: a fair start—and here came O'Brien, first wicket down, the place in the batting order we have always thought peculiarly Bradman's own. An aggressive batsman by nature, he had to restrain himself and help to wear the bowling down, and he never looked quite at home in the rôle.

Australia had scored 42 for one by the time the lunch interval arrived. The batsmen had survived the first shock treatment by Larwood and Voce (who loosed more short-pitched bumpers than his senior partner), and it seemed that they might now live on, gingerly coping with the lesser voltage of Allen, Bowes and Hammond.

But after lunch, the drama of the First Act was to unfold with dizzying speed. It began when O'Brien saw a short run from a ball played slowly in the general direction of Pataudi. The Nawab was a deceptive fieldsman; immobile or lolling one minute, a flash of activity the next. He sprang at the ball, whipped home his return, and O'Brien had lost his wicket in the most unsatisfactory way in which a newcomer to Test cricket can begin his career.

In came Bradman, cheered every step of the way. He took guard slowly, carefully, as was his way; stood for one moment in relaxation, and then darted his eyes round the field, making a quick mental note of the enemy's order of battle.

Then Bowes began his loping run to the wicket, towered and untangled his long arms, and shot forward a ball which he has since assured me was not the long-hop it may have seemed at the time. Bradman certainly was deceived into supposing it just such a thing. He drew back, squared his shoulders and let fly with a terrific hook designed to cause the crowd at square-leg to take cover for its very life. The ball beat him; he was but able to touch it, and edge it on to the top of his leg stump. I had seen Bradman go in this way against a West Indies team; but it had never occurred to me that his fondness for scoring to leg off the first ball he received would lead him to such a fate in a Test match against England.

Three wickets for 67: none of them to Larwood. Certainly the game was running England's way now. There were only McCabe and Richardson to help Fingleton drag the side to safety before the hutch was open; and though McCabe was always capable of any deed which might re-mould the shape of the game, Victor Richardson only once in this series of Tests was to look more dangerous than a club player with a magnificent eye defying an attack of superior sophistication and experience.

Meanwhile there was Fingleton to be got rid of. He was closing in on his half-century and so far had given no signs of mortal weakness. He played the fast bowlers, if not comfortably (and he was a batsman who never luxuriated at the wicket), at least without apprehension or hesitancy. He always looked a mechanical run-maker, created from a blue-print out of a Meccano set. Alone among Australians of his day, he had a defensive forward stroke which smothered the fast ball before it began to rise for ribs or wicket. With very strong forearms he could force a ball off his back foot, between point and cover, and though he indulged in no full-blooded pulls which made even the non-cricketer in the crowd tingle with the sheer human rapture of the achievement, he was by no means brittle on the on-side. An exceedingly difficult man to get out: though, when one came to look back on his innings with several healing years between, it was hard to recall exactly where the runs had come from. But it was very certain that they came.

He didn't, on this occasion, find the headstrong partner he was looking for in McCabe. This pocket Hercules played a few valiant strokes off Bowes and Hammond, but Jardine was quick to sense a weakness for an uncontrolled act, and in the fullness of time he himself closed his hands over a rather piano poke into the gully.

Up till the tea interval, the balance of the game had been fairly distributed between attack and defence; but there had been a feeling in the air that moral supremacy lay with the bowlers, and sooner or later they must have their way. The hour struck shortly after the tea interval. First Allen whipped home a ball past Fingleton's bat to trim the bails from the stumps. Then Voce took two wickets within the space of a few minutes. Richardson was caught by Hammond at deep square-leg, and Sutcliffe held a hard hit from Grimmett in the last over of the day.

Seven wickets for 194 left the game tilted England's way. But for the fact that Larwood had not given of his best, partly because his boots were giving him discomfort, the advantage would have been more marked. As it was, it was surprising to find that, on the pitch on which Barnes had won his greatest triumphs, the fast bowler had yet to take his first wicket. He speedily put this right next morning, wasting on O'Reilly and Ironmonger balls which might have been preserved for the top batsmen in the second innings.

Oldfield, cool and dapper, remained unbeaten. He looked, not for the first time in his career, one of the most trustworthy bats in the side. If, by general consent, he was considered an inmate of the hutch, he had his nose firmly on the wire-netting—if he was not actually nibbling out an escape route towards the aristocracy beyond. In the averages for this series he finished above Fingleton, Ponsford, O'Brien and Kippax; and if his academically faultless strokes had had the added weight of a follow-through, he would have ranked with the most dangerous Australian batsmen.

No one could have called the 228 runs facing England an

intimidating score. On a pitch which befriended batsmen, England was expected to top it by a couple of hundred at least.

But from the very first the team never looked like mastering the finest bowling they encountered on the tour. Wall and O'Reilly carried the day, and they might as well have been allowed to bowl unchanged through the English innings. Wyatt was groping and tentative and there were moments when Wall put his hand to his mouth as he watched his fastest ball almost fan the bails from the stumps. In the end the opening batsman departed miserably, the victim of a sad lapse of judgment: he raised his bat in the air and covered his wicket with his pads against O'Reilly's fastish leg-break. In this humiliating position he saw the umpire's hand raised against him as O'Reilly and the reticent Oldfield appealed in unison. That was one thing about Oldfield—if he joined an appeal, you could reconcile yourself to the justice of the decision given against you. He never asked questions of the umpire "on spec." Moreover, I have seen him many times sketch in the motions of breaking the wicket but decline to disturb a bail because he knew that the batsman had regained his ground by the fraction of a second. He was the fairest, as he was the most immaculate and most dangerous, wicket-keeper of the last quarter-century.

Things continued to go wrong for England. Wall broke through Hammond's defence and sent a stump jigging into the gully. Pataudi dragged a ball from O'Reilly, wide of the off stump, back on to his stumps. And Leyland, promoted to close the gap, hit away heartily until the Tiger wrecked his wicket while he was indulging in a dip which would have made Emmott Robinson cut him out of his will.

Even Sutcliffe was surviving more by luck than Yorkshire judgment. Once or twice O'Reilly let out banshee wails of appeal against him, but the umpires could not see it his way. And once, while Grimmett filled the strange and sad rôle of acting as change bowler while the chief agent of destruction had a rest, McCabe inexplicably dropped a chance from him in the slips.

The Ball that Swung a Test Match

As for the rest of the English batsmen, their display was pitiful. Jardine was caught by Oldfield, striking like a hawk at a sparrow, from a perfectly executed leg-glide off a long-hop from Wall. Ames was bowled while indulging in a wild slog at a good-length ball. And then Sutcliffe himself went, well caught by Richardson from a mistimed forcing stroke.

There were hopes that Larwood might stem the rot, but O'Reilly deceived him in the air and off the ground, and the day's play ended with the dismissal of Voce, after Allen had struck a few valiant blows scattering the fieldsmen who were crowding up towards the bat like poor relations closing in on the solicitor at the reading of the rich uncle's will.

At the close of play it was 161 for nine: in answer to Australia's 228. Feeble as it looked in itself, it was all the more paltry when one remembered that an hour or two previously 80 was on the board with only two batsmen back in the pavilion.

Moreover, no part of the English collapse could be attributed to original sin in the wicket, or to maliciousness on the part of the light, or to any other acts of God.

The batting had crumpled simply because the bowling had taken the wind out of it. Tim Wall, a much better bowler in Australia than was appreciated in England, had been tireless as ever and had developed a head of steam which suggested to a few gullible optimists that, if fast bowling could win Test matches, Australia had nothing to worry about.

Yet the main cause of England's collapse was the zeal and unvarying hostility of the Tiger. He was always too good to be hit off his length—both Leyland and Allen tried it, and both in due course paid the price. His accuracy was such that he could set an offensive field, and still bowl a maiden every other over.

Perhaps for the first time we noted those portents which in the decade to come were to be the very hallmark of his triumphs—the long, pump-handling run to the wicket, with the ball clenched in the fist, the body-swing at the crease, and the right arm rippling up, like a cobra writhing and rising to a snake-charmer's music. Then down would bang the big left foot, and over would sweep the arm: and out would shoot a ball, faster than any ball has a right to be with so sharp a break clamped upon it. And there would come the reflex-action dab on the principle of better late than never, and the ball would end in the hands of slip, doing a brisk knees-bend exercise almost perfunctorily at the sight of this fast-rolled leg-break. Or perhaps the wicket would be cracked apart; and there would be O'Reilly, unemotionally rubbing the sweat from his vast palm, preparatory to bowling another thirty overs just like the first thirty he had limbered up with after they had given him the ball, as soon as the sheen had been knocked off and it was of no use to the fast bowlers. Didn't he bowl till he had skinned his fingers raw in the last Test match before the Second World War? And even then he wasn't prepared to call it a day. How fascinating it was (and how typical of Australians) that he should come into the game, a fully developed figure of greatness, at the very hour when Grimmett's magic was beginning to wane.

He finished off England's first innings early on the third day when Allen, belligerent to the end, tried to hit him out of the ground.

After that, with a lead of 59, it was up to Australia; and miserably enough, in the presence of a record crowd of over 68,000, did the home team acquit themselves. It was not like them to be feeble when a crisis called for every quality of greatness they possessed, but they were feeble indeed on this critical day.

And by the day's end the advantage had see-sawed away from them. The first day had been England's: the second was Australia's: the third was England's again with an emphasis that suggested the advantage was decisive. But there was always a fourth day.

The story of the Australian second innings resolved itself into two parts: the glory of Bradman's one great innings against this particular array of bowlers; and the overwhelming performance by the English attack.

The first to do any overwhelming was Gubby Allen. He and he alone had very nearly broken down Fingleton's resistance in the first innings. His pace and penetrating qualities had all but prevailed against the one batsman who had contrived to give Australia her positive if slender advantage. This time Jardine brought Allen into action at once, instead of Voce. With wind and slope against him, he soon persuaded Fingleton, as in the first innings, to tickle at the going away ball. Up went Ames's great hands: and up went the high chorus of the slips.

Half an hour later the second fortress fell. O'Brien, all dash and sparkle, shot his forward stroke over Larwood's well pitched-up ball, and the bails sprayed the wicket-keeper's face.

As Bradman marched slowly to the wicket, he was advancing on a game that was wellnigh perfectly poised. Australia stood 86 runs ahead, with two wickets down in the second innings. There were almost two full days to go; the weather was idyllic—and the far from exhausted English fast bowlers were ravening to be at their man.

The innings Bradman played was, as I analyse it, the direct expression of the attitude of mind he held on the subject of leg-theory bowling. To him, this form of attack was a nine days' wonder; whereas, if he kept himself healthy and in one piece, he had ten years of cricket before him. The solution was, therefore, on no account to get seriously or permanently hurt by this new tactic, which would be forgotten long before the crowds assembled to cheer his great innings to come. But if it was fundamental not to get hurt, it was at least of secondary importance to hurt the attack itself. So Bradman set himself, not as at Leeds or Lord's a couple of summers earlier, to pile up the greatest possible aggregation of runs, but rather to flay the bowling with all his might for the comparatively short while a man, allowing himself no margin of error, might remain in enemy territory on such a mission.

Thus, he attacked from the first. He stepped back and hooked the rising ball that buzzed like a wasp past his ear. He played that fantasy of a stroke, half square-cut, half drive, that went faster to the boundary than any other shot in anybody else's locker. He used his feet audaciously. He was prepared to move away from the line of the ball on the leg stump, and cut it sumptuously through the desert once inhabited by the slips.

Larwood, bowling with five excellent fieldsmen packing his leg-field, never looked like storming past a defence that was never less than unmitigated attack, or full-blooded assault. Voce's bumpers were disposed of—leaving no heeltaps. Allen, who never used the packed leg-field, was dealt with as ruthlessly as the others, as if to show that the master played no favourites. Only Bowes, bowling uphill and with the wind in his face, once got a ball past him—but afterwards he paid a heavy price for that.

To support Bradman in the early stages of the innings there was Woodfull, cautious and apparently securely set. It was a surprise to all when he played an uppish defensive shot to a ball for once not fraught with hostility, and gave Allen a dainty catch at square-leg.

Later in the innings Richardson shared the counter-attack. A brave, determined batsman, he was not a master of the hook like Bradman and McCabe, but was ever ready to drive in front of the wicket and often found depopulated areas which yielded runs.

The innings ended on a note of melodrama. When Ironmonger, last man in, reached the wicket, Bradman still needed a couple of runs for his century. There were two balls of Hammond's over to be survived before he could get his chance: and Ironmonger was the sort of batsman for whom two balls were almost certain to be too many. Hammond, who had done invaluable work by bowling uphill to relieve the faster bowlers of a task none of them fancied, twice missed Ironmonger's wicket by the thickness of a sheet of paper; and tissue paper at that.

And then the Don was at last free to make or mar his own fortune against Bill Voce and his battery of bouncers. There was, of course, no mistake about the slash that carried him past the century and gave the crowd the excuse for the loudest cheer of the match—indeed of the season. The crowd could cheer itself hoarse, but the fact remained that 191 was a pitiful score for a side to make on so good a wicket.

The Ball that Swung a Test Match

England was well placed, with only 251 runs between them and victory, over a team boasting only four bowlers.

As the drama mounted to its close, every stroke and counter-stroke of strategy was noted and applauded. There went Jardine, astutest of captains, shrewdly opening his campaign with a change in the batting order. The situation was made for Sutcliffe and Leyland. The Yorkshiremen, if anybody, could worry through to victory: moreover everyone in the Australian team must realize, and perhaps be a little cowed by, the relentless challenge their opening partnership offered.

It seemed, too, that the risk was well taken. In the last hour of play the two men fought their way forward, grimly and gaily; Sutcliffe in particular batting with a confidence and skill that suggested he intended to see the thing out as a mere matter of business routine. When stumps were drawn he had scored 32 out of the 43 on the board. Next day England, with every wicket intact, would have to get a mere 208 to win. Who could doubt what the end must be?

And next day something happened which had been allowed for in nobody's calculations: the hearty, bonhomous wicket of the evening before instantaneously developed signs of something like senile decay. First-hand accounts of its condition vary with the part played by the cricketers involved. Bill O'Reilly has described it to me as the type of the wicket on which Australia hit up 404 on the last day at Leeds in '48: a wicket which made it possible for the ball to be spun. Douglas Jardine, in his fine account of the game, explains that his own innings on this pitch was limited to three balls, of which he smothered the first before it had turned more than four or five inches, while the second, left alone, broke a foot and a half, and the third turned nine inches before he touched it into the slips.

It was clear that, after an apathetic youth and a hearty middle-age, the wicket was finishing its life in a mood of arthritic crotchetyness. This gave an opportunity which O'Reilly was quick to seize. Here at last was the chance— the lost game could be won. While Leyland was batting buoyantly enough, Sutcliffe was demurely exploring the possibilities of expansion and development. Yet it was Sutcliffe who stood between Australia and victory: get rid of Sutcliffe and you had rolled up the English flank.

And that is precisely what Bill O'Reilly did. The ball that turned the trick was of perfect length and pitched on the leg stump, whipping across to hit the off bail while the batsman groped down the line of the wicket. After all these years O'Reilly still remembers it as about the best ball he ever bowled in his life: and the point is, of course, that he bowled it at the exact moment when the best ball of a bowling genius (and nothing less) could set his side on the high road to victory.

After that, winning the match was a routine job. The only possible batsman who might alter the shape of the game was Hammond. In the face of much ill-informed criticism, he attempted to hit the bowlers off their length in a death-or-glory innings. For a while he prospered; and then his bat failed to get properly under a quickening leg-break as it left the pitch, and the majestic mashie-shot ballooned into the deep, where O'Brien, with a quicksilver dart from the rim of the boundary, seized the shadowy chance.

Then, one by one, the hopes of the side came, half-saw, and were conquered. Of them all, only Wyatt and Allen gripped the imagination as counter-attackers with a mission. They went down making strokes to the end: and when, as in the first innings, O'Reilly claimed Wyatt as a leg-before victim, the game was virtually over. The last four wickets fell while 4 runs were added: Allen, being delectably stumped whilst prancing out to administer cavalier treatment to Ironmonger.

And so Australia, decisively beaten at Sydney, turned the tables hardly less decisively in the Second Test. The crowds streaming from the ground were buoyed up by a new hope; perhaps body-line had been mastered—perhaps by their win the Australians had shown the way back to the traditional cricket of their fathers.

And perhaps not.

Before body-line is done with a rubber will be won and lost, and a posse of county captains, young and old, will sit together in brooding debate; and a few vigorous West Indians will bounce balls round the lobes of Douglas Jardine's ears and Patsy Hendren will appear at Lord's in a crash helmet properly belonging to a Chelsea Arts Ball. And after that there will be no more body-line.

Meanwhile Australia have won a great Test; and all Melbourne has gone home happy. The players are happy, too; not least Don Bradman, for whom someone has taken up a collection of a hundred pounds in recognition of his contribution to victory. But if you are to reward people according to their deserts, I am not persuaded that the right man got the cherry on the cake on that particular occasion. Bradman was mighty; Bradman was invincible. In the second half of the game, when not another man of them all could scrape together 35, Bradman hit his superb century like a man from Mars toying with the playthings of a lesser star.

The game, however, was not won by Bradman, but by the bowler who took, in the match, ten wickets for 129 runs. That is, if such a game can be won by one man alone. If it can be won by one ball alone, it was won by the ball that kicked back from the on, to shave Herbert Sutcliffe's off bail from his wicket. No one raised a collection of a hundred pounds for the man who bowled this ball. No one splashed his name in headlines in bolder type than you use for abdications or atom bombs.

After all, he was only a bowler.

The Ball That Swung a Test Match

AUSTRALIA

FIRST INNINGS		SECOND INNINGS	
Woodfull, W. M., b Allen	10	c Allen, b Larwood ...	26
Fingleton, J. H., b Allen	83	c Ames, b Allen	1
O'Brien, L. P., run out	10	b Larwood	11
Bradman, D. G., b Bowes	0	not out	103
McCabe, S. J., c Jardine, b Voce ...	32	b Allen	0
Richardson, V. Y., c Hammond, b Voce	34	lbw, b Hammond	32
Oldfield, W. M., not out	27	b Voce	6
Grimmett, C. V., c Sutcliffe, b Voce	2	b Voce	0
Wall, T., run out	1	lbw, b Hammond	3
O'Reilly, W. J., b Larwood	15	c Ames, b Hammond ...	5
Ironmonger, H., b Larwood	4	run out	0
Extras (b 5, lb 1, w 2, nb 2) ...	10	Extras (b3, lb 1, w 4, nb 1	9
	228		191

ENGLAND

FIRST INNINGS		SECOND INNINGS	
Sutcliffe, H., c Richardson, b Wall	52	b O'Reilly	33
Wyatt, R. E. S., lbw b O'Reilly ...	13	lbw, b O'Reilly	25
Hammond, W. R., b Wall	8	c O'Brien, b O'Reilly ...	23
Nawab of Pataudi, b O'Reilly ...	15	c Fingleton, b Ironmonger	5
Leyland, M., b O'Reilly	22	b Wall	19
Jardine, D. R., c Oldfield, b Wall ...	1	c McCabe, b Ironmonger ...	0
Ames, L. E. G., b Wall	4	c Fingleton, b O'Reilly ...	2
Allen, G. O. B., c Richardson, b O'Reilly	30	st Oldfield, b Ironmonger...	23
Larwood, H., b O'Reilly	9	c Wall, b Ironmonger ...	4
Voce, W., c McCabe, b Grimmett ...	6	c O'Brien, b O'Reilly ...	0
Bowes, W. E., not out	4	not out	0
Extras (b 1, lb 2, nb 2)	5	Extras (lb 4, nb 1) ...	5
	169		139

Bowling Analysis

ENGLAND

	O.	M.	R.	W.			O.	M.	R.	W.
Larwood	20.3	2	52	2	...	...	15	2	50	2
Voce	20	3	54	3	...	...	15	2	47	2
Allen	17	3	41	2	...	...	12	1	44	2
Hammond	10	3	21	0	...	...	10.5	2	21	3
Bowes	19	2	50	1	...	...	4	0	20	0

AUSTRALIA

	O.	M.	R.	W.			O.	M.	R.	W.
Wall	21	4	52	4	...	...	8	2	23	1
O'Reilly	34.3	17	63	5	...	...	24	5	66	5
Grimmett	16	4	21	1	...	...	4	0	19	0
Ironmonger	14	4	28	0	...	...	19.1	8	26	4

Chapter Twelve

CLIFFORD BAX'S LAST MATCH

(1933)

A CURIOSITY about cricket is that it appeals to men who are brimming over with disinterest in every other sporting manifestation. Lyric poets, who shudder at football as a vulgar brawl, find an echo of the music in their own souls at the sight of Woolley's elegance or Keith Miller's Tudor gusto. Philosophers find a charm in the pattern of a game with uncharted rhythms that only balance into justice or injustice in retrospect. Men of action appreciate the strategies of the little battle. And many love the game for no reason at all: only vaguely conscious that what they are watching is part of the pageant of the English tradition. They are only hazily aware that larks are singing above the field where the least athletic may perform prodigies, and that strawberries will be served with nutty beer in the little tent at lunchtime, and that the evening will be mellowed by the friendliest and most absorbed talk of the week as the last stand is thrashed out, ball by ball, while Orion and the Pleiades wheel to the sky's summit and over towards the greening horizon.

Perhaps you would not have attributed a passion for the game to the last of the elegants, to share a place in his heart with John Webster, Leonardo, Socrates and Turgeniev, with Gustav Holst and a whole procession of beautiful women with pretty witty Nell at their head.

Clifford Bax has been a Buddhist for many years; he is an Old Master among (or above) our current dramatists, and a poet of exquisite distinction relished by those who have a palate for delectable cadences and the shrewd use of words. Is it possible that such a man is a cricketer, too?

And the answer is yes—cricket is in his blood and in the marrow of his bones for all that he is Shakespeare to the life, if the Droeshout bust or his own recently discovered presumed portrait of the Bard gives us any true picture of the man. He was a cricketer ever since a young man called John Simon, on vacation from Oxford where he played at Wadham with C. B. Fry, taught Clifford and Arnold Bax the rudiments of the game on Streatham Common.

Life was beginning in earnest for young Clifford. Though forbidden the theatre, he was—in his teens—writing his first plays. Quite soon he was to see his own early masterpiece *The Poetasters of Ispahan* performed as a curtain raiser at the Criterion. A great day that for the gangling young dramatist, perplexed like Wells's Mr. Kipps by the problem of what sort of footwear should be sported with the new dinner jacket. Should it be purple bedroom slippers, or were brown button boots *de rigueur*?

Anyway, the curtain-raiser was hugely successful. Before the evening was over the book-rights had been sold, and theatrical impresarios were bidding against each other for the coming man's next work. There were even murmurs in the wings about the sale of the American rights. This was encouragement indeed for an unsophisticated twenty-six year old with a background of study at the Slade and a single publication (*Twenty-five Chinese Poems*) to his credit. The next thing would be established and enduring fame as a dramatist. Well, Clifford Bax was to wait eleven years before his next play was produced in the commercial theatre. By the time he had reached the age of thirty-seven without solid achievements you would have written him off as a dilettante who was never going to make a mark in the world.

You would certainly never have supposed that his fortunes were to be changed as by a spell on the blustery day at Roehampton on which the late Nigel Playfair was one of an audience cupping its ears with gloved hands trying to listen to the words of Clifford's one-act play, *Square Pegs*. The dramatist himself sadly recognized that nature was implacably against him. If only there could have blown a west wind, of the kind Dunois prayed for on the Loire . . . oh well, there are many lives, and to be vexed with trivialities in this one will not improve the health of the undying soul.

And the next day there arrived a letter from Nigel Playfair. Would Mr. Bax be interested in preparing—re-writing, re-editing, adding to—John Gay's *Polly* for the Lyric Theatre, Hammersmith?

Mr. Bax was. The collaboration was triumphant. It was also the beginning of a new era, both in the fortunes of the new dramatist and even in the British theatre. For ten years at least Clifford Bax's elegant, exquisite talent decorated the stage to the delight of more educated audiences than could be found today. At first what he offered them was a *zabaglione*: frothy and bitter-sweet, not quite cloying and never insubstantial, but fare rather for the palate than for the appetite. There was the charm of *Midsummer Madness*, *Nocturne in Palermo*, *Mr. Pepys*. Delectable stuff—it melted on the tongue. A verse or two will set the tone.

> What shall we bring to you?
> What shall we sing to you?
> Where is a plot that has never been used?
> Yet if our venture is
> Doomed by the centuries,
> How shall we keep you awake and amused?
>
> There now! Already, see,
> Ripe for his bed is he;
> Look where Sir Gorgius nid-nods in a stall . . .!
> Best of world-brighteners,
> Prince of heart-lighteners!
> "Pappa" Goldoni—now quicken us all!

And then the fragile talent strengthened and matured. The painter on chicken-skin took to himself a larger canvas, robuster subjects, the blazing colour of imperial language. There came *The Venetian* (his own favourite work) and *The Rose Without A Thorn* (the public's). Outside the main line of development stood *Socrates*. James Agate picked it for his favourite, rating Bax's plays thus:

The Match I Remember

The Rose, c Morgan, b Agate 75.

Socrates, not out 100.

Of course no London impresario has ever been found to give *Socrates* a chance. You see, so profound a play obviously could never appeal to any audience except the topmost highbrows. So *Socrates* has never been produced: except to a packed house of Newcastle working-men—who greeted it with an ovation.

From *The Poetasters* to *The Rose* is two decades' span: the busiest of Clifford's life, yet the one in which he made time to found and play cricket with the most delightful of all clubs. The Old Broughtonians were born in 1911, getting their name from Broughton Gifford, the Somerset village where Clifford had his home and gathered his entire team around him to make forays against the neighbouring village pitches, to play cards or chess at night, and sleep in the huge attic that spanned the Elizabethan manor house much as the salon of Chenonceaux spans the Cher. The captain chose this method of centralization, because in two earlier seasons he had led teams to Norfolk, where the undisciplined players drifted away from the tour to spend afternoons with their girl friends, so that for the last of these matches only five Spartans reported for duty.

It was the best sort of club, the Old Broughtonians. You didn't have to have any special qualifications to belong to it, except the essential qualification of being the sort of person who ought to be a member. How on earth did the captain and sole selector tell whether one was that sort of person? Well, I suppose, a cricketer and clubman knows that sort of thing as instinctively as a lover knows the girl he wants to marry. In they came, the inevitable members, being— strangely enough—respectable bats and almost expert bowlers as well as good companions and fine talkers.

Of that first covey in the year 1911, there were many remarkable figures, some of whom were also quite good cricketers. There was Stacey Aumonier, for instance, chosen because he was interesting anthropologically as the worst slow bowler in the world. There was Herbert Farjeon, capable of hitting centuries and quixotic enough to allow himself to be moved from his appointed place to wicket-keeper, in which position, standing discreetly back, he took many catches off the seam bowlers in whom the team abounded. There was the son of the Bax family gardener, a brilliant fast bowler who deserves to be honoured as a pioneer of Socialism, for he demanded to be paid for his fort-night's cricketing holiday. There was Arnold Bax, not yet knighted nor Master of the King's Musick, but important enough in his way as a fast left-hander with a natural swerve.

There was Clifford himself, a hectoring batsman and a brilliant field. For years it was his major boast that he once hit a ball out of the Oval.

As the years passed, new strength, or at least new members were added to the club. One was a very distinguished writer of detective stories who, negligible as bowler and batsman, was played as a deep-fieldsman solely because his bladder was so weak that he had to be well placed for the dash behind the pavilion—punctually made every fourth over.

In 1913, J. C. Snaith, then an eminent novelist, joined the side. He had in his time bowled for Nottinghamshire, and was black-browed with grief when taken off in club games. His fastish left-arm bowling was by this time not very formidable, but his batting, which he despised, was magnifi-cent indeed—once, while scoring a century, he blocked a yorker to the boundary. He was so nervous that before going in he could hardly persuade his trembling fingers to buckle on his pads.

Snaith was an original mainly on account of his remark-able pessimism. He once sadly surveyed a stand of 112 in forty minutes by Clifford and Rudolph Lowe, an excellent cricketer and the author of a delightful anthology on the game. An ecstatic spectator turned to ask him what he thought of it. "They shouldn't sit on the splice, you know," was Snaith's comment, delivered with a funereal wag of the head.

He finally retired from the side with a letter of resig-nation which read: "I think you will be a happier party without me."

After Snaith came the poet Edward Thomas, a modest performer who liked to keep the score because he said that a score-sheet reminded him of a sonnet.

And then came the war. When the grounds around Bath—Melksham and Corsham, Lansdown and Grittleton—echoed again to the deep-throated cover-drives and falsetto late-cuts of the O.B.s a new generation had come to the wicket. In the first post-war season of '21 there were Harold Monro of the Poetry Book Shop and Alec Waugh, an excellent fast bowler and a hard-hitting batsman with a festive array of strokes. His enthusiasm was the chief reason for the Old Broughtonians' revival during the long week-end.

Newcomers in the second season were Eric Gillett, good enough to play for anybody's team, and Ralph Straus, who once, as technical adviser, succeeded in persuading a Hollywood film company not to allow the hero to bowl, catch and bowl, and run out the villain of their piece off the same ball.

Then came such proficients as Armstrong Gibbs, the composer; Kenneth Lindsay, M.P., a warrantable fast bowler; Keith Falkner, the singer, who once took twenty wickets in a tour at 5 runs apiece; Julius Harrison, conductor at the Worcester Festival, and B. W. O'Donnell, in command of the Irish Guards Brass Band.

"There were no painters in my team," the founder observes broodingly. "Only musicians and writers. I sometimes wonder whether we should have won more or fewer matches if we had discovered any painters who could be persuaded to be interested in cricket."

A quarter of a century ago two distinguished figures joined the side. One was Jack (later Sir John) Squire, who, in the intervals of running the *London Mercury* and saving Wren churches, captained a brother club known as The Invalids. With the Old Broughtonians he was given the exacting post of long-stop at both ends; moreover, he once made 10 at a time when runs were urgently needed.

His fellow new boy in the team was A. D. Peters, the literary agent, and a major power behind the scenes of the London theatre. Peters was a left-handed bowler of parts.

Shortly after the First World War he found himself having a holiday in a Somerset village where the event of the year, the great all-day cricket match with the neighbouring rivals, was in process of being planned. Was it possible that Mr. Peters played a little cricket himself? In that case would he care to play in the game, and bowl the opening over? With his first five balls Peters took five wickets. They took him off at the end of the over, alleging, on the strength of that sixth ball, that he was losing his form. The real reason, of course, was that he had already done far too much to spoil a battle royal planned to last till sunset.

With the Old Broughtonians his form was almost as imposing. He played his first game for the side at Box, and put on as second change took six wickets for 10 runs. That was in the season when the great Lansdown club, with a couple of county players, was handsomely beaten. Peters took six wickets for 63; but the high-light of the match was the scoring of 59 runs in seven minutes by Clifford himself. The Old Broughtonians published annual volumes recording their history—the full set today is worth a fortune among American bibliophiles. In the volume which deals with this match Ralph Straus not only vouches for the timing of Clifford's innings, but adds that the spectacle was so inspiring that it even moved the local reporter to stop playing shove-halfpenny and cast an occasional eye at the wicket.

That victory was one of the unforgettable days in the Old Broughtonian saga. But there were many such. There was, for example, the first match against the County Mental Hospital at Devizes, when a patient walked up and down juggling marvellously, ignoring both the desperately close struggle at the wickets and the sad listlessness of the spectators.

There were other strange stories and scenes crowded into the thirty years' history of the side. One of the most inexplicable incidents was the form in 1937 of one of my own oldest friends, J. R. H. Chisholm. For seasons John had appeared in the team, showing a form which he could be relied upon to maintain whatever the strength or weakness of the opposition. In 1934, for example, he had finished the tour with a batting average of 1; but this was only achieved, I hasten to add, because almost all his total was amassed in one great innings—in which he scored no less than 5.

But in 1937 there came a transformation scene. J. R. H. Chisholm finished (and on his merits) top of the batting averages. Nothing more remarkable has been seen in cricket, except possibly the rise of Glamorgan from abyss to zenith in the County Championship.

There are shortsighted critics who have attributed John's success to his cap, which happens to be that of the Batchelors Cricket Club, founded and captained by myself when I was young enough to know no better. The best part about that club was its cap: a confection of magenta, aspidistra green and white triangles. The last time I wore it in action the opposing wicket-keeper said (as I left after my fourth ball): "When you came in I supposed you were a Free Forester." I am assured, on good authority, that there was never any likelihood of this mistake being made about John Chisholm. He owed his position at the top of the Old Broughtonian averages to his skill as a stroke-player, not to loss of control by the bowlers as the consequence of a case of mistaken identification.

From 1911, when A. J. Waugh was the leading batsman with an average of 77, to the autumn of 1933—it was a long and golden chapter for the captain who had been taught to hold a bat when Queen Victoria was on the throne, before Mafeking had fallen or the Wright brothers had become airborne at Dayton, Ohio, while Irving was still appearing in Sardou's *Robespierre* at the Lyceum, and Swinburne was taking his morning walk from Number 2, The Pines to the Green Man on Putney Heath.

As he came to his last match of all, on the beautiful Corsham ground, then still ringed with elms, ghosts paced beside him. He remembered immortal days. The game in which he had shared in a record stand for the ninth wicket. And the game against the Queries in 1935 when the Old Broughtonians were set to get 255 in less than two hours—and won with half an hour to spare. And the match in which he and Rudolph Lowe added 112 runs while Snaith had shaken his sombre head—and how the two of them had bicycled home in the mellow evening, flushed with victory and the sunset glow. He remembered the genial loquacity of Lord Methuen on the edge of that same Corsham ground which made it a little difficult for a captain to concentrate on his strategic planning. And he remembered how, again at Corsham, a clergyman, by this time a bishop, had been bowled by a ring-tailed boomer from Willy Eden, to observe as he made for the pavilion: "You sim to hev pleed befah. . . ."

It was at Corsham, too, that Fred Hulbert had flourished in the long, long ago. Here, before the guns had sounded on the Marne, he had taken nine wickets against the Old Broughtonians, finishing up with six for 7 in his last wonder-ful spell. And beyond that, was he not the hero of Clifford's sonnet, mirroring the whole experience of those green-golden summers?

> I often think how lucky I was that day
> When, seven years old, I first saw bat and wicket,
> And learned to love—better than I learned to play—
> Our beautiful, difficult English game of cricket.
> And when I stuff my bag for the last time,
> As soon I must, with pads and boots and flannels,
> What sunny days, what friendships of my prime,
> What contests will remain in memory's annals!
>
> But no ground prettier than that Corsham field;
> No games more happy to think upon than those;
> And no man who more steadfastly revealed
> The spirit of England, whatever luck befell,
> Than gay Fred Hulbert, friendliest of all foes,
> A cricketer and a musician who used life well.

"But no ground prettier than that Corsham field." None more historic either, in this quiet backwater of the West. Hadn't W. G. come to play here at the age of fifteen, a year or two after he had watched William Clark's All-England Team, wearing top hats, play on the old ridge and furrow field behind the Full Moon at Stokes Croft, Bristol?

But the game was on at last. There would be all too much time for meditation later on.

First there was the toss to be won. For the eighth time running, Clifford won it. Really there was something to be said for urging the veteran to stay on as non-playing captain—perhaps even in Test matches. With his peculiar gift, any batsman worth an average of less than 40 should not grudge giving up a place to him.

Then to the wickets, with A. D. Peters, the captain-elect, beside him.

When you were in your forty-ninth year it was no joke to be facing bowling with an edge to it on a fast wicket. Holder and Hampton bowled well from the first over, and soon Peters was back in the pavilion.

But if the new captain fell, the old timer stuck around. It cannot be said that the off-drive was in the mint condition which had won respectful plaudits from the Hurns at Melksham from ten to twenty years back. There wasn't the same roystering straight-drive or quite the old gay leg-hit. But there were strokes still, handsome, mellow strokes that brought runs in their wake. And when at last the captain was caught for 22 he had done well enough to bring the Corsham spectators to their feet to cheer him back to the pavilion.

How well he had done was soon all too apparent. Riddle, who had taken his wicket, soon added to it those of Eric Gillett and R. O. Morris, despite the employment by the latter of a mahogany-coloured bat which he had used at New College in 1906—a vintage year for port also. Four for 57 was a woebegone position: for you must not suppose that the Old Broughtonians mixed with the sort of village team that found itself scratching a spade-shaped beard dubiously when faced with a total of 17.

But at this stage the British characteristic of refusing to know when one is beaten reared its pretty head. Patrick Knox-Shaw and Hugh Prew were the embodiment of the Nelsonian tradition on this particular occasion. They added 77 runs in three-quarters of an hour, Knox-Shaw hitting two full-pitches for sixes beyond the memory of the longest greybeard sunning himself at the foot of the tallest elm. The first of these majestic swipes soared over the stone wall circling the ground, over the road on the other side, and over a second wall, before it finally landed deep in the asparagus bed in the kitchen garden beyond.

After this little tornado there was not much batting to exult over, except from Kenneth Lindsay, whose innings might have been expressly designed as a reproach to his captain, who had long failed to recognize his batsmanlike qualities when flourished under his very nose. While others held a fort which had as great a lease of adventure and much less stability than those defended by Beaux Geste and Sabreur, Lindsay sabred his way through to lead the team to the safe side of 200. Batsmen who had had less distinguished experiences began to cluster round their captain, drawing his attention to aspects of technique not usually associated with this particular performer, except in theory. A late-cut reminded one austere critic of Percy Holmes when the bloom was on his game; others dissented, seeing in the curve of wrist and economic use of forearm and torso, an echo of an earlier master—subtle Bobby Abel.

At the innings' end came tea. After all these years no gourmet seems to have an exact menu printed on his memory, but there were certainly scones and blackberry jam, to say nothing of plates heaped with cheese and lettuces, and plum cake hard outside and succulent under the crust, and as many cups of rich, brown tea as glowing ladies could pass round and perspiring men could drink in that blissful quarter of an hour's ease.

At five o'clock, with a resplendent August evening gathering its stage effects in the sky, battle was rejoined. If Corsham really set about the bowling (and they were just the club to do such a thing) they might yet pull the game out of the fire. W. Holden began by lashing 13 runs off the first two overs—indeed, he seemed set for a dazzling century which would give his side victory with time to spare. But when he had rollicked his way to 28 out of the first 33 runs scored, he hit a whistling drive to silly mid-off. Clifford Bax was fielding there, perhaps as a sort of gesture of confidence in his suc-

cessor as captain, who was bowling. It was the sort of chance
he (let alone the rest of the side) would have forgiven himself
for not having attempted ten or twenty years earlier; indeed,
if he had escaped scatheless from such a bullet-swift volley
there would have been occasion for general congratulation.
But now—in the eleventh hour—he flung out his hand and
the great catch miraculously stuck.

In came Jim Newman, gigantic of shoulder, intent on belt-
ing the cover off the ball. His terrific drives, violent as the
kick of a racehorse, slammed the ball—an all but invisible
speck in its headlong race with Light—in the same general
direction. Again, out went the long arm; out shot the cool
fingers—and up went the catch against the blue and white
quilt of Wiltshire skyscape. You could watch Sydney Barnes
fielding at suicide point on the edge of the pitch for half a
dozen seasons without seeing him better two such catches. It
was the glorious *coup de théâtre* of a cricket career: thrice
blesséd is the captain who contrives such a curtain for his
last act.

With four wickets down for 39, the Old Broughtonians
had a right to look optimistic, even if they managed to look
surprised at the same time. But there the tide of glory rolled
home its last wave. The O.B.s were not to be carried farther
to the shore. Danger had gone: besides the captain's two
demoralizing catches, there had been Knox-Shaw's snapping
up at the wicket of a chance from Riddle, who four years
earlier had hit a whirlwind century against this team, and
was the chief remaining embodiment of danger.

With their first batsmen overthrown, Corsham fell back
on a valiant defence. Gingell and Gale held out in a stub-
born stand, and Fido stood firm afterwards.

As the game drew to an end, the captain, moved perhaps
by some sentimental motive which no mere analyst of tactics
could hope to plumb, threw the ball to R. O. Morris. Research reveals that this member of the side once took three
wickets several years earlier in a game against Newbury; but
this appears to have been the limit not only of his success
but of his appearance in this rôle since he bowled for the
Harrow eleven. Now, as a veteran, he seemed to the Corsham

team a puzzling bowler: "Puzzling, indeed, that he should
be a bowler at all," as one of them put it. He swiftly took
three wickets; and had he had five minutes more at his dis-
posal he might have brought the match to end in a sensational victory.

But, as it was, a calm, soul-satisfying draw closed the game
and the captain's career fittingly enough. There remained
only twilight and the return to Bath, to the farewell dinner
and the farewell speeches to round off the story of the twenty-
odd years of captaincy. Well enough—he was a greedy man
who would ask for more.

As the stumps were drawn, as the light faded over the
quiet field, Clifford remembered again the quintessence of
happiness and solace the game had brought him. Years ago,
prophetically enough, he had woven this evening's mood into
a poem.

When life was budding and I new-married, I made my
    home in a house that stood
Grey in the green of the Wiltshire meadows—a hoary
    dwelling of stone and beam;
And there, when summer had burst the poppy and skies
    were brazen, the men I loved—
Letting the world go by—would gather for days of cricket
    in field or park.

Days of delight! For delight unmeasured it was to fare
    through the morning lanes,
And hour by hour, as the sun went over, to strive for
    victory friend with friend;
Or, jogging home as the twilight settled on ancient village
    or farm, to see
The curtained windows, the candles lighted, the supper
    spread and the cider drawn.

Beautiful too were the nights that followed when, strolling
forth in a glad fatigue

And lazing long where the starlight glimmered on ghost-
like lilies that fringed the lawn,

We shared our thought or our laughter, forging a love
between us that years of change

Have left but stronger, alike responsive to this man's
learning or that man's wit.

I knew, indeed, as the days went by us, how none of all
that were yet to be

Could bring delight that was more unclouded. I did not
know that with every hour

We stored a joy that should last for ever—like Arab
merchants who fill their gourds

With crystal water from some white city and then set forth
to the desert sand.

And now that story was over. Well, there had to come an
end some day. Perhaps the time was at hand when poets and
musicians would not find time or peace of mind to play such
leisurely games through the last weeks of an English summer.
This sort of cricket, friendly and sweet tempered, suited to
the chivalry of the English countrymen, was not likely to last
for ever. The year was 1933. This very day over in Germany
a little man had sprung up who looked like Charlie Chaplin,
but who seemed to be roaring and rampaging in a style that
boded ill for chivalry and the English way of life.

The dusk had fallen. The moon was among the elms.
Good night, Corsham—and farewell.

Index

203

Index

scores century, 142
143, 144, 148, 152, 160—2, 164, 165, 171, 174, 175
Chester (*Umpire*), 22
Chipperfield, A. G., 91
Chisholm, J. R. H., 195, 196
Clark, William,
his All-England team, 197
Clay, J. C., 123
Cobden, F. C., 92, 102
Collins, H. L., 12, 14, 15, 18—20, 23, 28, 158, 159, 164, 166—8, 171
Compton, D., 44, 59
his modesty, 60
sets out for South Africa with M.C.C. (1948), 61
62, 65—7, 69, 70, 72, 73, 124, 126—128, 131, 133, 135, 136
Compton, L., 132, 134, 136
Constantine, L. N., 78—82, 86—9
Cooper, Gary, 141
Corrall, P., 124,
his benefit match, 125—35, 136
Corsham, Wilts, 196, 197, 202
Corsham C.C., 199—201
Cotter (*Australia XI*, 1911), 12, 29
Craig, H. S., 78, 79, 89
Crawford, J. N., 45, 46, 48, 133
Cristofani, D. R., 78, 80—2, 86, 87, 89
Crush, E., 96, 98, 101, 103
Currie Cup, the, 63, 65

D

Darling, J., 35, 107, 119
Davies, J. G. W., 79, 83, 86, 87, 89
Dawson, O. C., 63, 73
Denton, D., 27
de Trafford, C. E., 130, 133, 134
Docker, C., 43
Dollery, H. E., 92, 93, 95, 96, 99—101, 103
Dominions XI, 83, 89
Donnelly, M. P., 59,
scores century in 'Varsity match, 75
"the best bat in England," 76
his match of a lifetime, 77
78, 79,
hits twenty boundaries in three hours, 80
83, 85, 87, 89, 99—101
Donoghue, Pat, 139
Donoghue, Steve, 139
Douglas, J. W. H. T., 29, 30, 49, 157
Dovey, R. R., 95, 100, 101, 103
Ducat, A., 51—53, 58
Duckworth, G., 30, 31, 35, 39, 41, 112, 118, 121, 142, 147, 148, 152
Duleepsinhji, K. S., 142, 145, 146, 149, 152
Durston, T. J., 51—3, 58

E

Eden, Willy, 197
Edrich, W. J., 44, 79, 81, 82, 85, 86, 89, 94, 95, 99, 100, 103, 126, 130—3, 135, 136
Elder (*Umpire*), 36
Ellis, R. S., 81, 86, 87, 89
England, in 1930, 140, 141
England Sides v. Australia:
(1925-6), 14—25
(1928-9), 29—41, 109—21
(1930), 143—52
(1932-3), 173—88
England Sides v. Dominions:
(1945), 77—89
England Sides v. South Africa:
(1906), 45—8, 57
(1948), 62—73
Essex C.C.C., 49
Evans, A. H., 140
Evans, T. G., 62, 63, 70, 73, 101
Everett, S., 14

F

Fagg, A., 93, 96, 103
Fairfax, A., 108, 148, 150, 152
Falkner, Keith, 194
Fane, F. L., 46
Farjeon, Herbert, 192
Faulkner, G. A., 43—6, 137, 138, 145
Fell, D. R., 78, 79
Fender, P. G. H., 50—2, 54, 76, 94
Fido (*Corsham C.C.*), 200
Fingleton, J. H., 178, 179, 182, 183, 188
First Mrs. Fraser, The, 141
Fishlock, L. B., 79, 81, 84, 89
Fleetwood-Smith, L. O'B., 61, 82
Fog Lane, 85
Foster, R. E. ("*Tip*"), 30, 75, 76, 105, 173
Freeman, A. P., 50, 96, 138, 158, 160, 161, 163, 165—9, 171
Fry, C. B., 12, 44, 76, 115, 190

G

Gale (*Corsham C.C.*), 200
Gardner, F. C., 94, 99, 103
Gay, John, his *Polly*, 191
Geary, G., 13, 22, 23, 25, 30—2, 34, 35, 39—41, 108, 115, 121, 143
Gibbs, Armstrong, 194
Gilbert (*Australian bowler*), 106
Gillett, Eric, 194, 198
Gilligan, A. E. R., 104, 110, 157, 160, 165—169, 171
Gimblett, H., 79, 81, 84, 89
Gingell (*Corsham C.C.*), 200
Gladwin, C., 62, 63, 71—3
Glamorgan C.C.C., 105
Gloucestershire C.C.C., 105
Goddard, T., 123, 143, 148, 152
Googly bowling, 16, 22, 45, 51, 52, 81, 84, 110, 151
Grace, Dr. W. G., 11, 21, 31, 197
Gray, L., 124, 128, 129, 134, 136
Gregory, J. M., 13—9, 21, 23, 25, 30, 45, 106, 108, 158, 159, 161, 162, 165—9, 171

Index

Index

McCarthy, C., 61, 63, 64, 69, 70, 73
McCormick, E. L., 106
McDonald, E. A., 13, 106
Mailey, A. A., 14 15,
  his bowling style, 16
   22, 23, 25, 60, 79, 106, 108, 111,
  his painting, 155
  at his best, 156
  takes 9 wickets in an innings, 157
   158, 161, 164, 166—71, 173
Mann, F. G., 63, 67, 68, 70, 73, 124,
  126, 128, 131, 132, 136
Mann, F. T., 53, 55, 58
Mann, N. ("*Tufty*"), 64—6, 69, 73
Martin, J. W., 94, 103
M.C.C., 49, 57, 61, 123, 139, 154
Matches described (*see also under
  Test matches*):
  England v. Dominions (1945), 77—
   87: *scores*, 89
  Kent v. Warwickshire (1949), 92—
   102): *scores*, 103
  Middlesex v. Leicestershire (1949),
   124—35: *scores*, 136
  Middlesex v. Surrey (1920), 49—
   56: *scores*, 58
  Old Broughtonians v. Corsham
   (1933), 198—201
Matthews, T. J., 29
Mead, P., 11, 29, 42
Melbourne Cricket Ground, 11, 20, 29
  —31, 35
  record attendance at, 176
Methuen, Lord, 197
Middlesex C.C.C., 45, 49, 52, 53, 55,
  105, 124, 125, 127—35, 138
Middlesex v. Leicestershire (1949),
  124—35: *scores*, 136
Middlesex v. Surrey (1920), 49—56:
  scores, 58
Midsummer Madness, 191
Miller, K. R., 59, 79, 83—5, 89, 160,
  189
Mr. Pepys, 191
Mitchell, A., 139
Mitchell, B., 18, 62, 63, 65, 67, 70, 73
Monro, Harold, 194
Morris, R. O., 198, 200
Munden, V., 134, 136
Munnings, Sir Alfred, 83
Murrell, H. R., 52, 55, 58
Mussolini, Benito, 141
Mynn, A., 95

N

Nagel, L., 173—5
Newman, Jim, 200
New South Wales C.C., 173
New Zealand XI, 60
Nichols, M. S., 143, 148, 152
Night Like This, A, 141
Noble, M. A., 46, 157
Nocturne in Palermo, 191
Nothling, O., 109
Nottinghamshire C.C.C., 49
Nourse, A. D., 62, 63, 65, 67, 69, 71, 73

Nourse, Dave, 45—8, 63

O

O'Brien, L. P., 175, 177, 179, 183, 188
O'Donnell, B. W., 194
Old Broughtonians C.C., 192, 194—
  8, 200
Old Trafford Cricket Ground, 78, 81,
  85, 140
Oldfield, W. A., 16, 19, 23, 25, 30, 33
  39, 41, 114, 118, 119, 121, 161, 162,
  168, 170, 171, 179—81, 188
Oldroyd, E., 139
On the Spot, 141
Ord, J., 94, 99, 101, 103
O'Reilly, W. J., 82,
  "the Tiger," 172
  173, 174, 179, 180,
  his bowling style, 181, 182
  183, 185,
  the best ball he ever bowled, 186
  188
Oval Cricket Ground, 11, 14, 20, 21,
  26, 30, 44, 92, 133, 138, 193
Oval, The, Adelaide, 168
Oxenham, R. K., 29, 33, 35—7, 39,
  41, 114, 115, 117, 118, 121
Oxford University XI, 139
Oxfordshire C.C.C., 49

P

Palmer, C. H., 72
Palmerston, Lord, 95
Pataudi, Nawab of, 142, 149, 177, 180,
  188
Peach, H. A., 58
Peebles, I. A. R., 44, 137,
  launched by Plum Warner, 138
  plays for Oxford University C.C.,
  139
  140
  picked for England v. Australia
  (1939), 143
  144—52
Peel, R., 37
Pepper, C. G., 78—80, 84—7, 89
Perrin, P. A., 55
Peters, A. D., 194, 195, 198
Pettiford, J., 79, 89
Phantom of the Opera, The, 141
Phebey, A., 98, 99, 103
Phillipson, W. E., 79, 81, 86, 89
Playfair, Nigel, 190, 191
Poetasters of Ispahan, The, 190, 191
Ponsford, W. H., 14, 15, 17, 25, 30,
  143—5, 148, 151, 159, 163, 171,
  175, 179
Prentice, F. T., 127, 134, 136
Prew, Hugh, 198
Priestley, A., 144
Pritchard, D. E., 92—4, 97, 101, 108
Pritchard, T. (Warwick), 92—4, 97,
  101

Q

Queries C.C., 196

Index